Environmental and Animal Abuse Denial

Environment and Society

Series Editor: Douglas Vakoch

As scholars examine the environmental challenges facing humanity, they increasingly recognize that solutions require a focus on the human causes and consequences of these threats, and not merely a focus on the scientific and technical issues. To meet this need, the Environment and Society series explores a broad range of topics in environmental studies from the perspectives of the social sciences and humanities. Books in this series help the reader understand contemporary environmental concerns, while offering concrete steps to address these problems.

Books in this series include both monographs and edited volumes that are grounded in the realities of ecological issues identified by the natural sciences. Our authors and contributors come from disciplines including but not limited to anthropology, architecture, area studies, communication studies, economics, ethics, gender studies, geography, history, law, pedagogy, philosophy, political science, psychology, religious studies, sociology, and theology. To foster a constructive dialogue between these researchers and environmental scientists, the Environment and Society series publishes work that is relevant to those engaged in environmental studies, while also being of interest to scholars from the author's primary discipline.

Titles in the Series

Environmental and Animal Abuse Denial: Averting Our Gaze, edited by Tomaž Grušovnik, Reingard Spannring, and Karen Lykke Syse

Conservation, Sustainability, and Environmental Justice in India, edited by Alok Gupta

Secular Discourse on Sin in the Anthropocene: What's Wrong with the World?, by Ernst M. Conradie

Environment, Social Justice, and the Media in the Age of Anthropocene, edited by Elizabeth G. Dobbins, Maria Lucia Piga, and Luigi Manca

Global Perspectives on Eco-Aesthetics and Eco-Ethics: A Green Critique, edited by Krishanu Maiti and Soumyadeep Chakraborty

Australian Wetland Cultures: Swamp Thinking, edited by John Charles Ryan and Li Chen

Motor Vehicles, the Environment, and the Human Condition: Driving to Extinction, by Hans A. Baer

Environmental and Animal Abuse Denial

Averting Our Gaze

Edited by
Tomaž Grušovnik, Reingard Spannring,
and Karen Lykke Syse

LEXINGTON BOOKS
Lanham • Boulder • New York • London

Published by Lexington Books
An imprint of The Rowman & Littlefield Publishing Group, Inc.
4501 Forbes Boulevard, Suite 200, Lanham, Maryland 20706
www.rowman.com

6 Tinworth Street, London SE11 5AL, United Kingdom

British Library Cataloguing in Publication Information Available

Library of Congress Cataloging-in-Publication Data

Names: Grušovnik, Tomaž, editor. | Spannring, Reingard, editor. | Lykke Syse, Karen, editor.
Title: Environmental and animal abuse denial : averting our gaze / edited by Tomaž Grušovnik, Reingard Spannring, Karen Lykke Syse.
Other titles: Environment and society (Lanham, Md.)
Description: Lanham, Maryland : Lexington Books, [2021] | Series: Environment and society | Includes bibliographical references and index.
Identifiers: LCCN 2020038401 (print) | LCCN 2020038402 (ebook) | ISBN 9781793610461 (cloth) | ISBN 9781793610485 (pbk) | ISBN 9781793610478 (epub)
Subjects: LCSH: Denial (Psychology)—Social aspects. | Denialism. | Animal welfare. | Climate Change. | Environmental psychology. | Human-animal relationships.
Classification: LCC BF175.5.D44 E58 2021 (print) | LCC BF175.5.D44 (ebook) | DDC 179/.1—dc23
LC record available at https://lccn.loc.gov/2020038401
LC ebook record available at https://lccn.loc.gov/2020038402

Contents

Acknowledgments

We would like to express our gratitude to our institutions, Faculty of Education, University of Primorska, Institute for Educational Sciences, the Centre for Development and the Environment, University of Oslo, and the Austrian Science Foundation (FWF, grant number I 4342, 2019-2022), which generously support us and enable our work. We would like to cordially thank Nataša Demirović and Maša Pungartnik for their help with technical editing and indexing of the manuscript. Without versatile support and encouragement from Lexington Books, this book would have remained a wishful thought. We also deeply appreciate the dedication that the contributors to this volume showed for our project amid the unprecedented global pandemic and devastating wildfires.

Introduction

Denialism in Environmental and Animal Abuse

Tomaž Grušovnik, Reingard Spannring, and Karen Lykke Syse

Despite readily available facts and figures on climate change, environmental degradation, species extinction as well as animal suffering and death, we are still faced with the disbelief and inaction with respect to the existence, extent, and implications of the anthropogenic impact on the environment and non-human lives. The question about the barriers to pro-environmental behavior calls for complex answers. Although a copious amount of empirical and theoretical work has been carried out, the phenomenon remains difficult to grasp.

The oldest model explaining pro-environmental behavior, the "information deficit model,"[1] was developed in the early 1970s. It assumed a linear relationship between environmental knowledge, awareness, and concern on the one hand, and corresponding behavior on the other hand. From this rationalist perspective, lack of pro-environmental behavior would be remedied by education about environmental issues. This model was soon disproved by studies showing that an increase in knowledge and awareness did not lead to pro-environmental behavior. In their meta-analysis of the literature on pro-environmental behavior, or rather the lack of it, Kollmuss and Agyeman list internal factors such as biographic experience, motivation, environmental knowledge, attitudes, values, and awareness, as well as external factors such as institutional, economic, social, and cultural norms.[2] There can be various cognitive limitations to environmental awareness and behavior such as non-immediacy of many ecological problems, the protracted time frame of environmental change, and the complexity of systems. The affective side of environmental awareness, the emotional involvement that makes us care, depends on the ability to respond emotionally to an environmental problem. However, a caring response can be thwarted by resistance against information that does not fit our beliefs and mental frameworks and by information

1

that triggers troubling emotions such as fear, pain, sadness, anger, guilt, and helplessness. Strategies to manage this conflict and emotions include denial, rational distancing, apathy, and delegation.[3] They imply the refusal to accept reality and one's own involvement and responsibility in the respective dilemma and prevent people from responding to it in an appropriate way.

The present collection focuses on "denialism" as an umbrella term for social, cultural, and psychological mechanisms that help individuals and societies continue with their lifestyles despite facts and figures that point to detrimental consequences of their actions for both the environment as well as lives of animals. While the first reflections of the phenomenon of willful ignorance appeared already in antiquity and were an important part of the philosophy of such thinkers as Saint Augustine, Thomas Aquinas, Rousseau, Kant, and many others, the topic of denial started to feature prominently in the humanities, psychology, and other related disciplines only with Sigmund Freud. Freud used two terms for what is generally referred to as "denial," namely "Verleugnung" (disavowal) and "Verneinung" (negation). Even though his reflections still form an important part of the knowledge base in psychoanalytic theory,[4] other authors and their work on denialism have received more attention in sociology and other branches of psychology, for instance the cognitive paradigm. Undoubtedly, Leon Festinger's *A Theory of Cognitive Dissonance*[5] reframed how we understand "denialism" in the light of avoidance of sensitive information that threatens to undermine the consistency of our conceptual webs. Indeed, "cognitive dissonance" became an important theoretical vehicle for the explanation of environmental and animal denialism, as will become clear later in this volume, especially in Susanne Stoll-Kleemann's chapter. However, the interest in the concept of "denialism" has been rekindled in recent decades from a more socio-logical perspective with the publication of Stanley Cohen's classic *States of Denial*[6] and Eviatar Zerubavel's *The Elephant in The Room*,[7] to which Reingard Spannring and José De Giorgio-Schoorl's chapter title alludes. Cohen's analysis became prominent because of its political import and social implications. In it, Cohen famously analyzes three distinct forms of denial, literal (the claim that something is not true), interpretive (the facts are not denied but given a different meaning, for example, through euphe-misms), and implicatory (failure to acknowledge the implications and to respond appropriately). They also play an important role in John Sorenson and Atsuko Matsuoka's chapter, as well as Opi Outhwaite's analysis in the present volume. Similar to Cohen, Zerubavel dedicated his research to social and political dimensions of denial, focusing specifically on the genesis of the conspiracy of silence about what is in front of everybody's eyes. In addition to that, social and evolutionary biology also attempted to shed light on deni-alism in our everyday lives: Robert Triver's *The Folly of Fools* is one such brilliant example of explaining the roots of our self-deception that, according to Trivers, grow out of our evolutionary inclination to deceive others. In short, his argument is that by being self-deceived, a deceiver's behavior is less likely to give away typical clues that can be picked up by others.[8]

Because it is such an important vehicle to explain a wide variety of phenomena, it is unsurprising that denialism has also become prominent in environmental and critical animal studies. The history of denial of environmental problems is long and encompasses campaigns against the protection of natural areas and wilderness, the banning of synthetic pesticides such as DDT, and anti-science campaigns such as the cases denying acid rain and the ozone hole.[9] Several fields have contributed to our understanding of the phenomenon.[10] In the following section, we will briefly turn to four publications we deem particularly important.

Together with *Merchants of Doubt* by Naomi Oreskes and Erik M. Conway, focusing on parallels between tobacco smoking and climate change, Kari Norgaard's *Living in Denial* is one of the most substantial monographs published on environmental denialism. Analyzing implicatory denial, Norgaard found people in Norway believed in climate change and expressed concern about it, yet they lived their lives as if it was not happening. This allowed people to protect themselves from troubling emotions such as the fear of loss of ontological security, helplessness, guilt, and the threat to their individual and collective identities.[11] Individual emotion management, however, is always embedded in a social context that prescribes norms of emotion and cognitive scripts of "thought prevention," "perspectival selectivity," and "selective interpretation." Accordingly, collective denial functions both as a "cultural tool kit" to keep disturbing information at bay, and also secures non-mobilization that contributes to reproduce political and economic power structures and dominant ideologies.[12]

Environmental scientist Haydn Washington and cognitive scientist John Cook's book, *Climate Change Denial. Heads in the Sand*, also provides an influential analysis of denialism with respect to climate science.[13] They identify five types of denial arguments which claim that (a) scientific consensus on climate change is a "vast conspiracy to deceive,"[14] (b) there is no scientific consensus based on statements of nonexperts, (c) climate models are unreliable, (d) climate change occurs naturally, and (e) there is scientific evidence for the deniers' view ignoring the mainstream thrust of evidence. Science denial and the denial industry squarely fit Cohen's concept of literal denial, while Cohen's interpretative denial is exemplified by governments and business that pretend to take or limit action to the "politically feasible."[15] Drawing on discourse analyses, Washington and Cook further address the role played by the media that in the interest of sales figures and viewing rates project extreme minority opinions[16] that allow readers and audience to turn their gaze away, and cover up their ignorance of ecological complexities, dynamics, and values.

Arne Johan Vetlesen's book, *The Denial of Nature*, takes a more philosophical approach to environmental denialism, exploring, among other topics, the misplacement or misformulation of several theoretical dichotomies, including debates about instrumental versus intrinsic value of nature or culture versus nature. When pondering the "denial of nature," Vetlesen also points to a common misunderstanding, present also in some of the most prominent nature philosophers, such as J. Baird Callicott, namely that appropriate environmental action is not undertaken because "most of us are simply ill-informed."[17] To the contrary, Vetlesen observes that the media attention given to environmental problematics seems to:

> fail spectacularly when it comes to both (1) effecting a change in interest in environmental policies in general, and (2) effecting a change in people's behaviour. The researchers do find a correlation, but it is not the one Callicott would have us expect. Rather, it is the correlation between the expected increase in global temperature reported from the scientists and the increase in average holiday-related flights among, for example, Norwegians.[18]

Indeed, for Vetlesen it is hard for us to change our ways, especially if we have invested so much of who and what we are in our lifestyles that are now proclaimed unsustainable and consequently undesirable. As Vetlesen sees it, both theory as well as practice will have to be redefined and brought together to solve issues connected with this phenomenon. We invite readers to scrutinize the latest development in Vetlesen's thinking through his contribution to this volume.

When assessing the research in environmental denial in general, an overview of the literature prepared by Karin Edvardsson Björnberg, Mikael Karlsson, Michael Gilek, and Sven Ove Hansson is very helpful, showing that more than 100 papers were devoted to the issue in the last three decades. Nevertheless, there is still more work to be done to conclude and understand the peculiarities of denial, especially on environmental issues beyond climate change, particularly issues such as land and water, and biodiversity.[19] Indeed, the identification of global warming as the most urgent ecological crisis could push other ongoing ecological and ethical disasters, their interconnections and underlying causes into the background. By allowing a focus on technical solutions and the salvation of humankind, it conveniently supports the denial of the role of the anthropocentric and speciesist industrial-consumer society that claims entitlement to the entire planet in the demise of the Earth—as Helen Kopnina, Joe Gray, Haydn Washington, and John Piccolo explicate in this volume.[20]

This line of thinking is supported by a growing literature on the ceaseless commodification and exploitation of nonhuman animals. Authors rooted in animal ethics, critical animal studies, animal philosophy, and related fields use the concept of denialism, in particular to account for our increasing meat consumption and lack of empathy for the animals slaughtered in the industries despite the efforts of educators, activists, and academia[21] to raise the awareness of the harsh realities of the "Animal Industrial Complex." Indeed, several books have exposed the drastic consequences of ignorance, alienation, and distancing within the meat-processing industry and analyzed individual and collective denialism that help sustain our meat-intensive diets. In the mid-1980s, Noëlie Vialles's pivotal work, *Le sang et la chair* (1987), offered her reflections on the separation of animals from the end product of the slaughterhouse, providing ample space for reflection of denialism in these contexts.[22] In *Every Farm a Factory: The Industrial Ideal in American Agriculture*, Deborah Fitzgerald explains how preindustrial farms were turned into complex industrial systems, partly due to the harsh economic terms in the period between the World War I and the Great Depression.[23] Understanding the history of how animals have been commodified is important to comprehend how the alienation of animals and slaughterhouse workers has taken place, as Amy Fitzgerald later reflected.[24] Jennifer Dillard and Jocelyne Porcher exposed the devastating consequences that the alienation from animals can have for humans, especially those who for one reason or another are engaged in the slaughtering process.[25] In trying to explain the functioning of our meat-eating societies, Melanie Joy has established the concept "carnism," thus labeling the carnivorous ideology that facilitates denialism and the management of cognitive dissonance.[26] In the present volume, John Sorenson and Atsuko Matsuoka, as well as Karen Lykke Syse and Kristian Bjørkdahl elaborate on the different aspects of denial related to meat production and consumption. Martin Lee Mueller and Katja Maria Hydle provide insights into denial in the salmon industry. While different forms of animal exploitation are widely criticized and analyzed as an interconnected phenomenon, not much research has explicitly used the concept to look into cases other than meat production and consumption.[27] Reingard Spannring and José De Giorgio-Schoorl therefore address the denial of horse subjectivity in a critical analysis of social science literature on human–horse relationships in this volume and Opi Outhwaite analyzes denialism among judges in habeas corpus cases on behalf of individual chimpanzees.

There are different discourses and movements grappling with the phenomenon of denialism with respect to climate change, conservation, and animal rights that do not always relate to one another without friction. However, many authors argue for a common vision of an ecologically just world and meaningful life in more-than-human communities[28] and for an intersectional approach to social, ecological, and species justice.[29] The long history of the denial of animal minds, for example, is causally related to the destruction of the biosphere.[30] Presented in the mainstream discourse as stimulus-response-driven or genetically programmed automatons, who lack agency and experiential perspective, animals are the archetypal Other, inferior to humans and an object that can be exploited for work, consumer goods, entertainment, science, or killed and displaced at liberty. This instrumental relationship served as a blueprint for the subjection of Nature, which transformed "fish into fisheries, forests and trees into timber, animals into livestock, wildlife into game, mountains into coal, seashores into beachfronts, rivers into hydroelectric factories"[31] and converted the animals' homes into resources for unlimited human use and capitalist profit.

Denialism is an apt concept to scrutinize what and how human individuals and collectives ignore, marginalize, or actively foreclose in the realms of environmental and animal ethical issues. Following this line of thought, this volume seeks to provide a cutting-edge contribution to our understanding of denial with chapters from researchers in the natural and social sciences as well as the humanities, disclosing the multifaceted appearance of the concept by approaching it from different perspectives and in different settings. Since social, ecological, and species justice are so intimately interrelated, the chapters are not ordered along this differentiation, but rather according to disciplines, thereby foregrounding a variety of denialism processes and the richness of perspectives from which they can be illuminated.

The contributions start with Susanne Stoll-Kleemann's (social-)psychological chapter. It explores altering forms of denial, which extend as far as moral disengagement, in relation to not shifting high-carbon lifestyles in light of the exacerbating climate crisis. Recent and earlier studies on the "psychology of denial" have shown that individuals regard such behavioral shifts toward a low-carbon lifestyle as extremely daunting and, therefore, deploy a number of moral-disengagement mechanisms. The chapter dives deeper into various theories, mainly from (social) psychology, which explain well why denial is still so persistent, particularly in relation to action denial. The majority of theoretical insights demonstrate convincingly the central but so far widely neglected role of emotions and self-interest in explaining continuing denialism and moral disengagement vis-à-vis established facts on damaging effects of high-carbon behavior. Further, key psychological concepts pertinent to denial are moral disengagement and motivated reasoning, which contribute to engendering a confirmation bias as well as a failure to achieve higher stages of moral development.

Taking the response (or lack of such) to climate change in Norwegian society as a case in point, Vetlesen's chapter argues that the defense mechanism of denial plays out among individual citizens in ways that are deeply structurally as well as culturally shaped. Examples are given to show how the Western culture of entitlement, in general, and powerful commercial players, in particular, shape, channel and exploit the individual's need to keep at bay the anxieties prompted by ongoing environmental degradation. The upshot is that expression in public of the anxieties in question (including anger and sadness) are suppressed for lack of support within the community. Mechanisms of relativization and alienation are shown to be key to how, say, the oil industry and international airliners manipulate the concerned citizen's attempt to cope with living in a society of organized denial.

Tomaž Grušovnik presents an argument that stresses the importance of existential anxiety with finitude as one of the factors of denialism of animal morality. The main argument of Grušovnik's chapter exposes how our uneasiness with our own mortality taints our reflection of animal morality and helps to deny it. Indeed, the problem of the existence of animal morality turns out to be largely an existential question, not a behavioral or even a psychological problem, as animals are namely culturally associated with finitude and remind humans of their own contingent and fragile existence. To avoid this awareness, we are prone to draw a conceptual demarcation line between "humans" on the one side of the ontological divide and "animals" on the other. This line then serves as what Grušovnik coins an "existential buffer zone," by offering humans an escape route when faced with awareness of impermanence: the notion of our belonging to "humanity" offers us an intellectual safe haven when faced with the impending end of our individual existence. His analysis of the notion of "uncanny proximity" argues that it is precisely because animals are so uncomfortably close to us that we seek to avoid awareness of our mortal animal existence. Grušovnik's chapter then exposes how "ethics" serves as that crucial concept which inaugurates and preserves the conceptual human–animal divide: by possessing the ability to lead an "ethical" life humans become beings of "spirit" and supposedly escape their animality which holds them captive in the world of mortals. Ascribing "moral life" to animals is thus to many theoreticians a sacrilegious idea that threatens to destroy cultural defense against premonitions of finitude and this is why the idea of animal morality may become unbearable.

Adam See provides a further philosophical analysis of denialism in the context of animal ethics. While comparative psychologists and philosophers of animal minds have traditionally been concerned with the threat of anthropomorphic bias, the twenty-first century has ushered in renewed emphasis on a related type of bias: *anthropodenial*, an epistemic predisposition to discredit evidence for mental continuity hypotheses. See's chapter references the philosophical and scientific literature on the theory of mind and shared intentionality to critically evaluate our argumentative strategies commonly used to deny humanlike cognitive capacities to animals. The chapter concludes by critically addressing the tenacious influence of the "logical problem" as a de facto mode of animal minds skepticism, particularly in the literature on human cognitive uniqueness.

Craig Taylor's chapter offers an explanation to why many of us seem impervious and unmoved by the enormous suffering of animals being raised for slaughter, the issue that both wounds and isolates the writer Elizabeth Costello in J. M. Coetzee's *The Life of Animals*. As Taylor shows, it is not the fact that they suffer that we miss. Indeed, our sense of other humans is not founded on any thoughts we might have about cognitive capacities or nociception of our fellow humans. On the contrary, that another person is a human being, something that may become an object of moral concern, is founded on all of those immediate, natural, ways one reacts to others, ways of reacting that are not themselves based on prior thoughts we might have about others, but which partially constitute the conception of what it is to be a fellow human being. Drawing from Ludwig Wittgenstein's later philosophy, Taylor shows that our attitude toward each other as moral beings is an attitude toward a soul. That is, we do not believe or have an opinion that others possess some magic "thing" like a soul, but we respond to them in such a way.

These natural modes of responsiveness partially constitute our conception of a shared kind of fellowship that might both ground and sustain moral relations between us. In this respect, Taylor argues that much of our sense of what it is to have a shared moral life with others is taken for granted, in ways rarely reflected upon. However, to reflect on them in the way that Taylor's chapter encourages, let us understand what is missing in our moral relations with other animals; our shared (but importantly different) fellowship with them. The facts concerning our suffering and theirs rather than establish such fellowship obscure and deflect it.

Martin Lee Mueller and Katja Maria Hydle discuss denialism on the basis of an anthropological study on the salmon industry in Norway. Through the lens of the paradigm shift between Enlightenment and Enlivenment theory and practice, they interpret the organization of salmon farming and its epistemological and ontological implications, and argue that an industry marketed as "the future" of human–animal relationships—spearhead of the so-called blue revolution said to be currently underway—shows symptoms of a comprehensive, structural denial of lived reality. They document practices of denying the fishes' outer and inner nature, of denying the commonwealth of ecological entanglements, and of denying nature's tendency for steady-state housekeeping. Such practices alienate the human–animal life world both technologically and conceptually. What is at stake in contemporary farming practices is not merely a question of our attitude toward other living beings, but more fundamentally, who these others are allowed to be. Against this background, the authors develop the tenets of future enlivened economic practices, practices that successfully disentangle, reject, and ultimately overcome the multiple structural denials of contemporary feedlot industries.

Karen Lykke Syse and Kristian Bjørkdahl offer historical insights into the changing presentation of meat in Norway between 1950 and 2015 and its implications for denialism in the context of meat consumption. Today's consumers meet meat in shapes that look nothing like the animal from which it was carved. In short, the removal of a reminder of origin allows us to forget, conceal, neglect, and deny the animal that this meat once was part of. How and why did we end up denying our consumption of animals at the point of retail? What was the significance of the transition from the butcher's shop to the supermarket? Lykke Syse and Bjørkdahl's chapter presents snapshots from the history of how meat has been presented and sold in the case of one particular country, Norway, from 1950 to 2015. Based on primary and secondary historical sources, they document how meat has been presented at various stages of this period, why and how changes were made, how those changes made themselves felt in the advertising of meat, and how the public responded to these changing forms.

John Sorenson and Atsuko Matsuoka's chapter contributes to the political economy of denialism by examining strategies of the animal industrial complex, using examples from the United States and the United Kingdom. Understanding institutionalized denialism means identifying vested interests with direct financial stakes in perpetuating exploitation and commodification of nonhuman animals. Ideas about consuming animals are shaped by massive agribusiness interests that invest billions of dollars in advertising and marketing efforts to influence consumers' attitudes and understanding, as well as lobbying and political spending to ensure that their activities can continue unimpeded by exposure from animal and environmental activists. Drawing on the work of sociologist Stanley Cohen, the authors identify rhetorical techniques and stories that mobilize preexisting cultural attitudes and practices and recast the endless killing as part of the natural order as primary vehicles of denial. In this way, animal suffering and death disappear as a problem and hindrance to further consumption. The chapter concludes that it is important to include animal rights in the imagining of "an alternative ethical landscape" shaped by "a sense of responsibility for the safety of others" and a commitment to justice—regardless of species.

Helen Kopnina, Joe Gray, Haydn Washington, and John Piccolo critically turn to a growing discourse in conservation and sustainability, which claims that, despite the clear evidence of human-caused biodiversity loss, and rapidly declining environmental indicators, nature is, in fact, thriving. They argue that there are many reasons to be skeptical of optimism when it comes to conservation, and show that techno-eco-optimism is both misplaced and counterproductive for addressing society's great environmental challenges. Hence, they critique the ecologically dystopian future that would result from the strategies championed by techno-eco-optimists. Eco-optimism also disregards the broader ethical ramifications of species extinctions, being a strategy of denial. At the end the authors turn to an eco-realistic vision, presenting arguments for conservation grounded in ecological ethics.

Reingard Spannring and José De Giorgio-Schoorl examine how deep-rooted the objectification of horses is in the social science literature of horse–human relationships. Bringing the perspective of a critical and activist ethology into dialogue with the disciplinary approaches, concepts, and research practices applied in these studies of human–horse relations, a number of obstacles will be unveiled that reproduce the denial of horses as protagonists of their own life. These obstacles range from more visible anthropocentric and speciesist attitudes to some research-specific factors such as disciplinary blinkers, the concept of agency in itself and the lack of critical engagement with power relationships and their consequences. Together they corroborate a picture of horses who are tailored to fit our society and our desires as natural. The chapter sheds light on the necessity for a broader horizon, both intellectual and in terms of a practical ability to experience otherness and to create space for animal subjectivity. Subjectivity is thus not primarily a theoretical concept but an ethical foundation of what it means to be a subject and of the coexistence between horses and humans.

Finally, Opi Outhwaite draws attention to the increased engagement between law and "the question of the animal." As a discipline, law has tentatively recognized the "animal turn" while in legal practice an emerging jurisprudence addresses the position of animals in law, most prominently the possibility that animals be recognized as legal persons to afford individual nonhuman animals' certain legal rights. While an existing body of work has critiqued the merits and flaws of the legal and moral arguments raised, there has been little analysis of the ways in which judges in these cases approach these issues. This analysis is important because the law, including through judicial decision-making, has direct implications for the individual parties involved but also plays a role in shaping wider societal attitudes. At the same time, critical legal scholars recognize that law is not merely a neutral objective organizing force but can be a means of maintaining oppressive structures and hierarchies. This chapter brings new analytical insights to the field by applying the lens of denial to judicial decision-making in a series of related cases in which the writ of habeas corpus was sought on behalf of individual chimpanzees in order that their confinement may be challenged in court. An analysis indicates that three particular forms of denial can be identified—legalism, distancing, and an appeal to higher authority. These tactics prevent the petitions from succeeding, even where the legal merits of the arguments are at times recognized and where individual judges have expressed their sympathy (but, ultimately, helplessness) to the situation.

NOTES

1. Jacquelin Burgess, Carolyn M. Harrison, and Petra Filius, "Environmental Communication and the Cultural Politics of Environmental Citizenship," *Environment and Planning A* 30 (1998): 1445–60.

2. Anja Kollmuss and Julian Agyeman, "Mind the Gap: Why Do People Act Environmentally and What are the Barriers to Pro-Environmental Behavior?" *Environmental Education Research* 8, no. 3 (2002): 239–60.

3. Ibid.

4. For a detailed presentation of the concept of "denial" in psychoanalytic theory and practice, see Eli L. Edelstein, Donald L. Nathanson, and Andrew M. Stone, eds., *Denial: A Clarification of Concepts and Research* (New York, NY: Plenum Press, 1989). Also, Slavoj Žižek's reflections of contemporary society and politics draw heavily from "disavowal" (see, for instance, the chapter "The Political and Its Disavowals" in his *The Ticklish Subject: The Absent Centre of Political Ontology* (London: Verso, 1999)).

5. Leon Festinger, *A Theory of Cognitive Dissonance* (Stanford, CA: Stanford University Press, 1957).

6. Stanley Cohen, *States of Denial: Knowing About Atrocities and Suffering* (Cambridge: Polity Press, 2001).

7. Eviatar Zerubavel, *The Elephant in The Room: Silence and Denial in Everyday Life* (Oxford: Oxford University Press, 2006).

8. See Robert Trivers, *The Folly of Fools: The Logic of Deceit and Self-Deception in Human Life* (New York, NY: Basic Books, 2011).

9. Paul Ehrlich and Anne Ehrlich, *Betrayal of Science and Reason: How Anti-Environmental Rhetoric Threatens Our Future* (New York, NY: Shearwater Books, 1998); Haydn Washington and John Cook, *Climate Change Denial: Heads in the Sand* (New York, NY: Earthscan, 2011).

10. Social psychology: see, for example, Susanne Stoll-Kleeman, Tim O'Riordan, and Carlo C. Jaeger, "The Psychology of Denial Concerning Climate Mitigation Measures: Evidence from Swiss Focus Groups," *Global Environmental Change* 11, no. 2 (2001): 107–17; philosophy: see, for example, Arne Johan Vetlesen, *The Denial of Nature: Environmental Philosophy in the Era of Global Capitalism* (London: Routledge, 2015); Tomaž Grušovnik, "Environmental Denial: Why We Fail to Change Our Environmentally Damaging Practices," *Synthesis Philosophica* 27, no. 1 (2012); sociology: see, for example, Kari Marie Norgaard, *Living in Denial. Climate Change, Emotions, and Everyday Life* (Cambridge, MA: The MIT Press, 2011); linguistics: see, for example, Arran Stibbe, *Ecolinguistics: Language, Ecology and the Stories We Live By* (New York, NY: Routledge, 2015); ecocriticism: see,

for example, Brian Deyo, "Ecophobia, the Anthropocene, and the Denial of Death," *ISLE: Interdisciplinary Studies in Literature and Environment* 26, no. 2 (2019): 442–55; ecofeminism: see, for example, Val Plumwood, "Ecofeminist Analysis and the Culture of Ecological Denial," in *Feminist Ecologies. Changing Environments in the Anthropocene*, ed. Lara Stevens, Peta Tait, and Denise Varney (Cham, Switzerland: Palgrave Macmillan, 2018); natural sciences: see, for example, Washington and Cook, *Climate Change Denial*; science studies: see, for example, Naomi Oreskes and Erik Conway, *Merchants of Doubt. How a Handful of Scientists Obscured the Truth on Issues from Tobacco Smoke to Global Warming* (New York, NY: Bloomsbury Press, 2010).

11. Norgaard, *Living in Denial*, 80.

12. Ibid., 91–95.

13. Washington and Cook, *Climate Change Denial*.

14. Ibid., 44.

15. Ibid., 96.

16. Ibid., 93–94.

17. Vetlesen, *The Denial of Nature*, 8.

18. Ibid., 8.

19. See Karin Edvardsson Björnberg, Mikael Karlsson, Michael Gilek, and Sven Ove Hansson, "Climate and Environmental Science Denial: A Review of the Scientific Literature Published in 1990–2015," *Journal of Cleaner Production* 167 (2017).

20. See also: Eileen Crist, "Beyond the Climate Crisis: A Critique of Climate Change Discourse," *Telos* 141 (2007); Lynn White, "The Historical Roots of our Ecological Crisis," *Science* 155, no. 3767 (1967).

21. Reingard Spannring and Tomaž Grušovnik, "Leaving the Meatrix? Transformative Learning and Denialism in the Case of Meat Consumption," *Environmental Education Research* 25, no. 8 (2018).

22. Noëlie Vialles's *Le sang et la chair*, was originally published in French in 1987 and appeared in English translation in 1994 as *Animal to Edible* (Cambridge: Cambridge University Press, 1994).

23. Deborah Fitzgerald, *Every Farm a Factory: The Industrial Ideal in American Agriculture* (New Haven, CT: Yale University Press, 2003).

24. Amy Fitzgerald, *Animals as Food: (Re)connecting Production, Processing, Consumption, And Impacts* (East Lansing, MI: Michigan State University Press, 2015).

25. See Jennifer Dillard, "A Slaughterhouse Nightmare: Psychological Harm Suffered by Slaughterhouse Employees and the Possibility of Redress through Legal Reform," *Georgetown Journal on Poverty Law & Policy* 15, no. 2 (2008); Jocelyne Porcher, "The Relationship Between Workers and Animals in the Pork Industry: A Shared Suffering," *Journal of Agriculture and Environmental Ethics* 24 (2018).

26. Melanie Joy, *Why We Love Dogs, Eat Pigs, and Wear Cows: An Introduction to Carnism* (Cork: Red Wheel Weiser, 2011).

27. On denialism in other areas of the instrumentalization of animals, for example laboratory experiments, fur farming, as well as leisure industry, see Tomaž Grušovnik

and Maša Blaznik, "Denied Relationship: Moral Stress in the Vocational Killing of Non-Human Animals," in *Animals and Business Ethics*, ed. Nathalie Thomas (Dordrecht: Springer, forthcoming).

28. Paul Waldau, "Venturing beyond the Tyranny of Small Differences. The Animal Protection Movement, Conservation, and Environmental Education," in *Ignoring Nature No More. The Case for Compassionate Conservation*, ed. Marc Bekoff (Chicago, IL: University of Chicago Press, 2013); Josefine Donovan, "Sympathy and Interspecies Care: Toward a Unified Theory of Eco- and Animal Liberation," in *Critical Theory and Animal Liberation*, ed. John Sanbonmatsu (Lanham, MD: Rowman & Littlefield, 2001).

29. David Nibert, *Animal Oppression and Human Violence. Domesecration, Capitalism, and Global Conflict* (New York, NY: Columbia University Press, 2013); Anthony J. Nocella II, John Sorenson, Kim Socha, and Atsuko Matsuoka, eds., *Defining Critical Animal Studies. An Intersectional Social Justice Approach for Liberation* (New York, NY: Peter Lang, 2014).

30. Eileen Crist, "Ecocide and the Extinction of Animal Minds," in *Ignoring Nature no More. The Case for Compassionate Conservation*, ed. Marc Bekoff (London: University of Chicago Press, 2013).

31. Ibid., 55.

BIBLIOGRAPHY

Björnberg, Karin Edvardsson, Mikael Karlsson, Michael Gilek, and Sven Ove Hansson. "Climate and Environmental Science Denial: A Review of the Scientific Literature Published in 1990–2015." *Journal of Cleaner Production* 167 (2017): 229–41. doi:10.1016/j.jclepro.2017.08.066.

Burgess, Jacquelin, Carolyn M. Harrison, and Petra Filius. "Environmental Communication and the Cultural Politics of Environmental Citizenship." *Environment and Planning A* 30 (1998): 1445–60.

Cohen, Stanley. *States of Denial: Knowing About Atrocities and Suffering*. Cambridge: Polity Press, 2001.

Crist, Eileen. "Beyond the Climate Crisis: A Critique of Climate Change Discourse." *Telos* 141 (2007): 29–55.

Crist, Eileen. "Ecocide and the Extinction of Animal Minds." In *Ignoring Nature no More. The Case for Compassionate Conservation*, edited by Marc Bekoff, 45–63. London: University of Chicago Press, 2013.

Deyo, Brian. "Ecophobia, the Anthropocene, and the Denial of Death." *ISLE: Interdisciplinary Studies in Literature and Environment* 26, no. 2 (2019): 442–55.

Dillard, Jennifer. "A Slaughterhouse Nightmare: Psychological Harm Suffered by Slaughterhouse Employees and the Possibility of Redress through Legal Reform." *Georgetown Journal on Poverty Law & Policy* 15, no. 2 (2008): 391–408.

Donovan, Josefine. "Sympathy and Interspecies Care: Toward a Unified Theory of Eco- and Animal Liberation." In *Critical Theory and Animal Liberation*, edited by John Sanbonmatsu, 277–94. Lanham, MD: Rowman & Littlefield, 2001.

Edelstein, Eli L., Donald L. Nathanson, and Andrew M. Stone, eds. *Denial: A Clarification of Concepts and Research.* New York, NY: Plenum Press, 1989.

Ehrlich, Paul, and Anne Ehrlich. *Betrayal of Science and Reason: How Anti-Environmental Rhetoric Threatens Our Future.* New York, NY: Shearwater Books, 1998.

Festinger, Leon. *A Theory of Cognitive Dissonance.* Stanford, CA: Stanford University Press, 1957.

Fitzgerald, Amy J. *Animals as Food: (Re)connecting Production, Processing, Consumption, and Impacts.* East Lansing, MI: Michigan State University Press, 2015.

Fitzgerald, Deborah. *Every Farm a Factory: The Industrial Ideal in American Agriculture.* New Haven, CT: Yale University Press, 2003.

Grušovnik, Tomaž. "Environmental Denial: Why We Fail to Change Our Environmentally Damaging Practices." *Synthesis Philosophica* 27, no. 1 (2012): 91–106. https://hrcak.srce.hr/index.php?show=clanak&id_clanak_jezik=139410 &lang=en.

Grušovnik, Tomaž, and Maša Blaznik. "Denied Relationship: Moral Stress in the Vocational Killing of Non-Human Animals." In *Animals and Business Ethics*, edited by Nathalie Thomas. Dordrecht: Springer, forthcoming.

Joy, Melanie. *Why We Love Dogs, Eat Pigs, and Wear Cows: An Introduction to Carnism.* Cork: Red Wheel Weiser, 2011.

Kollmuss, Anja, and Julian Agyeman. "Mind the Gap: Why Do People Act Environmentally and What Are the Barriers to Pro-Environmental Behavior?" *Environmental Education Research* 8, no. 3 (2002): 239–60.

Nibert, David. *Animal Oppression and Human Violence. Domesecration, Capitalism, and Global Conflict.* New York, NY: Columbia University Press, 2013.

Nocella, Anthony J. II, John Sorenson, Kim Socha, and Atsuko Matsuoka, eds. *Defining Critical Animal Studies. An Intersectional Social Justice Approach for Liberation.* New York, NY: Peter Lang, 2014.

Norgaard, Kari Marie. *Living in Denial. Climate Change, Emotions, and Everyday Life.* Cambridge, MA: The MIT Press, 2011.

Oreskes, Naomi, and Erik Conway. *Merchants of Doubt. How a Handful of Scientists Obscured the Truth on Issues from Tobacco Smoke to Global Warming.* New York, NY: Bloomsbury Press, 2010.

Plumwood, Val. "Ecofeminist Analysis and the Culture of Ecological Denial." In *Feminist Ecologies. Changing Environments in the Anthropocene*, edited by Lara Stevens, Peta Tait, and Denise Varney, 97–112. Cham: Palgrave Macmillan, 2018.

Porcher, Jocelyne. "The Relationship between Workers and Animals in the Pork Industry: A Shared Suffering." *Journal of Agriculture and Environmental Ethics* 24 (2018): 3–17.

Spannring, Reingard, and Tomaž Grušovnik. "Leaving the Meatrix? Transformative Learning and Denialism in the Case of Meat Consumption." *Environmental Education Research* 25, no. 8 (2018): 1190–99.

Stibbe, Arran. *Ecolinguistics: Language, Ecology and the Stories We Live By.* New York, NY: Routledge, 2015.

Stoll-Kleeman, Susanne, Tim O'Riordan, and Carlo C. Jaeger. "The Psychology of Denial Concerning Climate Mitigation Measures: Evidence from Swiss Focus Groups." *Global Environmental Change* 11, no. 2 (2001): 107–17.

Trivers, Robert. *The Folly of Fools: The Logic of Deceit and Self-Deception in Human Life*. New York, NY: Basic Books, 2011.

Vetlesen, Arne Johan. *The Denial of Nature: Environmental Philosophy in the Era of Global Capitalism*. London: Routledge, 2015.

Vialles, Noëlie. *Animal to Edible*. Cambridge: Cambridge University Press, 1994.

Waldau, Paul. "Venturing beyond the Tyranny of Small Differences. The Animal Protection Movement, Conservation, and Environmental Education." In *Ignoring Nature No More. The Case for Compassionate Conservation*, edited by Marc Bekoff, 28–43. Chicago, IL: University of Chicago Press, 2013.

Washington, Haydn, and John Cook. *Climate Change Denial: Heads in the Sand*. New York, NY: Earthscan, 2011.

White, Lynn. "The Historical Roots of our Ecological Crisis." *Science* 155, no. 3767 (1967): 1203–7.

Zerubavel, Eviatar. *The Elephant in The Room: Silence and Denial in Everyday Life*. Oxford: Oxford University Press, 2006.

Žižek, Slavoj. *The Ticklish Subject: The Absent Centre of Political Ontology*. London: Verso, 1999.

Chapter 1

From Denial to Moral Disengagement

How Integrating Fundamental Insights from Psychology Can Help Us Better Understand Ongoing Inaction in the Light of an Exacerbating Climate Crisis

Susanne Stoll-Kleemann

THE ROLE OF DENIAL AND RELATED CONCEPTS IN THE CLIMATE CRISIS

It is obvious that the mitigation of dangerous climate change is imperative to limit severe and prolonged public health dangers, social and economic disruption, forced migration, and increased regional conflict, as well as vast swathes of destruction to biota and ecosystems.[1] Secure scientific evidence of climate change from all over the globe has become more universally accepted, including the encompassing broad public and political recognition of the virtually indisputable role of human influence.[2] As the climate crisis is mainly produced by the world's wealthiest countries, their high-income inhabitants, and a cross-national global elite, personal response to addressing it is presented here as being mainly a moral issue. The consequences of the climate crisis threaten the key human rights to life, health, and decent subsistence, as droughts, floods, and other natural calamities undermine food security. There is also widespread evidence that the obligation of nations to help their citizens avoid harm is regularly violated.[3]

Nevertheless, neither political responses such as the Paris Agreement, which aims to limit global temperatures "well below" 2°C above preindustrial levels, nor personal or further societal promises are sufficiently implemented.[4] This observation manifests itself in different forms of continuing climate denial, such as "climate silence" and "moral corruption." Being in denial in general can be understood as exhibiting a kind of "emotionally self-protective

17

self-deception"[5] to "close the mind off to unwanted conclusions."[6] Climate silence is defined as "socially constructed" or even a "conspiracy of silence" based on people tacitly agreeing to "outwardly ignore something of which they are all personally aware" and the factors that hinder action on mitigation and adaptation in the case of the climate crisis.[7] A concrete variety of climate silence is avoiding facing certain "more disturbing" implications of the climate crisis, which can be called "implicatory denial,"[8] that is, when "information is selected to fit existing perceptual frames and information which is too threatening"[9] and finally manifests itself in "silence about climate change's moral aspects."[10] This is explained in more detail later in the theoretical insights on motivated reasoning.

"Moral corruption" is a closely related phenomenon. Gardiner argues that even if people accept that climate change poses a serious moral challenge, our resolve to tackle it is threatened by "corruption that targets our ways of talking and thinking, and so prevents us from even seeing the problem in the right way."[11] This has been confirmed by Markowitz and Shariff, who discovered that climate change confuses information processing,[12] making it difficult to appreciate that there are indeed victims (in other places and in the future).

They also point to the justification called "blamelessness of unintentional action," in which the prospect of damaging outcomes is played down just because they are too unsettling to contemplate and are judged less harshly than equally severe but intentionally caused ones.[13] Shue introduced the very useful distinction into the discussion on climate change between subsistence and luxury emissions[14] as a moral problem: While individuals—of course—should not be blamed for the emissions produced in the course of meeting basic needs or that result from deficient infrastructure, they are, however, accountable for their profligate emissions because they have the freedom to decide to reduce "unnecessary" greenhouse gas emissions (GHG), for example by decreasing their consumption of animal products or flying less frequently.[15]

Against this background, the aim here is to illuminate the degree to which (social) psychological theories explain continuing high-carbon behaviors, often based on denial. Optimally, something can be learned from their application to climate change as a moral problem to help deflate denial and hence deflect high-carbon lifestyles.

EMPIRICAL EVIDENCE BASED ON DISSONANCE AND MORAL DISENGAGEMENT

In two studies on "the psychology of denial," the author and colleagues[16] empirically and theoretically investigated why Europeans continue to undertake high-emitting behaviors in light of the climate crisis.

In the first study, from 2001, based on focus-group research in Switzerland, four "interpretations" of perceived barriers to action were detected. (1) The tragedy-of-the-commons interpretation is the belief that any personal costs are greater than any benefits to others.[17] (2) The comfort interpretation reveals the reluctance to abandon habits and preferred lifestyles associated with self-identity. (3) The governance-distrust interpretation summarizes the observation that economic interests are predominant and powerful, accompanied by a feeling that government fails to deliver supportive politics and actions. (4) The managerial-fix interpretation describes the belief in technological solutions and regulatory innovation.[18]

In the current study, the relevance of social–psychological theories for explaining people's subdued climate-related behavior was shown, among them Festinger's theory of cognitive dissonance,[19] in which individuals experiencing dissonance seek resolution or denial. Festinger studied the psychological effects of new, inconsistent information on one's existing beliefs and observed a natural, psychological resistance to belief revision as a result of dissonant information.[20] What is important here is the emotional component in subjects' responses. Bardon summarizes Festinger's research and its importance for denial explanation as follows:

> Cognitively dissonant information can also be experienced as personally disruptive—undermining the comfort one feels in thinking one has a good grasp of things—and therefore be anxiety inducing. This discomfort spurs an unconscious drive to resolve the dissonance by discounting or otherwise dismissing information that contradicts existing beliefs. . . . Festinger found that cognitive dissonance can produce intense emotional discomfort when the particular change in thinking demanded by the dissonant information threatens a representation of reality to which the subject is emotionally attached. Information can be threatening to the self because it conflicts with one's desires, expectations, sense of control, or cultural or political identity.[21]

Recent research by Norgaard[22] on climate change denial details the role of emotions because they affect cognition, while playing down the roles of knowledge and caring. In particular, she identifies feelings of helplessness and guilt as reasons for climate-change denial. This is—on a more general level—confirmed by a review of recent studies that shows how emotions drive actual moral behavior and that emotions are instrumental in fueling real-life moral actions such as those on denial-driven high-carbon behavior.[23]

The second study—based on a representative nationwide online survey of 1,032 people living in Germany—showed that the overall majority of respondents (93.9%) think that people are or will be notably affected by climate change.[24] Nearly half the interviewees (47.9%) feel that they are already being affected by climate change, and only 6.1% think that climate change has no effect either on them or anyone else. The majority, 77 percent, expressed the opinion that not enough is being done to reduce climate change, 7.4 percent concluded that enough is being done, and 5.5 percent think that current efforts are doing more than is actually necessary. Partially contradictory, about 70 percent of the respondents blame advanced developed countries, business and industry, and society as a whole. About 60 percent think that politicians are responsible, and half (52%) regard each individual person as being responsible.[25]

In the second study, Festinger's theory was enriched by Bandura's psychosocial mechanisms of selective moral disengagement,[26] in which he describes selective disengagement of moral self-sanctions as an impediment to individual and collective action designed to reduce global warming and other moral problems.[27] Selective moral disengagement adopts a form of moral action framed as "the product of the reciprocal interplay of cognitive, affective and social influences" and "personal agency operates within a broad network of socio-structural influences."[28] By means of separating moral reactions from inhumane conduct and cutting out self-condemnation, this convinces people that ethical standards do not apply in a particular context.[29] Thus it involves a process of reinterpreting damaging behavior as being morally acceptable.[30]

Eight psychosocial mechanisms operate here at both the individual and social system levels (see figure 1.1). The first three operate where people

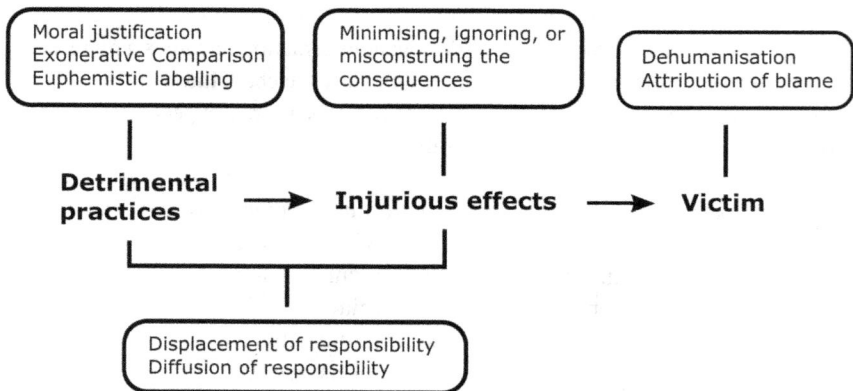

Figure 1.1   Psychosocial Mechanisms through Which Moral Self-Sanctions Are Selectively Disengaged from Detrimental Practices at Different Points in the Exercise of Moral Agency. See Albert Bandura, "Impeding Ecological Sustainability Through Selective Moral Disengagement," *International Journal of Innovation and Sustainable Development* 2, no. 1 (2007): 10. Graphic created by author.

translate harmful practices into worthy ones through social and moral justification, exonerative social comparison, and euphemistic language. Through two further mechanisms, called displacement and diffusion of responsibility, people are released from their personal accountability by shifting the responsibility to others. By diffusion of responsibility, moral control can be suspended by subdividing activities that seem harmless in themselves. The final two mechanisms are responsible for marginalizing and blaming the victims, for example, for worsening ecological conditions.[31]

Applying this theory to the data of the second survey, five of the eight psychosocial mechanisms described by Bandura (see earlier) are identified. The first and most widely used one was displacement of responsibility. Not surprisingly, politics and business and industry are seen as highly interwoven—almost always in a negative way—and are frequently mentioned together. In addition, a particular group—"the rich"—is characterized through the notion of being too greedy. A final subgroup frequently named is "egoistic people" who enjoy "too high a living standard" and who are seen as not being willing to change their lives because of ignorance and/or comfort requirements.[32]

These results confirm the two results of the 2001 study, namely the governance-distrust interpretation (government fails to deliver supportive politics and actions together with the observation that economic interests are predominant and powerful) and the comfort interpretation (reluctance to abandon habits and preferred lifestyles). The governance-distrust interpretation is even more pronounced in the repeated fusion of politics, business, and industry acting in a way that undermines democracy. Concerning the comfort-interpretation perspective, respondents today state more forcefully than in the 2001 study that it is the other people who are not prepared to change their luxury lifestyles and habits and who are a primary cause of emissions increases. In the present study, a minority assert that they do not want to change anything. That people blame other individual emitters is in line with attribution theory.[33] In particular, the two mechanisms called "fundamental attribution error," which refers to the tendency to overemphasize the role of personal traits in influencing the behavior of others, and "self-serving bias," where external circumstances, such as lobbying, bias and shape behavior to justify support of these reactions.[34]

Social, economic, and moral justifications constitute another disengagement mechanism that was discovered. Economic justifications are dominant as a subcategory, but examples of social and moral justifications can also be found, although to a lesser degree. An example of the first subcategory is the contention that "There are a lot of things that could be changed, but they are simply too expensive" (P983, P982).[35] Examples of social and moral justification are displayed in the following quote: "Protecting the climate leads to exclusion from your circle of friends" (P129, P861).

This reasoning is hard to change because people strive to preserve a sense of self-worth while causing harm through their activities.[36] One example is the (false) claim by members of some professional groups, such as scientists, who argue that very high-carbon behavior such as flying is "necessary," for example, to communicate research results personally at conferences, or that doing research in very distant places is a career-enhancing component of their work. In interviews, they greatly enjoy the privileges linked to their professional activity, including travel to interesting places.[37]

Disregard, distortion, or denial of harmful effects still forms an observable mechanism. When people act to serve their self-interest but produce damaging outcomes, they turn away from the harm they cause or seek to minimize it. They may also attempt to discredit the scientific evidence of harm. Although not many respondents to our present survey deny climate change as such, there are some who argue that warnings about a climate crisis are exaggerated and "scaremongering."[38]

The mechanism of diffusing responsibility for detrimental behavior, such as emitting GHG, as the most discussed issue in climate ethics (also known as the "individual causal inefficacy") is also a widely used argument of the respondents. Nevertheless, in this context, Peeters and colleagues rightly remark that the argument that "the greenhouse gases of any particular individual make no observable contribution to global warming . . ." is ". . . wrong because the expected amount of harm is greater than not emitting."[39]

The final mechanism, called exonerative (or advantageous) comparison, is used by respondents to emphasize the higher GHG emissions of China and/ or the United States compared with those of Germany, or to compare their behavior to people who practice a more luxury-carbon-intensive lifestyle. Merely pointing the finger at the worst offenders encourages comparison with people who emit more greenhouse gases to let the avoider "off the hook."[40] Overall, the conclusion is that there is still denial, but it becomes more indirect by favoring displacing responsibility or even assigning guilt to others (e.g., government, business and industry, lobbies, "the rich," the "egoistic people"), thus somewhat mitigating the refusal to be a first mover or to undertake more than merely low-cost behavior.

DIVING DEEPER INTO THEORETICAL ANALYSIS: THE ROLE OF MORAL DEVELOPMENT AND EMOTIONS IN MOTIVATED REASONING

Two more lines of theoretical insights, in addition to the mechanisms of selective moral disengagement and the closely related cognitive dissonance, help to provide better understanding of why individuals do not directly deny climate change but continue to contribute to the harm that the climate crisis causes by going on with their high-carbon lifestyles. One line of research is based on Kohlberg's well-known Theory of Moral Development.[41] The other line refers to "motivated reasoning," perfectly summarized in Adrian Bardon's recent, wide-ranging book *The Truth About Denial.*[42]

The Role of Moral Development

Kohlberg's Theory of Moral Development is very relevant for understanding the importance of individual differences within the psychology of climate change—including the role of denial—because it explains that moral reasoning, the basis for ethical behavior, is not achievable for everybody to the same degree, which presents a barrier caused by problematic self-centeredness to low-carbon behavior. Several new studies argue for the consideration of Kohlberg's theory toward explaining climate-(un)just behavior and environment-related behavior more generally.[43] This is the case because an individual's moral development influences personal norms, the influence of social norms on the person's behavior, the willingness to assume individual responsibility, and the cost–benefit calculation of a specific person.

The theory distinguishes six developmental stages, each more adequate at responding to moral dilemmas than its predecessor.[44] Kohlberg determined that the process of moral development was principally concerned with justice and that it continued throughout the individual's life.[45] The six stages of moral development occur in phases of pre-conventional, conventional, and post-conventional morality.[46] Kohlberg's scale is about how people justify behaviors and generally hypothesizes that moral behavior is more responsible, consistent, and predictable from people at higher (moral) levels. Although what is known as the "Kohlberg–Gilligan debate" on the role of gender is well-perceived in the various scientific communities, the majority of studies ultimately have demonstrated that no model is more powerful than Kohlberg's in explaining moral development.[47] A large number of empirical studies clearly prove that Kohlberg's various levels and stages, described in detail later, are universally applicable in very different cultural contexts. His theory has been tested successfully in the Bahamas, Mexico, Puerto Rico, Honduras, India, Pakistan, Indonesia, Israel, Turkey, Iran, Taiwan, Thailand, Japan, New Zealand, Nigeria, Iceland, the United Kingdom, Finland, Germany, and Poland.[48]

The pre-conventional level of moral reasoning is solely concerned with the self in an egocentric manner and focuses largely on external consequences. It is characterized by an obedience-and-punishment orientation at the first stage and a self-interest orientation ("What's in it for me?") at the second. Arguably, too many people stay on this level, constituting a major obstacle to change in regard to reducing denial and ultimately toward increased climate action. Low-carbon behavior is only adopted for egoistic motives such as fear of punishment or an anticipated benefit such as economic advantage.

The stages of the medium level, called conventional morality, are characterized by exponents' placing high relevance on the approval of others and maintaining good interpersonal relationships via social norms and conformity at stage three, and an authority and maintaining social order orientation at stage four. Most active members of society remain at this stage, at which morality is still predominantly dictated by outside forces.[49] Authority is internalized but not questioned, and reasoning is based on the norms of the group to which the person belongs. At this level, an individual obeys rules and follows society's norms, even when there are no consequences either for compliance or disregard. Adherence to rules and conventions is somewhat rigid, however, and a rule's appropriateness or fairness is seldom questioned.[50] Here, at least some opportunities to move people toward less harmful behavior can be identified, but only if social norms—which are currently too consumption oriented and directed toward high-carbon behavior—shift.

At the final level, called post-conventional morality, people live according to their own set of ethical principles, which include basic human rights such as life, liberty, and justice, and apply to all people worldwide rather than to a particular group (e.g., the family, the city of residence, and/or fellow citizens). Exponents' thinking follows the principle of global contexts, but they also act locally. To them, rules are not absolute dictates articulated by a political system and/or authority that must be obeyed without question. In addition, the individual is prepared to act to defend these principles, even if it means going against the rest of society and having to pay the consequences of disapproval.[51]

People who are at this final level must be regarded as the great hope for the shift from denial to morally more desirable low-carbon behavior because, according to Kohlberg, the probability of translating moral judgments into adequate action increases with the level of moral development achieved. At this final level, the correlation between judgment and action is at least 75 percent. Furthermore, people are prepared to overcome many more—and higher—situational barriers and to take all kinds of different "costs" into account to implement their moral judgment in actions. This is the case because the increasing consistency between thought and deed at each higher level leads to a reduction of behavior patterns such as moral disengagement being used as excuse.[52]

This is confirmed by Habermas, who remarked that the only individuals motivated by the "unforced force of the better argument" are those who can be identified as being on the post-conventional level and have something like a "post-conventional identity or mentality."[53] Individuals on the post-conventional level manifest much more independence from their emotions and desires, the expectations of others, cultural norms, and recognition structures because their moral development is based on a Weltanschauung whose focus tends away from self-centeredness, which results in their seeking the well-being of others in their actions. Their moral norms work as an authority that negotiates between multiple and contradictory interests and leads to a manageable structure. Although the majority of people apparently prefer post-conventional arguments to pre-conventional ones, for ideas to be transformed to action, the individual seems to need a certain moral competence that permits and facilitates post-conventional approaches.[54]

People on the post-conventional level can serve as role models for those on the conventional level because the latter mostly derive their moral views from those around them, and only a minority think ethical principles through for themselves.[55] Consequently, it is necessary to focus on post-conventional level people first, as they already are—and will continue to be—the first movers in the necessary moral and behavioral transformation. Although moral behavior can be motivated by external stimuli, for example, by educational institutions, the perception of practical examples and role models for morally right (here, low-carbon) behavior is of particular relevance because it reduces the costs of the change of one's own lifestyle and can even make change attractive if the pioneers are highly esteemed individuals.

Motivated Reasoning, the Role of Emotions, Social and Cultural Identity

The second important strand of research is summarized by Bardon in the convincing demonstration that the essence of "denial is the involvement of the emotionally motivated rejection (or embrace) of a factual claim in the face of strong evidence to the contrary."[56] Importantly, Bardon focuses a lot of attention on the phenomenon of motivated reasoning as the main driver of denial and shows that evidence from social psychology proves that information processing is often "motivated by emotions" because they are "an integral part of judgment, motivation, and belief at both the psychological and neurological levels. For example, we know that one's emotional state can affect how much attention is paid to aspects of a situation."[57]

The most obvious emotional factor that can implicitly bias information processing is self-interest, for example, to validate our moral worthiness, intelligence, and/or competence or to maintain beliefs and worldviews that favor the social group with which we identify. To the extent that one's self-concept is tied up with one's membership in a group, then evidence working either for or against the status of that group should be expected to trigger, respectively, a positive or negative emotional response.[58] Strongly related,

Sociologist Kari Marie Norgaard identifies "norms of attention" as protecting cultural identity, reducing dissonance, and alleviating negative emotions like guilt and insecurity.[59] Unfortunately, a person in a state of denial is motivated to stay in denial because maintaining beliefs is emotionally very satisfying and it is easy to continue on this path by treating incoming information in a biased manner. Overall, denial is about maintaining self-identity and self-worth and avoiding emotional distress brought on by the conflict between what one wants to believe and some incoming inconvenient information.[60]

Some hope is provided by Stone and Fernandez who conclude—after a detailed literature review—that people can be motivated by cognitive dissonance to perform pro-social behavior when the inconsistency they experience follows from an act of hypocrisy having its greatest effect when people publicly advocate the importance of the respective pro-social behavior and then are privately reminded of their own recent personal failures to perform the target behavior.[61]

CLIMATE CHANGE DENIAL AS CHANGING AND MULTIFACETED PHENOMENON

The majority of people, including the respondents of the two studies presented earlier, know and care about climate change and its harmful effects. Nevertheless, there is denial of appropriate climate action (low-carbon behavior), the reasons for which are located at different levels such as at that of individual egoism and self-interest and related comfort and habits. This confirms that the theories of Bandura (on Selective Moral Disengagement), Festinger (on Cognitive Dissonance), and Kohlberg (on Moral Development) have a high degree of explanatory power for climate action denial.

The summary of the empirical results of the two European studies should also have made clear that it is important to note that powerful political elites and economic lobbies, "deliberately misinform the public on various issues." In particular, "false claims about climate science by vested interests and their allies find a receptive audience in those with preexisting anti-government inclinations."[62] This is why the study of problems caused by the public and private misunderstanding of reality needs to look at psychological processes that allow bias and self-deception to thrive. "Denial is convenient, comforting, and occasionally even useful; but it also cripples our ability to face urgent public policy issues effectively, and thus stands in the way of essential social, political, and economic changes. It pollutes our culture and retards our individual intellectual and moral development."[63]

This applies significantly to the climate crisis, and it can be argued that to overcome the harmful effects of climate action denial, we have to understand the phenomenon of denial even better. Integrating insights from psychology is very helpful in this respect. We need a better understanding of the causes and mechanisms of denialism regarding the climate crisis, including profound comprehension of how people can progress as individuals and make better decisions for themselves. This, in turn, requires better understanding of the causes and mechanisms of denial as it manifests itself in the private sphere.

NOTES

1. Susanne Stoll-Kleemann and Tim O'Riordan, "Revisiting the Psychology of Denial Concerning Low-Carbon Behaviors: From Moral Disengagement to Generating Social Change," *Sustainability* 12, no. 3 (2020): 935.

2. Intergovernmental Panel on Climate Change, *AR5 Synthesis Report: Climate Change 2014* (Geneva, 2014), 48; Anthony Leiserowitz et al., *Politics & Global Warming, October 2017* (New Haven, CT: Yale Program on Climate Change Communication, 2017), 8.

3. Simon Caney, "Climate Change, Human Rights and Moral Thresholds," in *Climate Ethics: Essential Readings* (New York, NY: Oxford University Press, 2010), 163; Keely Boom, Julie-Anne Richards, and Stephen Leonard, *Climate Justice: The International Momentum Towards Climate Litigation* (Berlin: Heinrich Böll Foundation, 2016), 64; Stoll-Kleemann and O'Riordan, "Revisiting the Psychology of Denial," 2.

4. Albert Bandura, *Moral Disengagement: How People Do Harm and Live with Themselves* (New York, NY: Worth Publishers, 2016), 435; Tim O'Riordan, "To Shift or Not to Shift Emissions-Generating Behavior: This Is the Dilemma," *Environment: Science and Policy for Sustainable Development* 59, no. 6 (2017): 2.

5. Adrian Bardon, *The Truth About Denial* (Oxford: University Press, 2019), 2.

6. Ibid., 1.

7. Eviatar Zerubavel, *The Elephant in the Room: Silence and Denial in Everyday Life* (Oxford: University Press, 2008), 29.

8. Stanley Cohen, *States of Denial: Knowing About Atrocities and Suffering* (Cambridge: Polity Press, 2013), 109.

9. Ibid., 109.

10. Kari Marie Norgaard, *Living in Denial: Climate Change, Emotions, and Everyday Life* (Cambridge: MIT Press, 2011), 57.

11. Stephen M. Gardiner, *A Perfect Moral Storm: The Ethical Tragedy of Climate Change* (Oxford: University Press, 2011), 301.

12. Ezra M. Markowitz and Azim F. Shariff, "Climate Change and Moral Judgement," *Nature Climate Change* 2, no. 4 (2012): 243.

13. Markowitz and Shariff, "Climate Change and Moral Judgement," 244; Stoll-Kleemann and O'Riordan, "Revisiting the Psychology of Denial," 936.

14. Wouter Peeters et al., *Climate Change and Individual Responsibility: Agency, Moral Disengagement and the Motivational Gap* (London: Palgrave Macmillan

UK, 2015), 230; Henry Shue, "Subsistence Emissions and Luxury Emissions," *Law & Policy* 15, no. 1 (1993): 56; Henry Shue, "Climate," in *A Companion to Environmental Philosophy*, ed. Dale Jamieson (Malden: Blackwell, 2001), 451.

15. Stoll-Kleemann and O'Riordan, "Revisiting the Psychology of Denial," 3; Shue, "Climate," 451; Wouter Peeters, Lisa Diependaele, and Sigrid Sterckx, "Moral Disengagement and the Motivational Gap in Climate Change," *Ethical Theory and Moral Practice* 22, no. 2 (2019): 427; See also: Jonathan Gilligan et al., "The Behavioural Wedge: Reducing Greenhouse Gas by Individuals and Households," *Significance* 7, no. 1 (2010): 16; See also: Jeroen C. J. M. van den Bergh, "Environmental Regulation of Households: An Empirical Review of Economic and Psychological Factors," *Ecological Economics* 66, no. 4 (2008): 563.

16. Susanne Stoll-Kleemann, Tim O'Riordan, and Carlo C. Jaeger, "The Psychology of Denial Concerning Climate Mitigation Measures: Evidence from Swiss Focus Groups," *Global Environmental Change* 11, no. 2 (2001): 107; Stoll-Kleemann and O'Riordan, "Revisiting the Psychology of Denial," 1.

17. Robert Gifford, "The Dragons of Inaction: Psychological Barriers That Limit Climate Change Mitigation and Adaptation," *The American Psychologist* 66, no. 4 (2011): 293; Garrett Hardin, "The Tragedy of the Commons," *Science (New York, NY)* 162, no. 3859 (1968): 1248; Albert Bandura, "Selective Moral Disengagement in the Exercise of Moral Agency," *Journal of Moral Education* 31, no. 2 (2002): 114.

18. Stoll-Kleemann et al., "The Psychology of Denial," 107.

19. Leon Festinger, *A Theory of Cognitive Dissonance* (2nd edition) (Stanford, CA: University Press, 1962), 4.

20. Bardon, *The Truth About Denial*, 6.

21. Bardon, 6.

22. Norgaard, *Living in Denial*, 83; Kari M. Norgaard, "Making Sense of the Spectrum of Climate Denial," *Critical Policy Studies* 13, no. 4 (2019): 437.

23. Rimma Teper, Chen-Bo Zhong, and Michael Inzlicht, "How Emotions Shape Moral Behavior: Some Answers (and Questions) for the Field of Moral Psychology," *Social and Personality Psychology Compass* 9, no. 1 (2015): 1.

24. Stoll-Kleemann and O'Riordan, "Revisiting the Psychology of Denial," 6.

25. Ibid., 6.

26. Albert Bandura, "Impeding Ecological Sustainability Through Selective Moral Disengagement," *International Journal of Innovation and Sustainable Development* 2, no. 1 (2007): 10.

27. Andries de Smet, Wouter Peeters, and Sigrid Sterckx, "The Delegated Authority Model Misused as a Strategy of Disengagement in the Case of Climate Change," *Ethics & Global Politics* 9, no. 1 (2016): 11; Bandura, "Impeding Ecological Sustainability," 10.

28. Bandura, "Selective Moral Disengagement," 102.

29. Bandura, "Impeding Ecological Sustainability," 10; Bandura, "Selective Moral Disengagement," 102; Celia Moore, "Moral Disengagement," *Current Opinion in Psychology* 6 (2015): 199.

30. Peeters et al., *Climate Change and Individual Responsibility*, 229; Bandura, "Selective Moral Disengagement," 10; Moore, "Moral Disengagement," 2.

31. Bandura, "Impeding Ecological Sustainability," 19.

32. Stoll-Kleemann and O'Riordan, "Revisiting the Psychology of Denial," 8.

33. Fritz Heider, *The Psychology of Interpersonal Relations* (New York, NY: Wiley, 1958), 79.

34. Lee D. Ross, Teresa M. Amabile, and Julia L. Steinmetz, "Social Roles, Social Control, and Biases in Social-Perception Processes," *Journal of Personality and Social Psychology* 35, no. 7 (1977): 491.

35. Number of interview partner in Stoll-Kleemann and O'Riordan, "Revisiting the Psychology of Denial."

36. Albert Bandura, "Moral Disengagement," in *The Encyclopedia of Peace Psychology*, ed. Daniel Christie (Hoboken, NJ: John Wiley & Sons, 2011), 668.

37. Mari Wieland, *Die Kluft Zwischen Einstellung/Wissen und Verhalten im Nachhaltigkeitsbereich: Entstehung, Rechtfertigungsstrategien und Mögliche Lösungsansätze* (Master's Thesis, University of Greifswald, 2018), 42; Seonaidh McDonald et al., "Flying in the Face of Environmental Concern: Why Green Consumers Continue to Fly," *Journal of Marketing Management* 31, no. 13–14 (2015): 1503–28; Alcock et al., "Green on the Ground but Not in the Air: Pro-Environmental Attitudes are Related to Household Behaviours but not Discretionary Air Travel," *Global Environmental Change* 42 (2017): 136; Stefan Gössling, "Celebrities, Air Travel and Social Norms," *Annals of Tourism Research* 79 (2019): 102775; Stefan Gössling et al., "Can We Fly Less? Evaluating the 'Necessity' of Air Travel," *Journal of Air Transport Management* 81 (2019): 101722; Stefan Gössling and Iliada Stavrinidi, "Social Networking, Mobilities, and the Rise of Liquid Identities," *Mobilities* 11, no. 5 (2016): 723.

38. P9 in Stoll-Kleemann and O'Riordan, "Revisiting the Psychology of Denial," 9.

39. Peeters, Diependaele, and Sterckx, "Motivational Gap in Climate Change," 433.

40. Ibid., 435; Stoll-Kleemann and O'Riordan, "Revisiting the Psychology of Denial," 10.

41. Lawrence Kohlberg, "Moral Development and Identification," in *Child Psychology: The Sixty-Second Yearbook of the National Society for the Study of Education, Part 1*, ed. Harold W. Stevenson et al. (Chicago, IL: National Society for the Study of Education, 1963), 277.

42. Bardon, *The Truth About Denial*, 24.

43. Martin Pinquart and Rainer Silbereisen, "Entwicklung Des Umweltbewusstseins Über Die Lebensspanne," *Umweltpsychologie* 11, no. 7 (2007): 88; Oliver Stengel, *Suffizienz* (PhD diss., Wuppertal Institut für Klima, Umwelt, Energie GmbH, 2011), 27.

44. Lawrence Kohlberg, "Stages and Aging in Moral Development-Some Speculations," *The Gerontologist* 13, no. 4 (1973): 498.

45. Lawrence Kohlberg, *Essays in Moral Development, Vol. II: The Psychology of Moral Development* (New York, NY: Harper & Row, 1983), 540.

46. Lawrence Kohlberg, "Stages of Moral Development," *Moral Education* 1, no. 51 (1971): 76.

47. Georg Lind, *Ist Moral Lehrbar Ergebnisse der Modernen Moralpsychologischen Forschung* (3rd edition) (Berlin: Logos Verlag, 2015), 103.

48. Stengel, *Suffizienz*, 280.
49. Kohlberg, *Essays in Moral Development*, 558.
50. Ibid., 559.
51. Stengel, *Suffizienz*, 281.
52. Lawrence Kohlberg, *Die Psychologie der Moralentwicklung* (Frankfurt a. M.: Suhrkamp, 1996), 409, 464–7; Stengel, *Suffizienz*, 275.
53. Jürgen Habermas, *Theorie des Kommunikativen Handelns* (Vol. 1) (Frankfurt a. M.: Suhrkamp, 1981), 284; Stengel, *Suffizienz*, 275.
54. Stengel, 278.
55. Kohlberg, *Essays in Moral Development*, 602.
56. Bardon, *The Truth About Denial*, 2.
57. Ibid., 12; Tomaž Grušovnik and Ana Arzenšek, "Experiential Education Against Environmental Denial in Environmental Ethics Education: A Case Study," *Journal of Education, Culture and Society* 5, no.1 (2014): 105.
58. Bardon, 16.
59. Norgaard, *Living in Denial*, 112; Bardon, *The Truth About Denial*, 22.
60. Bardon, 23.
61. Jeff Stone and Nicholas C. Fernandez, "To Practice What We Preach: The Use of Hypocrisy and Cognitive Dissonance to Motivate Behavior Change," *Social and Personality Psychology Compass* 2, no. 2 (2008): 1047.
62. Bardon, *The Truth About Denial*, 3.
63. Ibid., 32.

BIBLIOGRAPHY

Alcock, Ian, Mathew P. White, Tim Taylor, Deborah F. Coldwell, Matthew O. Gribble, Karl L. vans, Adam Corner, Sotiris Vardoulakis, and Lora E. Fleming. "Green on the Ground but not in the Air: Pro-Environmental Attitudes are Related to Household Behaviours but not Discretionary Air Travel." *Global Environmental Change* 42 (2017): 136–47.

Bandura, Albert. "Selective Moral Disengagement in the Exercise of Moral Agency." *Journal of Moral Education* 31, no. 2 (2002): 101–19.

Bandura, Albert. "Impeding Ecological Sustainability Through Selective Moral Disengagement." *International Journal of Innovation and Sustainable Development* 2, no. 1 (2007): 8–35.

Bandura, Albert. "Moral Disengagement." In *The Encyclopedia of Peace Psychology*. Edited by Daniel Christie, 668–73. Hoboken, NJ: John Wiley & Sons, 2011.

Bandura, Albert. *Moral Disengagement: How People Do Harm and Live with Themselves*. New York, NY: Worth Publishers, 2016.

Bardon, Adrian. *The Truth About Denial*. Oxford: University Press, 2019.

Boom, Keely, Julie-Anne Richards, and Stephen Leonard. *Climate Justice: The International Momentum Towards Climate Litigation*. Berlin: Heinrich Böll Foundation, 2016.

Caney, Simon. "Climate Change, Human Rights and Moral Thresholds." In *Climate Ethics: Essential Readings*, 163–77. New York, NY: Oxford University Press, 2010.

Cohen, Stanley. *States of Denial: Knowing About Atrocities and Suffering*. Cambridge: Polity Press, 2013.

Festinger, Leon. *A Theory of Cognitive Dissonance* (2nd edition). Stanford, CA: Stanford University Press, 1962.

Gardiner, Stephen M. *A Perfect Moral Storm: The Ethical Tragedy of Climate Change*. Oxford: University Press, 2011.

Gifford, Robert. "The Dragons of Inaction: Psychological Barriers That Limit Climate Change Mitigation and Adaptation." *The American Psychologist* 66, no. 4 (2011): 290–302.

Gilligan, Jonathan, Thomas Dietz, Gerald T. Gardner, Paul C. Stern, and Michael P. Vandenbergh. "The Behavioural Wedge: Reducing Greenhouse Gas by Individuals and Households." *Significance* 7, no. 1 (2010): 17–20.

Gössling, Stefan, and Iliada Stravrinidi. "Social Networking, Mobilities, and the Rise of Liquid Identities." *Mobilities* 11, no. 5 (2016): 723–43.

Gössling, Stefan. "Celebrities, Air Travel, and Social Norms." *Annals of Tourism Research* 79 (2019): 102775–96.

Gössling, Stefan, Paul Hanna, James Higham, Scott Cohen, and Debbie Hopkins. "Can We Fly Less? Evaluating the 'Necessity' of Air Travel." *Journal of Air Transport Management* 81 (2019): 101722–44.

Grušovnik, Tomaž, and Ana Arzenšek. "Experiential Education Against Environmental Denial in Environmental Ethics Education: A Case Study." *Journal of Education, Culture and Society* 5 (2014): 99–110.

Habermas, Jürgen. *Theorie des Kommunikativen Handelns* (Vol. 1). Frankfurt a. M.: Suhrkamp, 1981.

Hardin, Garrett. "The Tragedy of the Commons." *Science (New York, NY)* 162, no. 3859 (1968): 1243–8.

Heider, Fritz. *The Psychology of Interpersonal Relations*. New York, NY: Wiley, 1958.

Intergovernmental Panel on Climate Change. *AR5 Synthesis Report: Climate Change 2014*, Geneva, 2014.

Kohlberg, Lawrence. "Stages and Aging in Moral Development-Some Speculations." *The Gerontologist* 13, no. 4 (1973): 497–502.

Kohlberg, Lawrence. "Moral Development and Identification." In *Child Psychology: The Sixty-Second Yearbook of the National Society for the Study of Education, Part 1*. Edited by Harold W. Stevenson et al., 277–332. Chicago, IL: National Society for the Study of Education, 1963.

Kohlberg, Lawrence. "Stages of Moral Development." *Moral Education* 1, no. 51 (1971): 23–92.

Kohlberg, Lawrence. *Essays in Moral Development, Vol. II: The Psychology of Moral Development*. New York, NY: Harper & Row, 1983.

Kohlberg, Lawrence. *Die Psychologie der Moralentwicklung*. Frankfurt a. M.: Suhrkamp, 1996.

Leiserowitz, Anthony, Edward Maibach, Connie Roser-Renouf, Seth Rosenthal, Matthew Cutler, and John Kotcher. *Politics & Global Warming, October 2017*. New Haven, CT: Yale Program on Climate Change Communication, 2017.

Lind, Georg. *Ist Moral Lehrbar. Ergebnisse der Modernen Moralpsychologischen Forschung* (3rd edition). Berlin: Logos Verlag, 2015.

Markowitz, Ezra M., and Azim F. Shariff. "Climate Change and Moral Judgement." *Nature Climate Change* 2, no. 4 (2012): 243–7.

McDonald, Seonaidh, Caroline J. Oates, Maree Thyne, Andrew J. Timmis, and Claire Carlile. "Flying in the Face of Environmental Concern: Why Green Consumers Continue to Fly." *Journal of Marketing Management* 31, no. 13–14 (2015): 1503–28.

Moore, Celia. "Moral Disengagement." *Current Opinion in Psychology* 6 (2015): 199–204.

Norgaard, Kari Marie. *Living in Denial: Climate Change, Emotions, and Everyday Life*. Cambridge: MIT Press, 2011.

Norgaard, Kari Marie. "Making Sense of the Spectrum of Climate Denial." *Critical Policy Studies* 13, no. 4 (2019): 437–41.

O'Riordan, Tim. "To Shift or Not to Shift Emissions-Generating Behavior: This Is the Dilemma." *Environment: Science and Policy for Sustainable Development* 59, no. 6 (2017): 2–3.

Peeters, Wouter, Lisa Diependaele, and Sigrid Sterckx. "Moral Disengagement and the Motivational Gap in Climate Change." *Ethical Theory and Moral Practice* 22, no. 2 (2019): 425–47.

Peeters, Wouter, Andries De Smet, Lisa Diependaele, Sigrid Sterckx, Robert H. McNeal, and Andries De Smet. *Climate Change and Individual Responsibility: Agency, Moral Disengagement and the Motivational Gap*. London: Palgrave Macmillan UK, 2015.

Pinquart, Martin, and Rainer Silbereisen. "Entwicklung Des Umweltbewusstseins Über Die Lebensspanne." *Umweltpsychologie* 11, no. 7 (2007): 84–99.

Ross, Lee D., Teresa M. Amabile, and Julia L. Steinmetz. "Social Roles, Social Control, and Biases in Social-Perception Processes." *Journal of Personality and Social Psychology* 35, no. 7 (1977): 485–94.

Shue, Henry. "Subsistence Emissions and Luxury Emissions." *Law & Policy* 15, no. 1 (1993): 39–60.

Shue, Henry. "Climate." In *A Companion to Environmental Philosophie*. Edited by D. Jamieson, 449–59. Malden: Blackwell, 2001.

Smet, Andries de, Wouter Peeters, and Sigrid Sterckx. "The Delegated Authority Model Misused as a Strategy of Disengagement in the Case of Climate Change." *Ethics & Global Politics* 9, no. 1 (2016): 1–21.

Stengel, Oliver. *Suffizienz*. PhD diss., Wuppertal Institut für Klima, Umwelt, Energie. Munich: Ökom, 2011.

Stoll-Kleemann, Susanne, and Tim O'Riordan. "Revisiting the Psychology of Denial Concerning Low-Carbon Behaviors: From Moral Disengagement to Generating Social Change." *Sustainability* 12, no. 3 (2020): 935.

Stoll-Kleemann, Susanne, Tim O'Riordan, and Carlo C. Jaeger. "The Psychology of Denial Concerning Climate Mitigation Measures: Evidence from Swiss Focus Groups." *Global Environmental Change* 11, no. 2 (2001): 107–17.

Stone, Jeff, and Nicholas C. Fernandez. "To Practice What We Preach: The Use of Hypocrisy and Cognitive Dissonance to Motivate Behavior Change." *Social and Personality Psychology Compass* 2, no. 2 (2008): 1024–51.

Teper, Rimma, Chen-Bo Zhong, and Michael Inzlicht. "How Emotions Shape Moral Behavior: Some Answers (and Questions) for the Field of Moral Psychology." *Social and Personality Psychology Compass* 9, no. 1 (2015): 1–14.

van den Bergh, Jeroen C. J. M. "Environmental Regulation of Households: An Empirical Review of Economic and Psychological Factors." *Ecological Economics* 66, no. 4 (2008): 559–74.

Wieland, Mari. *Die Kluft Zwischen Einstellung/Wissen Und Verhalten im Nachhaltigkeitsbereich: Entstehung, Rechtfertigungsstrategien und Mögliche Lösungsansätze.* Master's Thesis, University of Greifswald, 2018.

Zerubavel, Eviatar. *The Elephant in the Room: Silence and Denial in Everyday Life.* Oxford: University Press, 2008.

Chapter 2

Denial as a Sense of Entitlement

Assessing the Role of Culture

Arne Johan Vetlesen

The more serious the climate crisis becomes, accompanied by the stubborn failure to do something about it, the more important it is to understand the role played by denial. Is the human propensity for denial at the heart of the crisis? Is it one of the prime factors driving it, helping explain why it is that this much reported danger—anthropogenic climate change—is going from bad to worse before our eyes? Or would it be closer to the truth to suggest that denial, far from a cause, is an effect—a symptom—of the crisis unfolding, explaining why we remain so passive rather than what helped cause it in the first place?

In what follows I will argue that denial is not a matter of being either the one or the other—cause or effect. It is both. And it being both is what makes denial so difficult to grasp theoretically and so hard to confront psychologically and culturally. I shall argue that the individual's all-too-human need to engage in denial as a defense mechanism does not exhaust its importance— we also need to explore how and by whom denial is being promoted and exploited, and at what costs.

WHAT IS DENIAL?

Denial is commonly understood as a property of individual behavior: a psychological phenomenon of defense operative in an agent's inability or unwillingness to face reality. Uncomfortable facts and truths are not acknowledged, hence not acted upon in what would be considered a rational manner. Denial manifests itself as avoidance or evasion. And the more uncomfortable the reality denied, and the evidence that supports it, the more energy will denial command.

To understand the role of denial in our situation of climate change and multiple nature loss, however, we need to deindividualize it. I will do so by highlighting its connection to entitlement, the sense that I have the right to something, that I deserve something, and that no one has the right to deny it to me. Attempts to do so will meet with harsh responses of self-righteousness.

There are two dimensions to entitlement as conceived here: one narcissistic, playing itself out in the individual agent, the other cultural, playing itself out collectively, sustained by cultural patterns of socialization, and reproduced in societal systems such as education, economy, and law. It is the latter dimension in particular that demands our attention with respect to the well-known paradox of "knowing" about the (dangerous, uncomfortable) reality, yet continuing to behave as if not knowing—going on as before instead of changing one's ways, notwithstanding the dangers involved.

To get at how deep denial with regard to anthropogenic harm to the natural environment runs, we need to address the hyper-entitlement of Western culture originating in the industrial era and promoted in current capitalist consumerism. Speaking from the point of view of contemporary Norwegian society—and leaving aside for now the significance of class division and inequality—the sense of entitlement intended here is instilled from early on by way of socialization. The more particular, historically specific, point is that the self-esteem and identity of the child are wedded to its self-understanding as a consumer, hopefully a successful one at that. Gaining recognition from others and a sense of self-worth is from early childhood tied to the possession of consumer items: the purchase and display of a wide variety of such items actively mediate—channel, symbolize, signal—who I am and who I want to be, meaning be recognized as by significant others. Commodities serve as the go-between in setting up and negotiating social relationships, in communicating belongingness and shared values in the peer group and in the larger social landscape.[1]

Even though climate change and degradation of the natural world, such as loss of biodiversity, habitat, and species, are driven by many factors, each of them is tied up with current patterns of consumption within a growth-dependent economic system. The inbuilt demand for growth in production, distribution, and consumption results in systemic overshoot, that is, in overexploiting habitats and ecosystems to such an extent that their ability to replenish and so help sustain future humans (not to mention future animals) is in jeopardy. Socialized into consumers from early on, we are (to varying degrees, depending on class and socioeconomic position) implicated in this overshoot. To keep at bay unwelcome feelings of guilt, the fact of this implication creates a need for denial. Entitlement and denial work in tandem to protect us—as individuals and as the sort of society we are part of and help maintain—from caring about the harmful consequences of our lifestyle, a lifestyle characterized by the addictions that present-day consumerism produces consequences we are to a large degree informed about, making it difficult to plead ignorance and innocence. Clive Hamilton puts it well when he says that "in fact, denial is due to a surplus of culture rather than a deficit of information."[2] What, more precisely, is the culture in question?

A CULTURE OF ENTITLEMENT

To answer this question, I shall concentrate on the situation in my native Norway. In doing so, I will draw on American sociologist Kari Marie Norgaard's book *Living in Denial: Climate Change, Emotions and Everyday Life*, based on her fieldwork in a rural town she calls "Bygdaby" (later identified as Voss, close to Bergen).[3]

Norway is a good place to study denial because the contradiction between knowledge and action is particularly visible in a country combining, on the one hand, high levels of education, idealism, and appreciation of nature (tied to popular outdoor activities like hiking and skiing), and on the other, a vibrant petroleum-based economy, employing more than 200,000 people, including subcontractors. To put the importance of the oil and gas industry into perspective, Norgaard notes that as of 2009 (i.e., the time of her fieldwork), Norway was the world's fifth largest oil exporter and the second largest exporter of natural gas. She observes that in the ten years prior to her stay in Bygdaby, Norwegian oil and gas production increased threefold. In the same period the Norwegian government dropped the goal of capping national carbon dioxide emissions, instead opting to expand petroleum development and pursuing a strategy for trading emissions rather than reducing them outright.

What is the role of denial in the contradiction set out here? I mean this not simply as an empirical question—that is, precisely how big a role does denial have—but also as a conceptual one, bearing on what we mean by denial. There being different types of denial, which one is predominant in the case Norgaard is studying?

Sociologist Stanley Cohen's influential monograph *States of Denial* serves as the theoretical model for Norgaard's work. Cohen identifies three varieties of denial: literal, interpretive, and implicatory. *Literal* denial is "the assertion that something did not happen or is not true";[4] Norgaard points to global warming skeptics as a case in point. In *interpretive* denial, the facts themselves are not denied but are instead given a different interpretation, taken to mean something else; euphemisms such as "collateral damage" are used to alter, or downright dispute, the meaning of facts and events. But it is the third of Cohen's categories, *implicatory* denial, that Norgaard considers most relevant for her study. What is minimized here is not information, but "the psychological, political or moral implications that conventionally follow."[5] Norgaard writes that what she observed when living in Bygdaby, asking the residents to share their thoughts and feelings about climate change in their home area, was not "in most cases a rejection of information per se, but the failure to integrate this knowledge into everyday life or to transform it into social action."[6] She quotes the passage where Cohen gives some examples to highlight what he means by implicatory denial: "The facts of children starving to death in Somalia, mass rape of women in Bosnia, a massacre in East Timor, homeless people in our streets are recognized, but are not seen as psychologically disturbing or as carrying a moral imperative to act." Here, then, Cohen explains, "knowledge itself is not at issue, but doing the 'right' thing with the knowledge."[7]

As Norgaard argues later in her book, in the case of climate change, "literal and implicatory denial go hand in hand," mutually reinforcing each other. The fact that "nobody wants information about climate change to be true happens to fit perfectly with the agenda of those who have put forward the messages of skepticism in the media. These facts create exactly the kind of slippery condition that makes implicatory denial feel so natural."[8]

I think that Norgaard is mistaken in holding the examples Cohen gives of implicatory denial to fit with her own particular case, climate change. As borne out by the chosen examples—Somalia, Bosnia, and East Timor—as well as his book's subtitle, *Knowing about Atrocities and Suffering*, Cohen, writing against the backdrop of 1990s humanitarian disasters, had cases of orchestrated massacres in mind, indeed what amounted to genocide in the case of Bosnia. The knowledge that thousands of people were being killed raised questions about the willingness or lack of such, of so-called "bystanders" to intervene, to stop the perpetrators committing the crimes in question, to limit the suffering inflicted on innocents. "Denial" in such cases is about not heeding—not registering and not acknowledging—the moral demand that arises from knowing that atrocities are being carried out.[9]

In Cohen's formulation, implicatory denials come from "techniques for avoiding moral or psychological demands."[10] To avoid these demands amounts to denying the *significance*—the meaning, the consequences—of the reality at hand. Note that the facts of the matter and "even their conventional interpretations" are conceded, are not as such denied, in implicatory denial; only "their expected implications—emotional or moral—are not recognized."[11] Denial in all three versions, Cohen maintains, is always partial: "Some information is always registered." This "paradox or doubleness—knowing and not-knowing—is the heart of the concept."[12]

Culture plays a prominent role in Norgaard's approach, comparable to that played by ideology in Cohen's. She uses Ann Swidler's concept of culture as a "tool kit" of shared symbolic resources, a kit that members of Bygdaby would draw upon in the forms of "tools of order" and "tools of innocence" to "create distance from responsibility, to assert rightness or goodness of actions, to maintain order and security, and to construct a sense of innocence in the face of the disturbing emotions associated with [anthropogenic] climate change."[13] Echoing Hamilton's observation that "denial is due to a surplus of culture," Norgaard's aim is to show how public nonresponse to global warming—conspicuous as it may be to the outsider—is *produced through cultural practices of everyday life.*"[14] When people "actively normalize climate change," they do so by way of taking part in the cultural practices prevalent in their community. This means that denial, although observable in the distinct individual's behavior, is a thoroughly cultural and intersubjective phenomenon, something deeply—and most of the time tacitly—*shared* by the individuals constituting the community rather than something setting them apart. If anything, the stance that would allow one individual to stand out from the community would be that of *refusing to take part in denial*, hence of noncompliance, something that always comes with a cost.

Norgaard stresses the importance of locating emotions in a political-economic context, alluded to in her observations about Norway's prominent role as a major producer of oil. For ordinary Norwegians, and not only members of Bygdaby, there is a strong connection between the country's fifty years history as a world leading producer and exporter of oil, on the one hand, and the economic prosperity and high standard of living this has brought to the population as a whole during that period, on the other. What this means culturally is that utilizing fossil fuels accessed within Norwegian territory is regarded as having been immensely beneficial to "us all." What is referred to as the "oil adventure" is considered a strike of luck for which we all have to feel grateful, not least to the professions involved in the early phase, fraught with danger, risk-taking, and bold engineering entrepreneurship, exhibiting a laudable willingness to put the well-being of the country before everything else. Contemporary Norwegians from all walks of life and all parts of the country are placed in a position of debt to the generation who devoted themselves so unselfishly to helping improve the well-being of the whole nation, a sort of debt whose basis is economic but whose implications are psychological and moral.

This is my way of explaining the significance of culture here, not Norgaard's. Not that I think she would disagree with it. Even so, my impression is that Norgaard, living in the United States, has not quite grasped the extent to which contemporary Norwegians grow up with a sense of collective indebtedness to those who, for the last fifty years, have devoted themselves to the production of oil that every child is told has been absolutely crucial in helping build the prosperous Norwegian welfare state.

Let me connect this point with my observation that a sense of entitlement is something cultural. In exploring denial in present-day Norwegian society, we need to acknowledge, on the one hand, "the general egoism and hyper-entitlement of Western culture in the industrial era," that psychoanalyst Donna Orange talks about[15]; and on the other hand, the particular role that being a producer of fossil fuels is playing in Norway. We need to recognize how a national culture of indebtedness and gratitude to those (often family members) employed in the oil and gas industry goes hand in hand with the more general (Western) culture of entitlement in Orange's sense, a culture of which Norway is a part, and indeed was so also prior to the onset of the "oil adventure." Indeed, it is not only that the latter fits with the former; it also helps sustain and amplify it over the generations. This is illustrated in the Equinor (formerly Statoil) commercials targeted at Norwegian youth: supporting—and, if possible, joining—the oil industry is painted as being part of "tomorrow's heroes" and so as a matter of loyalty, of helping secure the welfare state and thereby one's country's future. Subtly or not, there is an element of emotional blackmail in this message "from the old to the young," casting, by implication, Thunberg-inspired critics of the oil industry as disloyal and not fully realizing what they do when they ignore their debt to those who built the welfare state they take for granted.

THE ROLE OF AMBIVALENCE

This constellation of entitlement and gratitude is important to keep in mind when we consider the specifically Norwegian way of handling the ambivalence addressed by so many scholars these days—namely that "while natural [environmental] damage may be experienced as a loss, the causes of the loss (e.g., industry) are also imbued with benefit, achievement or surplus. We partake of the fruits of industry whilst we may experience sadness or longing for the losses it incurs."[16] In my opinion a more profound notion than the much discussed one of cognitive dissonance,[17] *ambivalence* refers to simultaneously holding competing affective investments, be it love and hate or gratitude and anger. As Renee Lertzman found in her interviews with residents of Green Bay, an industrialized urban area in Wisconsin, United States:

> Ambivalence characterizes the mood with which participants tended to relate with the local industry and the local environments. On the one hand, many openly expressed disgust and shock towards the level of local water and air pollution, yet on the other hand they quickly shifted modes and contradicted themselves to provide excuses or rationales for the very issues they just reported unhappiness over.[18]

Typically, the respondents would say that industry is an evil, albeit a necessary one, hastening to add that "Green Bay is a good place to live." Environmental health problems that are initially acknowledged are disavowed a moment later, then acknowledged again, and so forth. As a rule, the admission of a blatantly negative feeling (anxiety, disgust, anger, sadness, hopelessness) toward man-made environmental harms will never be allowed to stand. Admissions will always be contradicted by assurances of a positive, upbeat kind.

Lertzman suspects that the negative feelings and the anxieties they produce are in a sense more true, more authentic, than the disclaimers, so that what strikes the observer as contradictory and confusing (going back and forth between opposite feelings) assumes the form of a persistent split in the person's psyche: where ambivalence runs as deep as this, never to be resolved, the price paid is inner conflict. The cohabitation of opposite feelings is no less torturous and exhausting for having an asymmetric rather than symmetric structure, insofar as the "positive" feelings are so much more welcome, culturally and socially speaking, than the negative ones, especially when they express anger or border on despair and depression. But it is not only that such a person will tend to adjust to the expected norms of his group by hiding his "negatives" and making sure to display his "positives" ("I'm sure it will work out"; "This is a wonderful place to live") but he will also engage in self-censorship, spending psychic energy to suppress the negative feelings and thoughts—a part of his emotional life that he not only wants to prevent others from seeing, but also does not want to acknowledge to himself either. Feelings that have nowhere to go must be disowned.

Lertzman's material from Wisconsin, United States, supplements Norgaard's from Bygdaby, Norway. In both countries and cases, experiencing industry as both benevolent and brutalizing contributes to a peculiar type of what Lertzman terms "industrial ambivalence" in which "we can be deeply attached to the very practices that are recognized as harmful and even damaging."[19] Indeed, how could we as individuals living in a place where environmental degradation takes place, accumulatively over the years and generations, *not* respond by being torn between our culture's overall narrative that "development" is a good thing, allowing us to "have it all" (if not all of it, than steadily more of it—what is called progress) and feelings of anxiety and despair when we—*simultaneously*—cannot but register the often eminently concrete loss that comes with the development and that seems to be the price to be paid, inevitably at that. Lertzman puts the two-in-one like this: "The Fox River is an ecosystem and a dumping site; it is abject and glittering, a gem or place of trauma. It contains shopping trolleys, PCBs, algae, fish, and mayflies. The river *is* both an ecosystem and a waste site. It is both industrial and natural."[20]

So when Norgaard's respondents insist that Bygdaby is a good place to live (despite the seasons becoming weird, with rain replacing snowfall in midwinter, disrupting all sorts of activities held dear and associated with the place and its particular qualities), or when Lertzman's respondents say the same about living in Green Bay (despite the river being polluted, fishing becoming forbidden, and swimming no longer attractive), what they say is true, but only partially so. It being only partially true is psychologically nonneutral: it is something that hurts, because something that should not be, evidence of a world gone wrong. Hence the loss involved is a difficult one twice over: painful in itself, subjectively so for objective reasons, yet at the same time socially discouraged, if not downright taboo: it is not a loss that can be socially processed and recognized. For lack of public recognition, the mourning (in Freud's sense) that would permit one to work through it by doing justice to the reality of the loss and what caused it cannot take place.[21] Perforce, then, the loss becomes melancholic, being attributed to unclear and to a large extent unacknowledged origins, evolving into what Lertzman describes as "a mood of sadness or vague disappointment."[22] Whereas mourning makes it possible to move on, even to grow in the wake of the loss suffered, melancholia is more of a dead end in that it sticks, disallowing the person to overcome it and to regain the energy lost.

Disappointment is an important factor here, expressed as a lack of comprehension as to how things were allowed to degrade and degenerate so badly— it is impossible to say this without thinking about Greta Thunberg's "How dare you?" directed at the betrayal by adults who have knowingly, and in a sense also willingly, spoiled the world left to their children.[23] "Did it really have to come to this"—be it the loss of snow (not to speak of wild animals) in Bygdaby or the pollution of the river in Green Bay; the river that used to be a place of joy and happiness and nothing else; the river, that is to say, that used to be the best place to go to in times of trouble, that would always, like other "good objects" in nature, be there as a guardian of reassurance and comfort but that now has turned into the opposite: no longer a source of comfort but itself a source/object of discomfort, of sadness because ruined in its original qualities, leaving so many people with the chilling feeling of being "homeless at home."[24] With the disappointment that this should come to pass questions arise, questions about whose responsibility it is that things have gone not from bad to worse, but from unambiguously good to *having that goodness spoiled* so as to become sources of anxiety and loss instead of enjoyment and happiness; of bad instead of good, of death instead of life. How to face a loss of such magnitude? How to do so without anger and a sense of injustice, of undeserved deprivation—whereby the "undeserved" is problematized by the fact of complicity, of being implicated, discussed earlier.

Adaptation is key to the answer. "I still love skiing!"; "It's still water, and I still love it!" People do their best to put on a brave face, convincing themselves that it is not that bad, or not all bad. Surely not everything is lost and one should get better at enjoying what is still, despite everything, left of the good object, the natural environment that was always near and dear. Lertzman speaks of this as "adjusting one's expectations," that is to say, "learning to live with disappointment."[25] What, more exactly, is this disappointment? It is, as Lertzman suggests, "a softening, a blunter edge than anger or outrage"; it has "a sadder quality, muted, and is entirely livable." As Sally, one of her respondents says, she can live with disappointment since "one adjusts."[26]

What we see in individuals whose life quality is clearly (one is tempted to say "undeniably") negatively affected by ongoing degradation of their natural environment, then, is a never-ending and as such psychically exhausting negotiation between awareness, shock, and disgust and the available modes of response or action. Culture enters into this in that it *blocks the types of communication and action that would be effective in solving the problem*, in addressing it and promoting efforts to get at its roots—located as they are in the deep structures, politically and economically, of the growth- and consumption-fixated societies we are part of. There is the ambivalence of being simultaneously aware and unaware of what is going on in terms of deterioration, of losses that are all too real and that multiply and grow, losses that cannot be fully acknowledged to oneself or shared in their full depth and gravity with others precisely because they originate so structurally and deeply, and are so real, so serious, and so generating of anxiety and despair. As we have seen, the result is adaptation in the form of lowering one's expectations so as to learn to live with disappointment, constituting what Lertzman observes as "a move inward, rather than outward, in terms of action."[27] Again, the responses seen in individuals like Sally must be recognized for what they truly are: denial and disavowal (knowing and not knowing at the same time concerning the same phenomenon) as culturally entrenched and so collective forms of defense. This being so, the apathy and resignation pointed to in individuals these days, and often explained in terms of cognitive dissonance (knowing but being unable to act on that knowledge), need to be deindividualized and to be seen not first and foremost as a more or less conspicuous absence of action, a deficit on the part of the individual, but as a defense mechanism, the upshot *not of a failure to be concerned but of being too concerned*, more so than is tolerated. We have to do with a defense resorted to in a situation where the individual is left alone, without the symbolic and affective support of culture and society that is needed to be able to face up to the reality at hand, one of loss.

UNDOING THE WRONGNESS OF
ENVIRONMENTAL HARM

Let us return now to the Norwegian context introduced earlier. If you are brought up in a cultural environment where gratitude is the norm with respect to the role of oil in building the welfare state you are fortunate enough to be born a member of, *refusing* to show such gratitude will come across as morally suspect. Should such refusal be openly displayed, it may be considered a downright provocation, prompting responses of anger. Sooner or later, such a person would be told "you should be ashamed of yourself, criticizing the country's fossil industry and by implication all who are part of it." Being a beneficiary of the prosperity facilitated by this industry over three generations, it would be hypocritical to take a negative attitude to it. Not only should one be ashamed of oneself when voicing criticism; one would also be told that doing so is really an instance of denial, of picturing as bad what is really good. Indeed, where would we have been, collectively and individually, without the benefits of oil?

This being how Norway's active role as a producer of oil and gas plays out in terms of patriotic identity formation among the three generations involved, something must be said about how that role is framed internationally. Across party lines, various Norwegian governments have argued that (I paraphrase) "since Norwegian oil and gas products are not the dirtiest in the international market, Norwegian oil and gas production is good climate policy internationally." This argument comes in two versions. In the first version, the claim is that oil and gas produced in Norway is cleaner than that produced in other countries and subject to other (presumably less rigorous) regulations. In the second version, the claim is that Norwegian natural gas emits less carbon dioxide than sources such as coal; therefore, in selling this excess energy to other nations, Norway is in fact helping reduce overall global emissions. The logic is that additional gas emissions *here* (in Norway) would be offset by reductions *there* (in other countries). In this way, what on the face of it appears to be a contribution to *increasing* emissions, ceases to qualify as such once the global picture as distinct from the local (national) one is taken into account. And the global has to be trump because it expresses the totality of emissions, being what counts.

To be sure, the claim that oil and natural gas produced in Norway is "cleaner" than that produced anywhere else in the world has been disputed by a number of scholars.[28] My present point, though, is a different one, bearing directly on the psychology of denial.

What is the element of denial in the reasoning just described? How is it possible to portray increase in carbon dioxide emissions as a contribution to their overall reduction, as a policy that is part of the solution?

To stick to the case of Norway's decision to continue being the world's fifth largest producer of oil, the element of denial I am referring to has three aspects.

The first aspect is to do with the long-standing practice of highlighting emissions from oil production at home over emissions caused by the use of that oil abroad, that is, in the countries around the world it is being exported to. Only when virtually all attention is paid to the domestic part, and none to the abroad one, can the picture of the policy involved as one conducive to solving the problem and so to be doing the morally right thing be maintained. As far as the actual consequences of the policy are concerned, however, this picture is a gross distortion, if not a blatant lie: the emissions abroad being ten times bigger than those at home, the former not the latter are clearly what we should focus on and what decides the environmental credentials (or lack of such) of the policy.

The second aspect is to do with the pride of place enjoyed by engaging in comparison—meaning the specific one of comparing existing Norwegian policies/practices with ones that are (or, if implemented, would be) worse than the Norwegian, worse in strictly comparative terms. The reasoning is as follows: if Norway were to significantly reduce its current activity (volume) of oil and gas production for international export, the vacant market role would be filled by fossil fuels production in other countries that would be much worse for the global environment. The finger is pointed at producers of coal, say, in China, suggesting that the dirtiest of the fossil energies would immediately take the place left vacant the moment Norway produces less oil and gas for export. To present this as being the "realistic" alternative is of course heavily biased in favor of the conclusion prepared for all along: that business as usual is the best policy in a regrettably imperfect world. So when current fossil production policies in Norway are assessed, comparing those fossil-based policies with *nonfossil* ones is not entertained. The exercise in comparison is self-serving and question-begging.

Finally, the third aspect is related to the second, being the more psychological and less technical of the two. What I have in mind is the policy of *offsetting*: I can pay a CO_2 offset company to "neutralize" my greenhouse gases. We have already seen what this amounts to: the increase of emissions here (at home, as a decision of ours, hence a matter of our responsibility) must be viewed in the light of helping reduce emissions elsewhere. In this way, offsetting allows us to do something that admittedly, on the face of it, may seem to be suspect, even downright wrong, but that, when considered in a larger context, can be viewed as right. We are induced to shift attention from the local and particular (what we do here and now) to the global. Bringing the totality to bear on the decisions made by particular agents (be it the country of Norway, be it myself as a citizen) has the effect of altering the action's quality from questionable to right.

As consumers we are invited to engage in this exercise all around the clock. Take the question of whether or not to fly to Thailand for the Easter holiday. Of course, I am aware that flying is not good for the climate; so too are all the commercial players involved. A good thing, then, that the international airline advertising the destination can inform me that they are just as keen as everybody else to take climate change seriously. They prove this by offering me, the likewise environmentally concerned customer, the option of offsetting the emissions that I cause by flying by buying a ticket a percentage of which goes to the planting of trees. As if by magic, the putative wrongness of my decision to fly is undone: I am assured that no action of mine is too small to qualify as part of the solution once the bigger picture is taken into consideration.

The subtleties of the logic into which the modern customer is lured, or more to the point, is being enrolled whether she wants to or not, are such as to elude us, if not all of the time, then most of it. No action is what it appears to be at first sight. Nothing is in itself wrong, environmentally speaking, which now means globally speaking.

RELATIVIZATION AND ALIENATION

At work here is a thoroughgoing relativization. Instead of my decision to act so and not so being what constitutes the entity to be judged, each and every decision on my part must now enter into a picture so big—so global, so encompassing, and "total"—that I cannot keep track of it. In my example, the airline company steps in to assume accountability for me, in my place and by proxy, as it were: I for one was reluctant to fly, as long as focused on flying as tantamount to help causing emissions and so to have an undeniable negative environmental impact. Thanks to offsetting, my flight contributes to help reduce global warming, since that is what planting trees is all about. Reassurance fosters a feeling of gratitude. Each flight taken with the "environmentally concerned" airliner will bolster my loyalty to the brand: we are in this together.

Apart from the sheer magic of *reducing emissions by way of causing them*, relativization amounts to a peculiar form of alienation. Being enrolled into the logic of offsetting means that I am deprived of ownership to my decisions and actions. Since every action of mine makes a difference (however small) within the overall, global context, and since it is the significance it carries *there*, as opposed to *here*, within my immediate context and concrete environment, that is highlighted, a divide is erected between what I do (which will always be particular in the given sense) and what I am being told qualifies as the relevant "facts" about the actual environmental impact of my action. Thus taken away from me, I am alienated from the only thing that traditional ethics will tell me I—and I alone—am responsible for: what I choose to do in a concrete situation involving alternatives.

That is not the whole story, though. The subtlety I alluded to has to do with the fact that for many of us, the alienation I have spoken about will not be felt as something negative, let alone problematic. To see why, we need to differentiate between two aspects.

First, being told that a decision of mine such as flying to Thailand can be a part of the offsetting arrangement that is becoming ubiquitous in current consumer life may strike me as the very opposite of alienation. By being given the freedom of choice to opt for offsetting, I feel empowered, confirmed in my agency, politically as well as morally. It feels good to be able to "do something" to sustain the environment—in this case, to help finance the planting of trees by flying.

At the same time, there is something at work here that pulls in the opposite direction: I may experience being enrolled into the logic of offsetting as losing ownership of my particular action, rather than having it confirmed. My sense of ownership is undermined in that what started out as emphatically *my* action vanishes into a context so vast that I have no chance to keep track of what my action's impact really amounts to. The loss of ownership effected means that I am alienated—split off—from what I do.

I said that the alienation in question need not be experienced as something negative. What did I mean by this claim?

Whereas to dump toxic chemicals into my local lake is clearly a piece of action for which I am unequivocally responsible, an action with straightforward (immediate) consequences in terms of its here and now (dead fish etc.), this does not hold for the case where my flight is subject to the logic of offsetting. If in the one case everything that I have to take into consideration is concrete, is part of my experience, and plays itself out within my time/space context, in the other such experiential qualities are eroded: no longer solid, but melting into air.

Enter the role assumed by other agents, immensely more potent ones than I will ever be. The modern "global" airline company comes to my rescue, assuring me that the decision I make will indeed have wider consequences, playing a role in the wider *Wirkwelt* (world of factual consequences) out there as distinct from my restricted, spatiotemporally local experiential *Merkwelt*.[29] What is truly reassuring about this is being told that the role my action is thus allowed to play is a *positive* one: my decision to fly is made into a contribution to reducing global emissions. Even though it remains the case that my action is "carried away" from me and so is rendered out of my reach, the loss of ownership (and in that sense alienation) that this implies will not be a problem for me—what I am inclined to find problematic about it is offset by the wider consequences, cast as positive.

What, then, is the significance of global commercial players such as airliners presenting themselves as part of the solution to the emissions problem?

I mentioned the importance of reassurance, that is, of being informed, in one advertisement after the other, that such global players do take the emissions problem seriously. By accepting the invitation to come on board (morally as well as literally) and be a part of their measures to solve the problem, I am led to thinking that, luckily, the system we have is one where everybody—not least the big players—is keen to take the responsibility that their position commands. In other words, I am encouraged to trust the system, to rest assured that it is in control of the problem and dedicated to solving it. Hence, I perceive no conflict of interest between the various agents, no inequality in power, resources, and the degree to which one is affected such as to hamper the problem-solving unanimously agreed to. Great or small, we are all on board. In this manner, powerful agents like international airliners recruit me, their customer, as an ally in denial: what is denied, on an individual as well as on a structural level, is the role of all involved, big or small, in causing the problem of climate change and nature loss; instead the whole narrative, of which one is part, is about helping solving the problem and fixing it. The denial born of the human psychological need to not-confront what is a deeply discomforting reality is actively nourished and exploited by agents like the airliners and for their particular ends.

A NON-SPLIT NATURAL LANDSCAPE

"Out of sight, out of mind." To see the relevance of this well-known and well-researched phenomenon for the present discussion, let us shift from the practice of flying to that of producing meat.

Again, various mechanisms of distancing are involved, ensuring that virtually no one who eats meat for dinner has had anything to do with the way in which what is on one's plate is actually being produced. Only a very limited number of people are involved—professionally, on a regular basis—with the work that needs to be done in order for me to pick a piece of meat from the supermarket shelf. The animals from which the meat is being made are indeed "out of sight, out of mind." This is true not only in a psychological sense. It is so also in terms of knowledge: the average consumer has virtually no knowledge about what goes into the sequence: animals—global agro-industrial production of meat by way of killing—buying and consuming the meat. In a society with the degree of specialization, division of labor, and general complexity and intransparency such as ours, there is simply no need for the consumer to have but a vague knowledge about the specifics of this sequence.

The main point is that knowing—being informed about the facts—is not required. There are so many things to pay attention to other than what goes into what one is eating. What I am getting at, then, is not only a tacit dimension in a psychological (individual) sense, but also in a structural one: the silencing of how the meat is being produced is embedded in the very structures involved in producing it—the structures coproduce and sustain the silencing of its own workings.

By silencing I mean the rendering invisible of the entire production chain.[30] Despite important differences, the similarity with the case of flying discussed earlier has to do with how the real-life consequences of my action—flying, eating meat—are kept in the background, outside the reach of my first-person experience and outside the frame of what I pay attention to. Crucially, it requires the anything but ignorant and noninterested effort of key players to help erect and maintain the "veil of ignorance" (John Rawls) outside which the ordinary consumer of the commodity in question (the flight, the meat) is discouraged from straying. To be sure, this is more easily done in the case of flying than in that of present-day agro-industrial meat production: whereas carbon emissions per definition are conceived as confined to no particular (experiential, tangible) here and now, the production of meat and the suffering caused to the animals involved—as well as the environmental costs of the production qua industrial enterprise, that is, the clearing of forests to facilitate feeding the ever-growing livestock[31]—are phenomena that do have a particular location in time and space, only in most cases and for most of the consumers, that location will be out of sight and so commanding no attention.

For all the importance of these effort-driven features on the commodity production side, however, there is also, and no less crucially, the role played by the consumers, a role vital to consolidate the whole supply–demand, producer–customer complex. The way this role is set up and enacted is profoundly bound up with the customers' sense of entitlement, bringing my analysis full circle.

As I indicated earlier, drawing on the work of Donna Orange, being socialized into the role of consumer in a present-day Western society, one championing anthropocentrism and the notion of human supremacy over all other creatures, means to take it for granted that nature is there for humans to exploit and that, provided that we can afford it, all sorts of commodities on the (legal) market are free for us to enjoy, whether it be flying to Thailand for my Easter holiday or eating red meat four days a week. This is not to say that no criticism of such consumer choices exists, or more generally of consumerism. Criticism there is, but the point is that the socialization into consumer serves to render most people immune to it, giving pride of place to freedom of choice and autonomy, the trump values presented as guaranteed by the free market. The effect is that the burden of argument rests with those voicing the criticism, daring to judge my actions on moral or political grounds, thereby interfering with my freedom and autonomy. Whereas insisting on one's right to enjoy individual freedom of choice involves no such burden at all. It is simply the culturally upheld default position, immensely powerful at that.

Psychoanalyst Sally Weintrobe directs our attention to the "mind share" sought in advertising, effecting "a colonized state" where "all our relationships in all our various and varied [internal, psychological] landscapes become narrowed down to just one kind of relationship"—namely, "one where we feel superior to the other and entitled to exploit and consume the other,"[32] whereby—as we have seen—the other can come in so many forms, ranging from animals to faraway places. She contrasts such colonization with what she calls a "non-split natural landscape," an open-minded and inclusive one where common ground is shared between humans and the myriads of nonhuman creatures and life forms, supporting feelings of empathy, humanness, and solidarity all across the board, celebrating differences rather than seizing on them as grounds for the superior/inferior, ends/means split. The shared landscape is meant to be a corrective to the predominant one that "imagines others in a faraway landscape where they are kept dehumanized, their significance is minimized and they are hermeneutically sealed off from being able to touch the self emotionally."[33] The goal of the landscape shift is to foster and provide mental space for awareness of conflict and issues of mourning, and for expressing something Western cultures have no word for, namely cross-species empathy: "When we know, in a feeling way, that we share the Earth with endangered and maltreated species, then we are liable to feel grief."[34]

By way of conclusion, let me quote psychoanalyst Donald W. Winnicott's statement that "defences are there for good purposes."[35] If denial, a mechanism of defense, helps sustain the lifestyle and patterns of behavior that drive climate change, then no "good" purpose is being achieved. Denial involves a refusal to face our vulnerability, our dependence, and our mortality. In its current cultural form, denial keeps us from confronting our addictions, those of power, technology, and material goods, the stuff on which so much (too much) of our sense of being alive, of being somebody, and of deserving recognition now relies. If the work done by denial to manage our inner conflict, centering on the anxieties born by our dependence as well as our addictions, takes pride of place over the outer conflict-cum-crisis in the natural world we are part of, whether we like it or not, then the consequences will be fatal, raising the question of whether we humans, in an attempt to rescue ourselves, ruin everything around us.

ACKNOWLEDGMENT

I wish to thank Zemir Popovac for his thoughtful comments to an earlier version of this text.

NOTES

1. See Benjamin Barber, *Consumed: How Markets Corrupt Children, Infantilize Adults, and Swallow Citizens Whole* (New York, NY: Norton, 2007); Juliet Schor, *Born to Buy* (New York, NY: Scribner, 2004).

2. Clive Hamilton, "What History can Teach Us about Climate Change Denial," in *Engaging with Climate Change: Psychoanalytic and Interdisciplinary Perspectives*, ed. Sally Weintrobe (Sussex: Routledge, 2013), 17.

3. Kari Marie Norgaard, *Living in Denial. Climate Change, Emotions, and Everyday Life* (Cambridge, MA: MIT Press, 2011).

4. Stanley Cohen, *States of Denial. Knowing about Atrocities and Suffering* (Oxford: Polity, 2001), 7.

5. Ibid., 8.

6. Norgaard, *Living in Denial*, 11.

7. Cohen, *States of Denial*, 8–9.

8. Norgaard, *Living in Denial*, 181.

9. See Arne Johan Vetlesen, *Evil and Human Agency* (Cambridge: Cambridge University Press, 2005), 235ff.

10. Cohen, *States of Denial*, 9.

11. Ibid., 22.

12. Ibid., 22.

13. Norgaard, *Living in Denial*, 11f.

14. Ibid., 207.

15. Donna Orange, *Climate Crisis, Psychoanalysis, and Radical Ethics* (New York, NY: Routledge, 2017), 65.

16. Renee Lertzman, *Environmental Melancholia: Psychoanalytic Dimensions of Engagement* (New York, NY: Routledge, 2015), 107; Linda H. Connor, *Climate Change and Anthropos: Planet, People and Places* (New York, NY: Routledge, 2016), 70ff.

17. See Per Espen Stoknes, *What We Think About When We Try Not to Think About Climate Change* (White River Junction, VT: Chelsea Green Publishing, 2016).

18. Lertzman, *Environmental Melancholia*, 107.

19. Ibid., 121.

20. Ibid., 121.

21. See Sigmund Freud, "Mourning and Melancholia," in *On Metapsychology* (Harmondsworth: Penguin, 2004 [1917]), 245–67; Ashlee Cunsolo and Karen Landman, eds., *Mourning Nature. Hope at the Heart of Ecological Loss and Grief* (Montreal: McGill-Queen's University Press, 2017).

22. Lertzman, *Environmental Melancholia*, 127.

23. Greta Thunberg, *No One is Too Small to Make a Difference* (New York, NY: Penguin, 2019).

24. Glenn Albrecht, *Earth Emotions* (Ithaca, NY: Cornell University Press, 2019).

25. Lertzman, *Environmental Melancholia*, 173.

26. Ibid., 176.

27. Ibid., 177.

28. See Arne Johan Vetlesen and Rasmus Willig, *Hva skal vi svare våre barn?* (Oslo: Dreyer, 2018).

29. To invoke a much used distinction in German philosophy, see Karl Otto Apel, *Diskurs und Verantwortung* (Frankfurt/M.: Suhrkamp Verlag, 1988).

30. See Arne Johan Vetlesen, *The Denial of Nature. Environmental Philosophy in the Era of Global Capitalism* (London: Routledge, 2015).

31. See Eileen Crist, *Abundant Earth. Toward an Ecological Civilization* (Chicago, IL: The University of Chicago Press, 2019).

32. Sally Weintrobe, ed., *Engaging with Climate Change* (London: Routledge, 2013), 205.

33. Ibid., 206.

34. Ibid.

35. Alexander Newman, *Non-Compliance in Winnicott's Words. A Companion to the Work of D. W. Winnicott* (London: Free Association Books, 1995), 129.

BIBLIOGRAPHY

Albrecht, Glenn. *Earth Emotions*. Ithaca, NY: Cornell University Press, 2019.

Apel, Karl Otto. *Diskurs und Verantwortung*. Frankfurt/M.: Suhrkamp Verlag, 1988.

Barber, Benjamin. *Consumed: How Markets Corrupt Children, Infantilize Adults, and Swallow Citizens Whole*. New York, NY: Norton, 2007.

Cohen, Stanley. *States of Denial. Knowing about Atrocities and Suffering*. Oxford: Polity, 2001.

Connor, Linda H. *Climate Change and Anthropos: Planet, People and Places*. New York, NY: Routledge, 2016.

Crist, Eileen. *Abundant Earth. Toward an Ecological Civilization*. Chicago, IL: The University of Chicago Press, 2019.

Cunsolo, Ashlee, and Karen Landman, eds. *Mourning Nature. Hope at the Heart of Ecological Loss and Grief*. Montreal: McGill-Queen's University Press, 2017.

Freud, Sigmund. "Mourning and Melancholia." In *On Metapsychology*, 245–67. Harmondsworth: Penguin, 2004 [1917].

Hamilton, Clive. "What History can teach Us about Climate Change Denial." In *Engaging with Climate Change: Psychoanalytic and Interdisciplinary Perspectives*, edited by Sally Weintrobe, 16–32. Sussex: Routledge, 2013.

Lertzman, Renee. *Environmental Melancholia: Psychoanalytic Dimensions of Engagement*. New York, NY: Routledge, 2015.

Newman, Alexander. *Non-Compliance in Winnicott's Words. A Companion to the Work of D. W. Winnicott*. London: Free Association Books, 1995.

Norgaard, Kari Marie. *Living in Denial. Climate Change, Emotions, and Everyday Life*. Cambridge, MA: MIT Press, 2011.

Orange, Donna. *Climate Crisis, Psychoanalysis, and Radical Ethics*. New York, NY: Routledge, 2017.

Schor, Juliet. *Born to Buy*. New York, NY: Scribner, 2004.

Stoknes, Per Espen. *What We Think About When We Try Not to Think About Climate Change*. White River Junction, VT: Chelsea Green Publishing, 2016.

Thunberg, Greta. *No One is Too Small to Make a Difference*. New York, NY: Penguin, 2019.

Vetlesen, Arne Johan. *Evil and Human Agency*. Cambridge: Cambridge University Press, 2005.

Vetlesen, Arne Johan. *The Denial of Nature. Environmental Philosophy in the Era of Global Capitalism*. London: Routledge, 2015.

Vetlesen, Arne Johan, and Rasmus Willig. *Hva skal vi svare våre barn?* Oslo: Dreyer, 2018.

Weintrobe, Sally, ed. *Engaging with Climate Change*. London: Routledge, 2013.

Chapter 3

Skepticism and Animal Virtues

Denialism of Animal Morality

Tomaž Grušovnik

SKEPTICISM, ANIMAL PAIN, AND ANIMAL MORALITY

The idea that animals are "moral patients" or beings "whose *treatment* may be subject to moral evaluation"[1] is by now "a reasonably orthodox one."[2] However, as Grace Clement notes, "almost all of those on *all* sides of the animal rights debate seem to take for granted that non-human animals are not moral agents."[3] Such asymmetry between recognizing animals as moral patients and acknowledging (at least certain) nonhuman species as "moral agents," beings "whose *behavior* may be subject to moral evaluation,"[4] is odd. Not only because the concepts "moral agent" and "moral patient" are often coterminous but also because it seems natural that as soon as one recognizes the complexity of animal mental life, one will also start pondering about the motives of animal behavior. Indeed, the structure of the philosophical question about the (moral) motives of animal behavior can be seen as analogous to the question about the ability of animals to feel pain, since both deal with what is traditionally described as "mental life" or "mental states" of animals. Briefly put, the denialism regarding animal moral agency can be analyzed in the same way as one should deal with the skeptical question, "Can animals feel pain?" The asymmetry between recognizing animals as moral patients and acknowledging nonhuman moral agency[5] can thus be viewed as a dichotomy that is a consequence of broader cultural and philosophical presuppositions (including denialism) influencing our understanding of animal lives as well as the concept of "morality."

The main line of the argument presented in this chapter resembles my past efforts that analyzed the skeptical structure and existential framework of the question regarding the existence of animal pain.[6] As I tried to show, a postulated skeptical uncertainty regarding animal pain should not be seen as a consequence of epistemological defects or insufficient information, but as a strategy of avoiding the troublesome knowledge about the severity of animal suffering. To explain this point, I often refer to the work of Stanley Cavell, and specifically to his understanding of the cause of skepticism as an interpretation of "a metaphysical finitude as an intellectual lack."[7] According to this understanding, skepticism transposes existential anxiety onto an epistemological level. Thus, it turns out that precisely because *we are always already intimately aware* of the extent of suffering that we are prone to *deny or question it*. Accordingly, we provide ourselves with a possible escape route from pressing ethical issues that surround us in our everyday lives.

There are at least two empirical facts that strongly corroborate the idea of an already existent knowledge about the severity of animal suffering: the architecture and urban setting of the slaughterhouse as a specific modern institution, and trauma experienced by slaughterhouse workers. Regarding the first, one can refer to Amy Fitzgerald's work on the social history of slaughterhouses where it becomes clear that this institution was and still is located in such a way that it helps removing animal slaughter from the view of the public: "The geography and architecture of slaughterhouses served then, as they do now, to avoid a 'collective cultural guilt.'"[8] Noëlie Vialles also points out that the architecture of the slaughterhouse intentionally obfuscates who does the killing and that the process of slaughtering is divided into many parts so that it becomes harder to pinpoint who actually does the killing.[9] Since the experience of guilt presupposes moral unsettledness, one can infer that our knowledge of animal suffering must obviously already be present. This, however, is still more evident when considering the psychological damage suffered by slaughterhouse workers. As a number of authors have shown,[10] prolonged exposure to extreme violence by slaughterhouse workers results in trauma related to post-traumatic stress disorder (PTSD). In fact, for most humans it is practically impossible to engage in violence toward animals without prior "psychic numbing."[11] This again testifies to the fact that humans do not have problems understanding animal pain behavior *as suffering*. To the contrary, as Melanie Joy shows in her book on "carnism" as our meat-eating ideology, we go to great length to avoid this awareness with the help of mechanisms that are used to resolve our cognitive dissonance between our beliefs that animals suffer and our carnivorous habits. The question "Can animals feel pain?" is nothing but another mechanism of avoiding this moral pitfall: it transforms our uneasy certainty into an epistemological problem similar to the famous philosophical "problem of other minds." This problem, however, is not something one can resolve with scrupulous philosophical argumentation, but with one's attitude toward others, or with what Cavell calls "acknowledgment": "the presentness of other minds is not to be known, but acknowledged."[12]

At the first glance, the question "Can animals be moral?" is not the same as asking whether they can feel pain. Morality presupposes much more than mere experience of pain. Even if, for instance, worms can feel pain, it is very doubtful that they can act on moral grounds, since they probably lack a rich mental life, which is necessary for deliberate and purposeful action that is essential for moral agency. However, the picture changes if we switch from life forms with poor cognitive abilities to species exhibiting complex behavioral patterns. Here it seems natural to presuppose that animals do not exhibit only such abilities as nociception but also forethought and character traits such as compassion, care, and even a sense of justice. Indeed, if one were a strict adherent to the rule of minimal anthropomorphism—the methodological principle forbidding any description of animal behavior with words that are used in reference to human behavior—one would end up without any criteria for judging the conduct of other humans and even one's own actions. As a number of authors have pointed out, the principle of parsimony in explanation, as well as the basic evolutionary principle, postulating that one should not assume categorical leaps between closely related species, forces us to consider behavior of animals that are closely related to humans as relatively similar to human behavior.

Considering this argument, as well as overwhelming ethological evidence in favor of animal moral agency, it is poignant to ask why academia, and especially philosophy, still finds it difficult to acknowledge animal morality. As I am trying to show in the second section, one should look for the reason of this avoidance in Cavellian "causes of skepticism," namely our fear of finitude and contingency. The work of past and contemporary philosophers shows that our attachment to "morality" and "ethics" as exclusively human characteristics grows out of our fear of our finitude: by postulating that humans have access to the realms of "culture" and morality, we try to transcend our natural embeddedness, culturally associated with cycles of birth and death. Indeed, the human–animal boundary can in this respect be understood as "an existential buffer zone," an artificial conceptual demarcation running between the "animal" and the "human," offering humans consolation when faced with awareness of impermanence and fragility of existence. Thus it turns out that such dualisms do not emerge from our observations of human cultures and the world. Instead, this binary human–animal thinking is projected onto biological reality prima facie, making it difficult to establish a fruitful and purposeful conversation between the "deniers" and "advocates" of animal moral agency: "This suggests that the two sides in this debate are ultimately divided not by judgments about the quality of particular arguments, but by background assumptions about the nature of the differences between humans and animals."[13]

UNDERSTANDING ANIMAL MORAL BEHAVIOR

As seen earlier, we should recognize questions about the existence of animal pain and animal moral agency as consequences of skeptical doubt. In both cases, we are presented with overwhelming evidence in favor of the existence of both. We have seen that the structure and geography of slaughterhouses and the psychological harm suffered by slaughterhouse workers leave little room for doubt about our awareness of the reality of animal suffering. In a similar vein one can say that ethological observations, as well as our everyday encounters with animals, including our way of speaking about these encounters, leave little room for postulating categorical difference between animal behavior and human moral conduct. In this section, I will thus briefly touch on Marc Bekoff's and Frans de Waal's research about animal moral conduct, as well as on a reflection about our everyday language that refers to animal behavior to show that we can justifiably speak about animal morality. Then, I want to develop further the idea outlined earlier, namely that the rejection of our everyday system of understanding animals implies traditional philosophical skepticism about other minds.

In *The Animal Manifesto*, Marc Bekoff is adamant on showing that animals can act on what we can best describe as moral reasons:

> lots of scientific research and anecdotal evidence is emerging that shows that animals—rather than being inherently cruel—instead have a natural inclination to work cooperatively and to respond with compassion and empathy. Faced with the pain of others, animals act in ways that display empathy, caring, a moral intelligence, and even a sense of justice.[14]

Here one should not only have in mind animals helping other animals within the same group but also helping "foreign" organisms, belonging to different species. This observation is of great importance, since now it cannot be argued that animals are only capable of expressing interspecies altruism, which can be well accounted for by the standard evolutionist interpretation. Indeed, as Cynthia Willett points out in her book *Interspecies Ethics*, "The development of social codes for fair play among wolves and other social carnivores establishes the basis for a radically egalitarian solidarity across and indefinite range of species."[15] Drawing from Bekoff, Willett thus points out four different characteristics of play that can be seen as a basis for "social equality." The first two are well-known phenomena of "role reversal" (e.g., dominant carnivore rolling over on her back, exposing her belly to a trusted playmate) and "self-handicapping" (soft bites of play-fighting), while the other two features entail specific gestures (e.g., bows) and social contagion of a shared mood.[16] Similar to Bekoff and Willett, primatologist Frans de Waal also lists several characteristics, observed in animals (mainly primates), which can be under-stood as elementary constituents of moral conduct, grouped into four main categories: sympathy-related traits, norm-related characteristics, reciprocity, and "getting along" (i.e., peacemaking, negotiating, and avoiding conflict).[17]

In addition to this ethological evidence, our everyday encounters with animals—and our speaking about their behavior—support the idea of animal morality. Indeed, in our everyday situations we have no problems ascribing moral virtues (such as "friendliness," "compassion," "caring," etc.)—and vices—to animals. It seems that understanding sentences like "Don't worry, this dog is friendly," or "Careful! This cat can be moody!" is in fact vital for one's safety. Claiming that we always commit mistakes when referring to the mental states of animals, succumbing to naïve anthropomorphism would itself be a mistake. For as John A. Fisher claims, "unless we also wish to reject our ways of understanding each other, there is a problem in rejecting the system for understanding animals."[18] Discarding all statements that use human moral terms when referring to animal behavior as unjustified anthro-pomorphism thus ultimately leaves us without criteria for judging human moral conduct. Indeed, understanding animal behavior is epistemologically on a par with understanding the behavior of fellow humans. As Clement notes, de Waal argues that "just as we must refer to our own experiences to help us understand the experience of other humans, we must refer to our own experiences to help us understand the experiences of other animals."[19]

One is, of course, tempted to say that other humans can *speak* and *tell us* what their intentions are. But the skeptical problem of other minds is, as philosophy has taught us, not solved by invoking our ability to speak the same language, for now one can plausibly ask *how exactly do we know that other people are referring to the same experience when using words about inner mental states?* As Ludwig Wittgenstein showed in his late philosophy, the only way out of this skeptical grip is the rejection of "private language argument," showing that the meaning of the words lies not in our reference to "inner mental states," but in praxis, as the famous paragraph § 43 of *Philosophical Investigations* concludes: "The meaning of a word is its use in the language."[20] In concrete terms, this means that we *learn* the meaning of concepts that refer to mental states from praxis, from our everyday encounters with other humans *as well as* animals. One could hardly express this point better than Raimond Gaita:

> such concepts, I have suggested, are formed in responses to animals and to human beings together . . . When dogs respond to our moods, to our pleasures and fears, when they anticipate our intentions, or wait excitedly to see whether we will take them for a walk, they do not assume that we are sensate being with intentions. I imagine it was the same for us in our primitive state. Out of

such unhesitating interactions, between ourselves, and between us and animals, there developed—not beliefs, assumptions, and conjectures about the mind but—our *very concepts* of thought, feeling, intention, belief, doubt, and so on. Misunderstanding this, captivated by a picture of ourselves as spectators, certain about our own minds but driven to hypothesizing about whether there may be other minds, we have misconstructed the natural history of the development of our concept of the mind.[21]

Thus, it seems that Fisher is right when saying that by rejecting our ordinary verbal references to animal behavior we end up in a state analogous to Cartesian "other minds skepticism." As Roger Crisp also notes: "Any reason we have to doubt the existence of the minds of animals also gives us a reason to doubt the existence of the minds of other humans. We are faced with a choice between attributing mental states to animals and solipsism or skepticism concerning other minds generally."[22]

As I already mentioned, the worry not to ascribe humanlike mental states to animals stems from the so-called principle of parsimony as a methodological rule. According to this principle, one has to explain phenomena with fewest possible assumptions. In the context of animal behavior research, this principle is normally applied so it prohibits the use of terms that are employed in explanation of human behavior, since this implies anthropomorphic assumption, according to which animal mental life resembles human. In animal psychology it thus became known as Morgan's Canon, saying that no animal behavior may be interpreted at a higher level when it can be interpreted at a lower one.[23] However, as Cavalieri notes, it could turn out that strict application of the principle results, perhaps for some paradoxically, in explanation of animal behavior in human terms:

In other words, from many sides it has been underlined that a criterion of parsimony can favor a simple interpretation at a higher level rather than a complicated explanation at a lower level. Imagine that an animal exhibits a highly versatile behavior, capable of adapting itself to varied and unexpected circumstances. On the basis of the behaviorist interpretation of the canon, we would find here a behavioral repertoire consisting of an extremely complex series of subprocedures started by specific stimuli. However, it is plausible to maintain that, in such a case, the appeal to a certain degree of rationality, capable of setting out a strategy and of modifying it with respect to a given number of changes, represents a definitively simpler and more elegant solution.[24]

This again forces us to conclude that describing appropriate animal conduct as "moral agency" represents the best possible explanation of certain behavioral phenomena in the animal kingdom.

Here I wanted to demonstrate that there are sound reasons to suppose that it is quite rational to ascribe moral agency to animals: first we dealt with some ethological observations yielding insight into behavioral traits that represent a basis of morality across biological species; second we saw that in ordinary language we have no significant problems when referring to animals as "virtuous," and so on; third, we demonstrated that denying animals moral agency implies skepticism about other minds and consequently leaves us without criteria for judging moral behavior of humans; and, finally, we saw that according to evolutionary and methodological principles we are perfectly justified to presuppose contextualized animal moral agency. Given this over-whelming evidence, it is thus remarkable that a substantial part of academia is still relatively slow in acknowledging (at least certain) animals as moral agents. This can lead us to suppose that the reasons for denying animal moral agency lie outside the actual observations of animal behavior and interspecies interactions. Indeed, it seems that such worldviews accept human–animal boundary as a dogma. As Clement notes: "Thus, the insistence that we rule out all plausible non-moral explanations of apparently moral actions before we can know that a nonhuman animal is a moral agent may be the result of accepting a human–animal dualism as a default position."[25]

EXISTENTIAL BUFFER ZONE, UNCANNY PROXIMITY, AND DENIAL OF ANIMAL MORALITY

After presenting reasons for the acknowledgment of animal morality, I finally turn to the analysis of skepticism regarding animal moral behavior. As the first section tried to point out, the "causes of skepticism" should not be looked for in epistemological defects, but in our strategies of avoiding the awareness of finitude. Indeed, as Cavell sees it, skepticism is a transformation of unsettling existential certainty into an epistemological issue, making what appears uneasily certain as "doubtful." The Cavellian insight is reminiscent of Hegel's remark that sometimes "fear of error, makes itself known rather as fear of the truth."[26] Bearing this in mind, the skeptical question regarding animal moral agency reveals itself a consequence of our avoidance of knowledge. My main hypothesis here is that animals are unacknowledged as "moral agents" because the concept of "morality" remains reserved for human beings as something that raises us above their merely contingent "natural" existence. The human–animal boundary in the realm of ethics thus protects the idea of "human dignity," which is culturally conditioned and defined in opposition to what is "animal" and "natural." Still in other words, the concepts "morality" (or "ethics") and "culture" serve as human tickets to transcendence, which are our special metaphysical ingredient that cuts us off from the fragile continuity in the natural world. This is the reason why I am referring to the human–animal boundary as the "existential buffer zone,"[27] an imagined categorical line that intellectually protects us from our awareness of our finite fate that we share with other animals.

There is, however, another point to be made here before moving on to the analysis of relevant philosophical passages that corroborate this claim: the question is why we choose to compare ourselves to something that is so *similar* to us when we want to point out our *difference*? Why do we insist on comparing ourselves with animals and not with, say, inanimate entities (such as rocks and mechanisms) when trying to demonstrate our superiority? My answer to this question is what I call "uncanny proximity" between humans and animals: it is precisely because we appear to be so similar to our animal relatives—to their vulnerable and mortal corporeal existence—that we feel the transcendental urge to distance ourselves from their finite nature, trying to overcome it by various intellectual maneuvers. It is precisely because "the animal" is our *genus proximus* in the classical (and also chauvinistic and sexist) definition of "Man," that *differentia specifica* has to be added to it in the form of the famous adjective "rationale." The uncanniness of the proximity thus grows out of our awareness of animal finitude, since that reminds us of our own contingent life. As Lori Marino and Michael Mountain point out, "we tend to deny our biological identity or creatureliness and distance ourselves from the other animals, since they remind us of our own mortal nature."[28]

The idea that humans are unjustified in ascribing immortality to themselves while simultaneously denying it to the animals is an ancient one. It can already be found in Pliny the Elder's famous *Naturalis Historia* where the historian complains that humans go to great lengths in trying to reserve eternity for themselves, which is curious, since many animals live much longer than humans, and yet we do not foretell "the like immortality to them."[29] This impulse, however, persists to this day and can be found in many philosophical passages throughout Western intellectual history.

In what follows we will look at four different authors who vividly demonstrate our uneasiness with uncanny proximity to animal mortality, thereby asserting categorical difference between animals and humans. Our first example comes from Descartes's *Discourse on the Method*. In this, the French philosopher distances humans from animals precisely to secure our eternal life, emphasizing that "when we know how much the beasts differ from us, we understand much better the arguments which prove that our soul is of a nature entirely independent of the body, and consequently that it is not bound to die with it."[30] Similarly to Descartes but with greater idealistic vigor, Immanuel Kant in famous passage from the *Critique of Practical Reason* again tries to secure human worth by alienating our species from the natural world:

Two things fill the mind with ever new and increasing admiration and rever-ence, the more frequently and persistently one's meditation deals with them: *the starry sky above me and the moral law within me* . . . The first sight, of a count-less multitude of worlds, annihilates, as it were, my importance as an *animal creature* that, after having for a short time been provided (one knows not how) with a vital force, must give back again to the planet (a mere dot in the universe) the matter from which it came. The second sight, on the contrary, elevates infi-nitely my worth as that of an *intelligence* by my personality, in which the moral law reveals to me a life independent of animality.[31]

The explicit connection between ethics, human transcendence, and animal mortality is, however, still more vivid in contemporary examples. In his short book titled *Ethics*, French philosopher Alain Badiou adopts the following exceptionalism of the human subject:

The fact that in the end we all die, that only dust remains, in no way alters Man's identity as immortal at the instant in which he affirms himself as someone who runs counter to the temptation of wanting-to-be-an-animal to which circum-stances may expose him.[32]

In a very similar vein, another French contemporary author distinguishes "Man"[33] from animals and natural processes:

For man is the antinatural being par excellence. This is even what distinguishes him from other beings, including those who seem the closest to him: animals. This is how he escapes natural cycles, how he attains the realm of culture, and the sphere of morality, which presupposes living in accordance with laws and not just with nature.[34]

Badiou as well as Luc Ferry need the concept of "animal" to define their concept of "Man" in opposition to it. What is still more important, however, are specific characteristics of these concepts, revolving around contingent mortality and transcendent ethics. Within such conceptual frameworks, the phrase "animal moral agency" necessarily appears as an oxymoron, since animals are by definition excluded from the realm of transcendence. The human–animal boundary serves the purpose of an existential buffer zone, protecting the "Man" from the knowledge about "his" uncanny proximity to the "animal." To such authors the idea of animal moral conduct sounds almost sacrilegious, since it attacks their central claim about the nature of human identity and dignity. This, then, is the cause of the skeptical conun-drum about "animal minds" and the doubt about the existence of animal behavior that can be best described with ethical vocabulary. Of course, not everybody is so adamant at denying animal moral agency as these authors are, but nonetheless one should not neglect their historical importance and intellectual influence: the ideas of Descartes and Kant have shaped the way we think about ourselves and the world surrounding us for centuries, and it is hard to disregard this cultural influence. Indeed, the presence of these presuppositions may even be something we are unaware of, thus causing our unconscious bias toward other species. This is, in fact, very similar to what a number of authors refer to as "speciesism," a term coined by Richard Ryder in 1970s.

ETHICS, RULES, AND THE ALTERNATIVE CULTURAL IMAGINATION OF ANIMAL MORALITY

We saw in previous sections that questions like "Can animals feel pain?" or "Are animals moral agents?" can easily be answered by observing animals and interacting with them. If these questions persist despite these observable facts, this must be beyond what we can refer to as "empirical demonstration." Indeed, we saw that the human–animal dualisms often enter discussions about the possibility of animal moral agency a priori, without any substantial backup from the natural sciences. We traced the reasons for this dualistic intellectual framework back to our "human condition"—our awareness of the contingency of life. Since the corporeal existence of animals reminds us of our own fragile existence, of our uncanny proximity to the natural world, we are prone to find refuge in the realms of "ethics" and "morality." Ascribing these to the animal kingdom would undermine our stake in transcendence.

There is, however, one often employed philosophical argument against animal morality that has not been mentioned so far and is common even among thinkers who generally support animal ethics by acknowledging animals as moral patients. The argument has to do with the idea that human morality consists primarily in practical application of universal rules or postulates, arrived at with rational analysis. Since animals are largely not capable of abstract thinking—so the argument goes—they in turn cannot be regarded as true moral agents. Animal behavior may resemble human conduct, but since it is not guided by abstract thinking, which is necessary for understanding universal moral rules, animals cannot offer *justifications* of their behavior. This picture of moral agency is what I like to call "rationalist morality," and has advocates even among philosophers like Peter Singer: "The notion of living according to ethical standards is tied up with the notion of defending the way one is living, of giving a reason for it, of justifying it."[35] This reason, however, cannot be just any reason; it has to be a reason that stems from an abstract, universal standpoint: "Ethics requires us to go beyond 'I' and 'you' to the universal law, the universalizable judgment, the standpoint of the impartial spectator or ideal observer, or whatever we choose to call it."[36] Without going too deep into the critique of this argument, let me point out that all theories of rationalist morality generally suffer from what is known as Wittgenstein's "rule-following paradox." The consequence of this paradox, mentioned in the famous paragraph § 201 of *Philosophical Investigations*, is a simple fact that at a certain point I must simply follow rules "blindly," that is, without "choosing" to obey them: "When I obey a rule, I do not choose. I obey the rule *blindly*."[37] Rules namely always already presuppose that we *understand* their content, that we know *how to apply* them. If we say that we know how to apply them according to new abstract and universal rules, then we end up in infinite regress, giving so to speak "one interpretation after another, as if each contended us at least for a moment, until we thought of yet another standing behind it."[38] Therefore, rule-following cannot ultimately be seen as a consequence of rational deliberation, but of a "custom,"[39] a "way of life." Here, however, the distinction between "acting in accordance with rules" and "acting on the basis of rules" disappears. Indeed, the rule-following paradox lets us see that our conduct is much more a matter of our ways of living and speaking than of our abstract ratiocination. In fact, what we call "rationality" simply cannot be removed from our "form of life."

There were, to be sure, many intellectuals and texts in history that had no issues with ascribing intelligence and morality to animals. It is true that many of those authors and literary sources considered animals only as illustrations of human vices or virtues: the famous series of *Bestiaria*, Western medieval manuscripts stemming from *Physiologus*, dedicated to the depiction of animals, is such an example. Pliny the Elder in his already mentioned *Natural History* also offers descriptions of animals with their character traits that strongly resemble moral virtues. Outside the Western tradition, Indian intellectual history offers similar descriptions of animals that can be found in *Panchatantra* and *Jataka* stories. However, it would be wrong to assume that all ancient texts reflected animal subjectivity from such a blatantly anthropomorphic perspective. Indeed, many paragraphs from the Daoist canon can be considered as early examples of reflection of animals' unique subjectivities, perhaps akin to Gilles Deleuze and Félix Guattari's attempt at constructing what they call "Becoming-Animal."[40] One such example of an attempt at understanding animal cognitive faculties from a non-anthropomorphic viewpoint in the Western tradition is Plutarch's *De sollertia animalium*, a text on the intelligence of animals written probably in the second-century CE. Curiously enough, Plutarch there advocates an argument that is in a sense quite similar to Fisher's and Gaita's reflections presented earlier. As Judith Mossman points out, Plutarch seems to claim that "the fact that . . . terms [describing animal mental processes] can be used of animals and have a recognisable application for the reader in itself stacks up the argument against the Stoics,"[41] who insisted that these notions can only be analogies or similes of "true" human cognition. Combining Plutarch's ideas with the Pliny's insight into the inconsistency of ascribing immortality to humans while denying it to animals, one could provocatively assert that the outline of the main argument of this chapter was already presented in late European antiquity and that these authors managed to reflect animal subjectivities with more acumen than, for instance, Cartesian philosophy. While this might indeed be a bit risky hypothesis, one can at least say that historical cultural imagination of animal subjectivity was variegated and complex: it did not rely only on strict opposition between humans and animals and it does provide us with an alternative way of thinking about more than human morality.

Finally, I want to wrap up this chapter by pointing out that the idea that our attitude toward animal morality should not be analyzed only from epistemological and methodological viewpoint but also from existentialist perspectives that emphasize our anxiety with our own mortality. As Marino and Mountain point out drawing from Ernest Becker and Terror Management Theory, "much of human behavior is motivated by anxiety, however unconscious, about personal mortality and that mortality salience is a specific driver of attempts to alleviate this anxiety."[42] It is thus perfectly imaginable that our attitude toward the environment is equally marked by our avoidance of the awareness of finitude. Perhaps our exaggerated hope that "green capitalism" with its "technological innovations" will be able to save both, the planet and our increasing growth is also connected with our escapism, our refusal to acknowledge limitedness and finitude of our existence. We do not avert our gaze only when it comes to problems connected with animal exploitation and their emotional as well as cognitive abilities but also when sociopolitical and environmental issues are at stake. To demonstrate this would, however, demand a new chapter. Luckily, some of the other texts in this volume address the latter cases.

NOTES

1. Paola Cavalieri, *The Animal Question: Why Nonhuman Animals Deserve Human Rights* (Oxford: Oxford University Press, 2001), 29. All italics appear in the works cited.

2. Mark Rowlands, "Animals That Act for Moral Reasons," in *The Oxford Handbook of Animal Ethics*, ed. Tom L. Beauchamp and Raymond G. Frey (Oxford: Oxford University Press, 2013), 521; David DeGrazia, *Taking Animals Seriously— Mental Life and Moral Status* (Cambridge: Cambridge University Press, 1996), 199.

3. Grace Clement, "Animals and Moral Agency: The Recent Debate and Its Implications," *Journal of Animal Ethics*, vol. 3, no. 1 (2013): 9.

4. Cavalieri, *The Animal Question*, 29.

5. For the purpose of this chapter, I use the concepts "morality," "ethics," and "moral agency" interchangeably.

6. Cf.: Tomaž Grušovnik, "The Avoidance of Moral Responsibility Towards Animals: Coleridge's 'The Rime of the Ancient Mariner' and The Human–Animal Boundary," in *The Human–Animal Boundary: Exploring the Line in Philosophy and Fiction*, ed. Nandita Batra and Mario Wenning (Lanham, MD: Lexington, 2018).

7. Stanley Cavell, *The Claim of Reason: Wittgenstein, Skepticism, Morality, and Tragedy* (Oxford: Oxford University Press, 1979), 493.

8. Amy Fitzgerald, "A Social History of the Slaughterhouse: From Inception to Contemporary Implications," *Human Ecology Review*, vol. 17, no. 1 (2010): 60.

9. Noëlie Vialles, *Animal to Edible* (Cambridge: Cambridge University Press, 1994).

10. Jennifer Dillard, "A Slaughterhouse Nightmare: Psychological Harm Suffered by Slaughterhouse Employees and the Possibility of Redress through Legal Reform," *Georgetown Journal on Poverty Law & Policy*, vol. 15, no. 2 (2008); Jocelyne Porcher, "The Relationship Between Workers and Animals in the Pork Industry: A Shared Suffering," *Journal of Agriculture and Environmental Ethics*, vol. 24 (2018); Melanie Joy, *Why We Love Dogs, Eat Pigs, and Wear Cows: An Introduction to Carnism* (San Francisco, CA: Conari Press, 2010).

11. Joy, *Why We Love Dogs*, 18–21.

12. Stanley Cavell, *Disowning Knowledge in Seven Plays of Shakespeare* (Cambridge: Cambridge University Press, 2003), 95.

13. Clement, "Animals and Moral Agency," 9.

14. Marc Bekoff, *The Animal Manifesto—Six Reasons for Expanding Our Compassion Footprint* (Novato, CA: New World Library, 2010), 80–81.

15. Cynthia Willett, *Interspecies Ethics* (New York, NY: Columbia University Press, 2014), 75.

16. Ibid., 78–79.

17. Frans de Waal, *Good Natured—The Origins of Right and Wrong in Humans and Other Animals* (Harvard, MA: Harvard University Press, 1996), 211.

18. John Andrew Fisher, "A Myth of Anthropomorphism", in *Readings in Animal Cognition*, ed. Marc Bekoff and Dale Jamieson (Harvard, MA: MIT Press, 1996), 3, 11.

19. Clement, "Animals and Moral Agency," 8.

20. Ludwig Wittgenstein, *Philosophical Investigations* (Oxford: Basil Blackwell, 1958), § 43.

21. Raimond Gaita, *The Philosopher's Dog: Friendship With Animals* (New York, NY: Random House, 2005), 62–63.

22. Roger Crisp, "Evolution and Psychological Unity," in *Readings in Animal Cognition*, ed. Marc Bekoff and Dale Jamieson (Harvard, MA: MIT Press, 1996), 310.

23. Cavalieri, *The Animal Question*, 14.

24. Ibid., 14–15.

25. Clement, "Animals and Moral Agency," 9.

26. Georg Wilhelm Friedrich Hegel, *The Phenomenology of Mind*, vol. 1, tr. J. B. Baillie (New York, NY: Routledge, 2014), 75.

27. Cf. Grušovnik, "The Avoidance of Moral Responsibility."

28. Lori Marino and Michael Mountain, "Denial of Death and the Relationship between Humans and Other Animals," *Anthrozoös*, vol. 28, no. 1 (2015): 5.

29. Pliny the Elder, *Natural History*, vol. 2, tr. Philemon Holland (London: Barclay, 1847), 248–9.

30. René Descartes, *Discourse on the Method. The Philosophical Writings of Descartes*, vol. 1, tr. Robert Stoothoff (Cambridge: Cambridge University Press, 1985), 141.

31. Immanuel Kant, *Critique of Practical Reason*, tr. Werner S. Puhlar (Cambridge: Hackett Publishing Company, 2002), 203.

32. Alain Badiou, *Ethics—An Essay on the Understanding of Evil*, tr. Peter Hallward (London: Verso, 2001), 12.

33. Perhaps it is worth adding here that this term is in itself a rather sexist concept, which ties in well with human–animal dualistic thinking, where "man," "human," "reason," and "culture" stand on the one side and "woman," "animal," "emotion," and "nature" on the other side of the conceptual divide. That the oppression of women and nature shares the same roots was well explored already by Theodor Adorno and Max Horkheimer in their *Dialectic of Enlightenment* (tr. Edmund Jephcott (Stanford, CA: Stanford University Press, 2002), 203–12; section "Man and Beast"), and has, as is generally known, became one of the central theoretical building blocks of ecofeminism.

34. Luc Ferry, *New Ecological Order*, tr. Carol Volk (Chicago, IL: University of Chicago Press, 1995), xxviii.

35. Peter Singer, *Practical Ethics* (Cambridge: Cambridge University Press, 1993), 10.

36. Ibid., 12.

37. Ludwig Wittgenstein, *Philosophical Investigations* (Oxford: Blackwell, 1998), § 219.

38. Ibid., § 201.

39. Ibid., § 199.

40. See Irving Goh, "Chuang Tzu's Becoming-Animal," *Philosophy East and West*, vol. 61, no. 1 (2011).

41. Judith Mossman, "Plutarch on Animals: Rhetorical Strategies in 'de Sollertia Animalium'," *Hermathena*, vol. 179 (2005): 148.

42. Marino and Mountain, "Denial of Death," 8.

BIBLIOGRAPHY

Adorno, Theodor, and Max Horkheimer. *Dialectic of Enlightenment.* Translated by Edmund Jephcott. Stanford, CA: Stanford University Press, 2002.

Badiou, Alain. *Ethics—An Essay on the Understanding of Evil*. Translated by Peter Hallward. London: Verso, 2001.

Bekoff, Marc. *The Animal Manifesto—Six Reasons for Expanding Our Compassion Footprint*. Novato, CA: New World Library, 2010.

Cavalieri, Paola. *The Animal Question. Why Nonhuman Animals Deserve Human Rights*. Oxford: Oxford University Press, 2001.

Cavell, Stanley. *The Claim of Reason: Wittgenstein, Skepticism, Morality, and Tragedy*. Oxford: Oxford University Press, 1979.

Cavell, Stanley. *Disowning Knowledge in Seven Plays of Shakespeare*. Cambridge: Cambridge University Press, 2003.

Clement, Grace. "Animals and Moral Agency: The Recent Debate and Its Implications." *Journal of Animal Ethics*, vol. 3, no. 1 (2013): 1–14.

Crisp, Roger. "Evolution and Psychological Unity." In *Readings in Animal Cognition*, 309–21. Edited by Marc Bekoff and Dale Jamieson. Harvard, MA: MIT Press, 1996.

DeGrazia, David. *Taking Animals Seriously—Mental Life and Moral Status*. Cambridge: Cambridge University Press, 1996.

Descartes, René. *Discourse on the Method. The Philosophical Writings of Descartes*, vol. 1, 111–51. Translated by Robert Stoothoff. Cambridge: Cambridge University Press, 1985.

Dillard, Jennifer. "A Slaughterhouse Nightmare: Psychological Harm Suffered by Slaughterhouse Employees and the Possibility of Redress through Legal Reform." *Georgetown Journal on Poverty Law & Policy*, vol. 15, no. 2 (2008): 391–408.

Ferry, Luc. *New Ecological Order*. Translated by Carol Volk. Chicago, IL: University of Chicago Press, 1995.

Fisher, John Andrew. "A Myth of Anthropomorphism." In *Readings in Animal Cognition*, 3–16. Edited by Marc Bekoff and Dale Jamieson. Harvard, MA: MIT Press, 1996.

Fitzgerald, Amy. "A Social History of the Slaughterhouse: From Inception to Contemporary Implications." *Human Ecology Review*, vol. 17, no. 1 (2010): 58–69.

Gaita, Raimond. *The Philosopher's Dog: Friendship With Animals*. New York, NY: Random House, 2005.

Goh, Irving. "Chuang Tzu's Becoming-Animal." *Philosophy East and West*, vol. 61, no. 1 (2011): 110–33.

Grušovnik, Tomaž. "The Avoidance of Moral Responsibility Towards Animals: Coleridge's 'The Rime of the Ancient Mariner' and The Human–Animal Boundary." In *The Human–Animal Boundary: Exploring the Line in Philosophy and Fiction*, 81–95. Edited by Nandita Batra and Mario Wenning. Lanham, MD: Lexington, 2018.

Hegel, Georg Wilhelm Friedrich. *The Phenomenology of Mind*, vol. 1. Translated by J. B. Baillie. New York, NY: Routledge, 2014.

Joy, Melanie. *Why We Love Dogs, Eat Pigs, and Wear Cows: An Introduction to Carnism*. San Francisco, CA: Conari Press, 2010.

Kant, Immanuel. *Critique of Practical Reason*. Translated by Werner S. Puhlar. Cambridge: Hackett Publishing Company, 2002.

Marino, Lori, and Michael Mountain. "Denial of Death and the Relationship between Humans and Other Animals." *Anthrozoös*, vol. 28, no. 1 (2015): 5–21.

Mossman, Judith. "Plutarch on Animals: Rhetorical Strategies in 'de Sollertia Animalium'," *Hermathena*, vol. 179 (2005): 141–63.

Pliny the Elder. *Natural History*, vol. 2. Translated by Philemon Holland. London: Barclay, 1847.

Porcher, Jocelyne. "The Relationship Between Workers and Animals in the Pork Industry: A Shared Suffering." *Journal of Agriculture and Environmental Ethics*, vol. 24 (2018): 3–17.

Rowlands, Mark. "Animals That Act for Moral Reasons." In *The Oxford Handbook of Animal Ethics*, 519–46. Edited by Tom L. Beauchamp and Raymond G. Frey. Oxford: Oxford University Press, 2013.

Singer, Peter. *Practical Ethics*. Cambridge: Cambridge University Press, 1993.

Vialles, Noëlie. *Animal to Edible*. Cambridge: Cambridge University Press, 1994.

Waal, Frans de. *Good Natured—The Origins of Right and Wrong in Humans and Other Animals*. Harvard, MA: Harvard University Press, 1996.

Willett, Cynthia. *Interspecies Ethics*. New York, NY: Columbia University Press, 2014.

Wittgenstein, Ludwig. *Philosophical Investigations*. Translated by G. E. M. Anscombe. Oxford: Basil Blackwell, 1958.

Chapter 4

Human Uniqueness, Animal Minds, and Anthropodenial

Adam See

Contemporary philosophers and scientists remain widely resistant to attributing humanlike cognitive capacities to nonhuman animals, particularly great apes, for reasons that are often not based on compelling empirical or theoretical grounds. Anthropomorphic bias is clearly capable of clouding our theories of animal minds; so too is "anthropodenial"[1] or "anthropectomy,"[2] an epistemic predisposition to discredit evidence for mental continuity hypotheses, or more generally, "a blindness to the humanlike characteristics of other animals."[3] Bernard Rollin, for instance, questions the tendency of "empirically-oriented philosophers and biological and psychological scientists to be agnostic if not downright atheistic about animal mind."[4] Anthropodenial arises in several flavors of skeptical argumentation and strongly influences the popular corner of the animal minds literature dedicated to questions of human uniqueness.

Twenty-first-century comparative cognition has seen a "virtual epidemic of new theories of human cognitive uniqueness," in the form of "sweeping characterizations of the differences between humans and other species."[5] The aim of this chapter is to survey and critically evaluate four argumentative strategies commonly used to deny humanlike cognitive capacities to animals. Importantly, these lines of argumentation are not inherently problematic; in each case, I provide examples of constructive and nonconstructive uses.

1. *Denial by Disparate Contexts*: To demonstrate the presence of capacity X in a nonhuman species, members of that species must perform a wide variety of different types of behaviors in different contexts associated with X. The number and/or types of contests need not be stated.

2. *Denial by Cognitive Simplicity*: To demonstrate the presence of capacity X in a nonhuman species, it must first be shown that their X-like behaviors could not also be caused—or, that it is less likely that they are caused—by "simpler" (i.e., less advanced, complex, etc.) capacities.
3. *Denial by Redefinition*: To demonstrate the presence of capacity X in a nonhuman species, it must first be shown that the behavioral repertoire of the species in question can accommodate a more exclusive definition of X.
4. *Denial by Human Ability*: To demonstrate the presence of capacity X in a nonhuman species, it must first be shown that the species in question can perform token behaviors commonly associated with X when humans do X.

Arguments of this nature often arise in response to legitimate concerns about avoiding anthropomorphic overinterpretations of animal behavior. Unfortunately, they have been used by philosophers and primatologists alike to stalemate once-promising research programs such as those hypothesizing theory of mind and joint attention in chimpanzees. To grasp how these arguments function in the human uniqueness literature to deny mental capacities to animals, some background on contemporary animal minds skepticism is necessary.

THE LOGICAL PROBLEM

Discussions among philosophers and primatologists regarding social cognition have long taken place under the influence of the *logical problem*. In its basic form, the logical problem states that since all we can observe is an animal's behavior, it is difficult (if not impossible) to determine whether an animal is predicting the behavior of others by means of mental state attribution, for example, of their underlying intentions, desires, and beliefs, *or* by means of associative or conditioned response mechanisms formed by experience with various bodily and societal cues, for example, facial expression/ orientation, gait, gestures, vocalizations, erect hair. As Kristin Andrews describes this impasse, "given that mindreaders use observable cues to infer the existence of mental states, how can we experimentally distinguish a predictor who uses only those observable cues from a predictor who also attributes mental states?"[6] In the chimpanzee mindreading literature, the logical problem rests on the task of designing experiments capable of distinguishing behaviors indicative of "two very general and opposing theories" of socio-cognitive mechanisms: behavior-reading hypotheses and mindreading hypotheses.[7]

Premack and Woodruff popularized these debates by speculating "about the possibility that the chimpanzee may have a 'theory of mind,' one not markedly different from our own."[8] Based on their experiments, they concluded that chimpanzees are mindreaders in the minimal sense of attributing goals and intentions to others. Fletcher and Carruthers call this "stage 1 mind reading," which they contrast with "stage 2 mind reading," namely, the ability to attribute "reality incongruent mental states" such as false beliefs to others.[9] The original mindreading skeptics such as Daniel Dennett justifiably noted that (what are now called) behavior-reading hypotheses can in principle "'handle' all ape behavior."[10]

In addition to this threat of global skepticism, much of the mindreading research in the 1990s was highly critical of Premack and Woodruff's hypothesis. Provocative experiments by Povinelli and Eddy, for instance, showed that chimpanzees beg for food indiscriminately from a human with a bucket covering their head, and from a human without, thereby suggesting that chimpanazees do not attribute mental states such as 'seeing' or 'attention' when begging for food.[11] Soon after, however, experimenters garnered results highly suggestive of mindreading hypotheses by designing experiments that mimicked scenarios chimpanzees actually experience in the wild. Brian Hare and colleagues allowed chimpanzees the ability to employ deceptive tactics when competing for food by placing various barriers between them, controlling what each chimpanzee could and could not see.[12] During various competitive trials, the actions of subordinate chimpanzees *were* affected by what dominant chimpanzees could and could not see, as well as whether their opponent possessed or lacked prior knowledge of the food source.

In response, it became clear that two distinct groups had formed: those—like Hare—who saw these numerous food competition experiments as evidence for mindreading, and those—sometimes called "killjoys"—for whom Hare's experiments failed to overcome the logical problem. To Povinelli and Vonk, the chimpanzees' behavior is better explained with the learned behavioral rule: "Do not go after food if a dominant who is present has oriented towards it."[13] By the twenty-first century, long-standing demands for parsimonious explanations—for example, complementary behavior-reading hypotheses—and for additional experiments—for example, can chimpanzees pass a false-belief test?[14]—had developed such that this debate no longer appeared amenable to empirical resolution. Indeed, Povinelli and Vonk's claim that:

The problem we face is not primarily an empirical one. Instead, the most pressing problem is to come to grips with the fact that the experimental results from the kinds of techniques that are currently in vogue cannot add a single bit of evidence in unique support of the conclusion that chimpanzees reason about mental states—*any* mental states.[15]

Povinelli and Vonk did not offer experimental guidance. Indeed, it seemed that no experiment could effectively demonstrate mindreading in chimps, not just those "currently in vogue." They admit as much: to them, the logical problem is ultimately not an empirical problem.

The logical problem is *a conceptual problem masquerading as an empirical problem.* Conceptual problems are "higher order questions about the well-roundedness of the conceptual structures (e.g., theories) which have been devised to answer the first order questions."[16] Such problems rarely arise from the subject-matter itself (the domain of empirical problems), but from the foundational assumptions and epistemic constraints from which researchers approach that subject matter. In mindreading debates, in addition to empirical questions concerning the relevance of the behavioral, biological, and neuroanatomical facts about chimpanzee and human social behavior, there is the epistemic (conceptual) question here as to how much, and what kind, of evidence will suffice to demonstrate the conclusion that apes attribute mental states to others. In a progressive research program, there can be large-scale disagreement over what the evidence tells us and how much is sufficient, and there can be—*should* be, ideally—competing hypotheses to explain the data/ behavior in question. This is the nuts and bolts of a normal, healthy situation in the natural sciences, but this is not the case in the mind-reading literature, where "the worry arises that no experiment can in principle avoid these alternative explanations."[17] The logical problem presently borrows as much from the philosophical problem of other minds as it does from the underdetermination of theories by evidence.

What is more, Laudan describes a particularly damning set of conceptual problems that arise when "basic categories of analysis are vague and unclear."[18] Ambiguities in defining and distinguishing cognitive processes decrease their empirical tractability and, at worst, can lead to theories incapable of making novel predictions. Consider behavior-reading hypotheses. Unlike mindreading hypotheses, they are unfalsifiable, that is, "too under-specified to make determinate predictions," and ad hoc, that is, explanations "can always be constructed after the fact," which is how Povinelli and colleagues employ them.[19] This evaluative process is not empirical; rather, it constitutes an ongoing game of positing hypothetical non-mentalistic explanations for animal behavior, none of which are capable of predicting novel behaviors distinct from mindreading hypotheses. The latter, in contrast, constitute "a progressing research program, issuing in a stream of positive results and increasingly precise theories."[20] Nonetheless, routine deference to the illusory simplicity of behavior rule hypotheses has foreclosed empirically tractable hypotheses about chimpanzee social cognition.

We need not be concerned that "complementary" hypotheses exist to explain a given phenomenon; we should expect it. What we should be concerned with is which hypothesis best accounts for the current collection of data such that we might provide reasonable *arguments to the best explanation*. Rather than focus solely on crucial experiments as the basis for optimism about the future of the mindreading research program,[21] researchers should pull congruous evidence from a wide variety of sources and develop what Whewell called a "consilience of inductions."[22] In contrast, consider the shared assumptions of Povinelli and Lurz. From the perspective of the logical problem, *twenty* extant studies suggestive of mindreading abilities—so long as they all admit of complementary behavior-reading hypotheses—are ultimately as valueless as a single such study. This state of affairs explains the popular presumption that crucial experiments are necessary to progress the literature. Lurz et al., for instance, claim that "the best way forward at this point is neither to believe nor to deny the existence of animal mindreading, but to suspend judgment on the issue until tests have been carried out that overcome Povinelli's problem."[23] In the sections that follow, I show how this well-intentioned "agnosticism" is manifest in practice as denialism.

DISPARATE CONTEXTS

There is a sense in which the skeptic's demand is not unreasonable. As Penn and Povinelli assert, "demonstrating that a nonverbal subject possesses an explicit mental state concept requires 'triangulating' across disparate protocols and showing that the subject cognizes the common causal role played by a given mental state across perceptually disparate task contexts."[24] If a challenge is raised to a human uniqueness claim that *cannot* demonstrate these conditions, this strategy functions in a very simple, effective manner: *collect more evidence to eliminate confounding variables*. The ability to provide suggestive evidence for a hypothesis across a wide variety of experimental contexts is clearly an experimental virtue not only in the animal minds literature, but also in scientific method generally. That said, due to the tenacity of the logical problem it is also evident that this strategy can be overused and turned into a go-to mode of skepticism to shoot down practically any experiment or compilation of evidence. How many distinct experimental contexts are sufficient to demonstrate a mindreading hypothesis? What type of contexts will suffice? These are crucial questions that those who take the logical problem seriously lack answers (Penn and Povinelli, ironically, provide a case in point).[25] With respect to those who propose specific crucial experiments to solve the logical problem,[26] their proposals have *also* been shown to likely allow for complementary behavior-reading hypotheses.[27]

The "agnosticism" advocated by Lurz and colleagues includes Call and Tomasello's claim, published on the thirtieth anniversary of Premack and Woodruff's article, that the collective experimental literature strongly suggests that chimpanzees "understand others in terms of a relatively coherent perception–goal psychology in which the other acts in a certain way because she perceives the world in a certain way and has certain goals of how she wants the world to be."[28] Despite disagreement over whether the logical problem can be overcome, "In a broad construal of the phrase 'theory of mind' . . . the answer to Premack and Woodruff's pregnant question of 30 years ago is a definite yes." A decade later, the evidence is even greater. Ever since Dennett's response[29] to Premack and Woodruff,[30] nonlinguistic iterations of the *false-belief test*—a litmus test for theory of mind in human infants—have been proposed to evaluate mindreading in chimpanzees. While chimpanzees have failed a variety of false-belief tests since the 1980s, this changed in 2017 with two empirical studies suggestive that great apes are capable of attributing false beliefs to others.[31]

There is good reason to accept the hypothesis that chimpanzees understand others in terms of a perception/goal psychology, and perhaps also something like a belief/desire psychology. In contrast, for Lurz and colleagues even the claim that chimpanzees are capable of attributing perceptual states to others, like *seeing*, is worthy is rejection.[32] Social behaviors indicative of such attributions can be more parsimoniously explained, they argue, with learned behavioral rules: the behavior of others is predicted entirely by means of inferences drawn from past bodily and facial orientation, for example, instead of chimps holding the propositional attitude *X sees Y,* the same behavior(s) can follow from them making inferences of the sort *X has a "direct line-of-gaze" to Y*, which does not entail mental state attribution.

Lurz et al. do advocate scientific fallibilism about animal mindreading, but their position is not standard in at least three respects. First, they portray these debates as if one must either totally affirm or totally deny chimpanzee mindreading hypotheses,[33] rather than viewing them in terms of varying probability based on evidence. Second, they place far too much emphasis—indeed, *all* their emphasis—on the success of crucial experiments as the only motivator of progress in mindreading debates, whereas the history of science suggests that crucial experiments rarely fill this role.[34] Third, in adopting strict "agnosticism," they implicitly reject how progress *is* most often made in the history of science: arguments to the best explanation drawn from a consilience of inductions, such as the wealth of evidence informing Call and Tomasello's more progressive position, decades after the debate began, that chimps arguably possess abilities for stage 1 mindreading.[35]

Against the wealth of positive support for these abilities, Penn and Povinelli argue that there is a "lack of evidence for anything even remotely resembling a theory of mind among nonhuman animals."[36] What is going on here? Oddly enough, they argue both that the past twenty-five years of evidence suggestive of chimpanzee mindreading is insufficient, while at the same time ostensibly denying that *any* evidence would likely suffice to solve the logical problem. Cecilia Heyes rightly claims that while the animal minds literature from 1978 to 2000 showed "considerable promise," more recent debates have been mired with theoretical and methodological problems indicative of a "declining research program" that now "seems to be in trouble."[37] I will now explain what I take to be the root of the logical problem.

COGNITIVE SIMPLICITY

Once a proponent of animal minds skepticism,[38] Heyes has more recently expressed her growing concerns with the "current of opinion in the study of comparative cognition suggesting we should assume that animals have simple minds," arguing that an ontology informed by a behavioristic "simple mindedness" has not aided the discipline, as "[i]n the most extreme cases, the claim that animals have simple minds amounts to the claim that associative learning is the only way in which animals can think about the world."[39] This de facto acceptance of "simple mindedness" in animal research has encouraged either/or dichotomies between association and cognition, which Heyes suggests are a major reason for the "decline" in the mindreading research program.[40]

A variety of disciplines are now considering more than ever the apparent fact that "complex" or "intelligent" behavior in human beings—perhaps even the majority of such behavior in daily life—is the product of mechanisms once thought to be "simple." Shannon Spaulding, for instance, convincingly argues that "mindreading is a rarely used, specialized skill,"[41] and as Andrews notes, "if other species predict, manipulate, deceive, compete, and so forth without mindreading, then we have no reason to think that humans need to do so."[42] The emerging picture is that associative learning plays a critical role in complex human behaviors that *appear* motivated by cognitive mechanisms (presumably) like mindreading.[43]

Increased emphasis on blurring the lines between associative and cognitive mechanisms is not good news for those hoping to "solve" the logical problem in research programs like theory of mind. This debate has traditionally relied on—and indeed, requires—rigid distinctions precisely of this kind, that is, mindreading hypotheses evoke "mentalistic" mechanisms while behavior-reading hypotheses evoke "simple-minded" associative mechanisms. The reason for this problematic assumption can be traced back to Morgan's Canon in the late nineteenth century and its constant misinterpretations throughout the twentieth century.[44] According to Lloyd Morgan, "In no case may we interpret an action as the outcome of the exercise of a higher psychical faculty, if it can be interpreted as the outcome of the exercise of one which stands lower in the psychological scale."[45]

The principle of cognitive simplicity (PoCS) encourages researchers to adopt two outmoded ontological assumptions shared by both Morgan's Canon and—I argue—the logical problem. First, *simplicity* entails associative mechanisms and *complexity* entails cognitive mechanisms; second, that there exists a relatively unproblematic cognitive hierarchy in nature wherein the mechanisms underlying animal behavior can be ordered by complexity.[46] As Elliot Sober argues, the ontological assumptions underlying Morgan's Canon clash with evolutionary theory and do not, strictly speaking, rest on principles of parsimony.[47] Parsimonious explanations are those that postulate comparatively *fewer* entities than competing explanations, but Morgan's Canon does not preference theories of this nature; it preferences theories that postulate comparatively "lower" faculties or processes in terms of a *scala naturae* (or otherwise hierarchical view) of cognitive complexity. As Louise Barrett likewise notes:

> Morgan's canon implicitly assumes a *scala naturae* in terms of the expected distribution of cognitive endowments across the animal kingdom. . . . Assuming that, for example, chimpanzees will show many of the precursors to human cognition because they are our closest living relatives assumes that . . . we moved up the ladder and left the chimpanzee stuck on a lower rung . . . Such assumptions . . . pervade comparative studies. The possibility that these creatures may possess some unique skills of their own is rarely, if ever, entertained.[48]

Morgan himself acknowledged this issue, and while he remained convinced that animal behavior should be explained with associative mechanisms, by his own admission: "I am very far from wishing to occupy the false position of dogmatic denial of rational powers to animals."[49] Unfortunately, as a growing number of commentators now accept, "the Canon has often served as a convenient justification for a priori resistance to attributions of mental states to animals."[50] The logical problem likewise shares this fate.

The logical problem does not simply describe an impasse between competing sorts of theories; this problem is related to the PoCS in that both are constrained by arguments from parsimony and bear normative weight: because behavioral rules are assumed to be less cognitively taxing, it is scientifically irresponsible to attribute a theory of mind to chimpanzees.[51] In line with Sober's critique of Morgan's Canon, when the logical problem tacitly adopts this normative role it assumes outmoded assumptions about evolutionary biology. The logical problem uses human cognitive capacities as the "gold standard"[52] for what qualifies as "complex" or "cognitive" means of responding to environmental problems. Recalling Barrett's point, unique skills that other species may use to solve similar problems, and which may entail a high degree of complexity in their own right, are fallaciously ignored by means of a false dichotomy. For example, rather than "Ask[ing] ourselves 'What kind of a theory of mind is adaptive for chimpanzees to acquire?' and 'When do they use it?'"[53] mindreading is traditionally defined exclusively in terms of attributing propositional attitudes to others.[54]

By virtue of dropping the de facto orthogenetic perspective, that is, that of "a single evolutionary trajectory culminating in *Homo sapiens*,"[55] these sorts of questions immediately relieve some of the logical problem's force. Without the orthogenetic lens, new interpretive possibilities emerge that transcend the theory of mind *or* "simple mindedness" dichotomy endemic to traditional formulations of both the PoCS and the logical problem.

For example, in the concluding section of *Do Apes Read Minds?* Andrews suggests the need for "a new research program" that, in contrast with the sorts of questions motivated by the dominant cognitivist framework of the past sixty years (such as the title of her book), urges researchers and philosophers alike to think beyond understanding apes as "containers for sets of propositional attitudes," and—instead—view them "holistically" with personalities, life histories, "smells, tics, cultures, status, and various idiosyncrasies."[56] Such a perspective is "consistent with a developmental picture" wherein, as the "social domain expands," "psychological profiles" are formed by means of a "combination of automatic processes" and "general principles . . . generated from previous individual personality profiles." Andrews is concerned that "mindreading accounts miss the richness and variety in our social interactions," and thus proposes a research program that views apes in a way that "better reflects the way we relate with other people."[57] The outmoded ontological assumptions on which the logical problem rests make it inimical to such a project.

REDEFINITION BY HUMAN ABILITY

Philosophers and scientists should expect new evidence to lead to refined definitions of core concepts. It is easy to imagine cases where animal behavior satisfies criteria for possessing a certain characteristic, for example, culture, only to have that concept redefined in light of the fact that there *do* seem to be relevant differences between, say, human and chimpanzee material culture. If the original definition was insufficient to capture those differences, the literature might be advanced by narrowing—and thus clarifying—its application. There are, then, problematic and unproblematic types of orthogenetic perspectives in comparative cognition. If our goal is to determine (1) the origins of a human characteristic, or (2) whether or not a species possesses or lacks a human characteristic, it might be reasonable to define cognitive concepts at the highest level of human ability. Unfortunately, the most complex of human faculties are often used as the "gold standard" to define the "true" or "real" meanings of core cognitive concepts, thereby denying their application to the behavior of nonhuman species.[58]

An argument repeatedly touted by Micheal Tomasello and colleagues, for instance, is that humans are the only species that "truly" cooperates because they alone possess a "socio-cognitive infrastructure" for shared intentionality, and thus uniquely engage in *"truly joint* joint attention."[59] The concept of shared intentionality is often used as a description of the logic underlying arguably the most complex form of communication: recursive mindreading, that is, A understands that B understands that A wishes B to attend to C. Put as such, C represents "the human capacity to establish common ground between interlocutors," and this third piece of the "referential triangle" is "a crucial aspect of human cooperative communication."[60] Under this definition, to engage in joint attention *is* to engage in shared intentionality. In line with my critique of overly exclusive definitions of theory of mind, Skyrms claims that "cooperation often involves various kinds of feedback mechanisms, but recursive mindreading, higher-order intentions, and mutual belief are only relevant concepts in very special cases."[61] To posit a single socio-cognitive mechanism responsible for all joint attentional activities, and then to *define* that mechanism in terms of the most complex form of human cooperation, is a clear case of *anthropofabulation*, that is, "our tendency to tie the competence criteria for cognitive capacities to an exaggerated sense of typical human performance."[62]

This move is also indicative of what Buckner calls *semantic anthropocentrism*: "precisifying vaguely-defined psychological terms to human-level ability."[63] The intimate relationship between semantic anthropocentrism and anthropofabulation—and between the Human Ability and Redefinition strategies—is highlighted by Griffin,[64] who identifies a "double standard" in comparative cognition wherein definitions for concepts applied to animal minds are derived from "the most complex levels of understanding known to human thinkers" often "meeting these requirements would eliminate many members of our own species." For Tomasello, while apes *appear* to engage in joint attentional activities, their inability for recursive mindreading necessitates that we relegate those behaviors to qualitatively different *kinds* of interactions than those of humans whenever they engage in similar activities, for example, active/tailored teaching among chimpanzees.[65] My point is not that chimpanzees possess shared intentionality (that seems unlikely); it is that joint attention should not be defined *as* shared intentionality.

In a highly influential paper, Bates et al. define joint attention as the ability for two or more individuals to "co-orient" toward a shared goal or locus.[66] Pointing gestures only acquire their meaning if both participants "share" a common focus of attention. Insofar as they utilize pointing gestures as means to reach desired ends, apes *do* point effectively.[67] If effective pointing requires joint attention, then apes engage in joint attention. Tomasello and colleagues have modified the standard definition of joint attention to better support their philosophical claims about human uniqueness. This leads them to an unparsimonious explanation of all joint attentional human activities. If you and I are having a conversation and I suddenly direct your attention to a speedily approaching bus with my finger, I do not, at least consciously, run through any recursive logical processes in my mind. Human beings clearly have the *ability* for recursive mindreading, but Tomasello assumes that it is occurring *somewhere beneath every interaction* indicative of joint attention. Shared intentionality is not merely a description of *how* humans communicate (as used in the philosophy of action literature). As Racine notes, in Tomasello's account, shared intentionality is now "reified" into a unique "adaptation" or "cognitive machinery" that makes possible, that is, plays a *causal* role in, the phylogenetic and ontogenetic development of these communicative abilities.[68] Redefinition by Human Ability has driven Tomasello's uniqueness claim onto precarious ontological foundations.

Tomasello and colleagues are investigating worthwhile questions about the origins of human communication. There is nothing inherently wrong with using the observation that our closest living ancestors appear to "lack" X as an explanatory device for identifying major differences in their X-related skill sets and ours. To the contrary, there are clearly questions that are best approached in this way. Consider Preston and de Waal's "perception–action model" for understanding the evolution of empathy.[69] The authors offer a "Russian doll"—style account of how all species with mirror neurons (among other neuroanatomical features) possess a basic capacity for "emotional contagion," while only those species that additionally have a theory of mind additionally possess the capacity for empathy. Preston and de Waal's orthogenetic approach to the question "Is empathy uniquely human?" does not tacitly evoke *scala naturae* implications of "higher" (empathy) and "lower" (emotional contagion) capacities. This is a responsible use of the orthogenetic perspective as it opens up more questions of potential continuities than it closes off, for example, "what are the rudiments of a theory of mind?" rather than "do chimpanzees lack (an adult human) theory of mind?"

Beginning inquiry from an orthogenetic perspective is more problematic when the impetus for erecting a cognitive hierarchy is to defend human uniqueness claims. We need to be far more cautious when attempting to explain the *lack* of (what appears to be) a uniquely human behavior in other

species *in terms of* their *lack* of (what appears to be) a uniquely human mechanism. Much can go wrong by drawing this sort of inference, not the least of
which being that just because a chimpanzee, for example, does not perform
behavior X (which is associated with mechanism Y in humans), this does not
necessarily imply that Y is absent in chimps, that is, perhaps chimps use Y
for other purposes and there are ecological, societal, or anatomical reasons
for why they do not do X. It is precisely this argumentative move that rests
at the crux of the aforementioned joint attention debates, where "top-down"
orthogenetic approaches readily lend themselves to semantic anthropocentrism and anthropofabulation. Terms like *"truly joint* joint attention" evoke
scala naturae assumptions and are inimical to gradualist approaches to mental processes that, for instance, focus on the comparative development of joint
attention in infant humans and chimpanzees.[70]

LOOKING FORWARD

Lori Gruen aptly describes a "bar-raising dialectic" endemic to debates about
human uniqueness wherein, "even in the face of clear evidence establishing
continuities between human skills and the skills used by some non-humans,
skeptics either deny it actually happened or minimize the significance of that
activity."[71] I have evaluated four such modes of skepticism.

There do exist progressive strategies for positing uniqueness claims about
humans. Before we say that animals "lack" X and navigate their environment
with minimal to no cognitive tools, we should ask: Has X been defined too
exclusively? Does X arise in degrees in human development, and if so, how
might this influence our discussions of X's possible presence in animals?
Does X have functionally analogous counterparts in the animal kingdom, and
if so, might it be more accurate to say that humans have *one kind* of X—a
particularly complex one—rather than argue that nonhuman animals lack X
entirely? Philosophers would not struggle so much to argue that X is uniquely
human if they had more options waiting in the wings to explain animal
behavior without X; that is, besides associative mechanisms, instincts, and
the obdurate, fuzzy and ultimately ad hoc "behavior-reading hypothesis." In
the mindreading and joint attention debates, the problem is not the inaccessi-
bility of the animal mind; it is the challenge of explaining minute differences
between human and animal behavior without first charting out the similarities
implicit in these gray areas.

Likewise, to be grounded in scientific fallibilism rather than philosophical
skepticism, the logical problem must be allowed to arise on a case-by-case
basis in gradients of incredulity, for example, one should be *more skeptical*
that chimpanzees are stage 2 mindreaders than stage 1 mindreaders, but not

feel compelled to reject the latter claim on principle. Such "all or nothing" assumptions reliably engender denialism. If its obstinacy endures, the logical problem must be amenable to arguments to the best explanation fueled by a consilience of inductions.

NOTES

1. Frans de Waal, "Are We in Anthropodenial?" *Discover*, vol. 18, no. 7 (1997): 50–53.
2. Kristin Andrews and Brian Huss, "Anthropomorphism, Anthropectomy, and the Null Hypothesis." *Biology and Philosophy*, vol. 29, no. 5 (2014).
3. De Waal, "Are We in Anthropodenial," 51.
4. Bernard Rollin, "Animal Mind: Science, Philosophy, and Ethics," in *Animal Minds and Animal Ethics*, ed. Klaus Petrus and Markus Wild (Verlag, Bielefeld: Transcript Press, 2013), 15.
5. Sara Shettleworth, "Modularity, Comparative Cognition and Human Uniqueness." *Philosophical Transactions of the Royal Society B: Biological Sciences*, vol. 367 (2012): 2794.
6. Kristin Andrews, *Do Apes Read Minds?* (Cambridge, MA: MIT Press, 2012).
7. Robert Lurz, Sharisse Kanet, and Carla Krachun, "Animal Mindreading: A Defense of Agnostic Optimism." *Mind and Language*, vol. 29, no. 4 (2014).
8. David Premack and Guy Woodruff, "Does the Chimpanzee Have a Theory of Mind?" *Behavioral and Brain Sciences*, vol. 4 (1978): 515.
9. Logan Fletcher and Peter Carruthers, "Behavior-Reading versus Mentalizing in Animals," in *Agency and Joint Attention*, ed. Janet Metcalfe and Herbert S. Terrace (New York, NY: Oxford University Press, 2009).
10. See, for example, Daniel Dennett, "Beliefs about Beliefs," *Behavioral and Brain Sciences*, vol. 4 (1978): 569.
11. Daniel Povinelli and Timothy J. Eddy, "What Young Chimpanzees Know About Seeing." *Monographs of the Society for Research in Child Development*, vol. 61 (1996).
12. See, for example, Brian Hare, Josep Call, Bryan Agnetta, and Michael Tomasello, "Chimpanzees Know what Conspecifics Do and Do Not See." *Animal Behavior*, vol. 59 (2000); Brian Hare, Josep Call, and Michael Tomasello, "Do Chimpanzees Know What Conspecifics Know?" *Animal Behavior*, vol. 61 (2001).
13. Jennifer Vonk and Daniel Povinelli, "Similarity and Difference in the Conceptual Systems of Primates: The Unobservability Hypothesis," in *Comparative Cognition: Experimental Exploration of Animal Intelligence*, ed. Edward A. Wasserman and Thomas R. Zentall (New York, NY: Oxford University Press, 2004).
14. Dennett, "Beliefs about Beliefs."
15. Vonk and Povinelli, "Similarity and Difference," 11.
16. Larry Laudan, *Progress and Its Problems: Towards a Theory of Scientific Growth* (London: Routledge, 1977), 45.

17. Kristin Andrews, *The Animal Mind* (New York, NY: Routledge Press, 2015), 147.

18. Laudan, *Progress and Its Problems*, 79.

19. Fletcher and Carruthers, "Behavior-Reading," 461.

20. Ibid.

21. See, for example, Lurz et al., "Animal Mindreading."

22. William Whewell, *The Philosophy of the Inductive Sciences, Founded Upon Their History* (London: John W. Parker, 1840).

23. Lurz et al., "Animal Mindreading," 450.

24. Derek Penn and Daniel Povinelli, "The Comparative Delusion: Beyond Behavioristic and Mentalistic Explanations for Nonhuman Social Cognition," in *Agency and Joint Attention*, ed. Janet Metcalfe and Herbert S. Terrace (New York, NY: Oxford University Press, 2013), 73.

25. Ibid.

26. See, for example, Robert Lurz, "Belief Attribution in Animals: On How to Move Forward Conceptually and Empirically," *Review of Philosophy and Psychology*, vol. 2 (2011): 19–59; Lurz et al., "Animal Mindreading."

27. Andrews, *The Animal Mind*, 148.

28. Josep Call and Michael Tomasello, "Does the Chimpanzee Have a Theory of Mind? 30 Years Later," *Trends in Cognitive Sciences*, vol. 12 (2008): 191.

29. Dennett, "Beliefs about Beliefs."

30. Premack and Woodruff, "Does the Chimpanzee Have a Theory of Mind?"

31. David Buttelmann et al., "Great Apes Distinguish True from False Beliefs in an Interactive Helping Task," *PLos One*, vol. 12, no. 4 (2017); Christopher Krupenye et al., "A Test of the Submentalizing Hypothesis: Apes' Performance in a False Belief Task Inanimate Control," *Communicative & Integrative Biology*, vol. 10, no. 4 (2017).

32. Lurz et al., "Animal Mindreading."

33. Ibid., 450.

34. Imre Lakatos, "Science and Pseudoscience," in *Philosophy in the Open*, ed. Godfrey Vesey (New York, NY: Open University Press, 1974); Laudan, *Progress and Its Problems*.

35. See Call and Tomasello, "Does the Chimpanzee Have a Theory of Mind?"

36. Penn and Povinelli, "The Comparative Delusion," 68.

37. Cecilia Heyes, "Animal Mindreading: What's the Problem?" *Psychonomic Bulletin & Review*, vol. 2 (2015): 313.

38. See, for example, Cecilia Heyes, "Theory of Mind in Nonhuman Primates," *Behavioral and Brain Sciences*, vol. 21 (1998).

39. Cecilia Heyes, "Simple Minds: A Qualified Defense of Associative Learning," *Philosophical Transactions of the Royal Society B: Biological Sciences*, vol. 367 (2012): 2695.

40. See Heyes, "Animal Mindreading."

41. Shannon Spaulding, "Embodied Cognition and Mindreading," *Mind & Language*, vol. 25, no. 1 (2010).

42. Andrews, *Do Apes Read Minds?* 219.

43. Heyes, "Simple Minds," 2697.

44. Elliott Sober, "Comparative Psychology Meets Evolutionary Biology: Morgan's Canon and Cladistic Parsimony," in *Thinking with Animals: New Perspectives on Anthropomorphism*, ed. Lorraine Daston (New York, NY: Columbia University Press, 2005); Simon Fitzpatrick, "Doing Away with Morgan's Canon," *Mind and Language*, vol. 23 (2008).

45. Conwy Lloyd Morgan, *An Introduction to Comparative Psychology* (London: W. Scott, 1894), 53.

46. Irina Meketa, "A Critique of the Principle of Cognitive Simplicity in Comparative Cognition," *Biology and Philosophy*, vol. 29, no. 5 (2014).

47. Sober, "Comparative Psychology Meets Evolutionary Biology."

48. Louise Barrett, *Beyond the Brain: How Body and Environment Shape Animal and Human Minds* (Princeton, NJ: Princeton University Press, 2011), 220.

49. Morgan, *An Introduction*, 53–54.

50. Fitzpatrick, "Doing Away with Morgan's Canon," 225; Sober, "Comparative Psychology Meets Evolutionary Biology."

51. See, for example, Shettleworth, "Modularity, Comparative Cognition and Human Uniqueness."

52. Marc Bekoff and Jessica Pierce, *Wild Justice: The Moral Lives of Animals* (Chicago, IL: Chicago University Press, 2009).

53. Christophe Boesch and Hedwige Boesch-Achermann, *The Chimpanzees of the Taï Forest: Behavioural Ecology and Evolution* (Oxford: Oxford University Press, 2000), 243.

54. See Andrews, *Do Apes Read Minds?*

55. Bekoff and Pierce, *Wild Justice*, 49.

56. Andrews, *Do Apes Read Minds?* 206–11.

57. Ibid., 206–11.

58. Bekoff and Pierce, *Wild Justice*.

59. Michael Tomasello, *The Origins of Human Communication* (Cambridge, MA: MIT Press, 2008); Melinda Carpenter and Josep Call, "How Joint is the Joint Attention of Apes and Human Infants?" in *Agency and Joint Attention*, ed. Janet Metcalfe (New York, NY: Oxford University Press, 2013).

60. Emilie Gentry, Christof Neumann, and Klaus Zuberbühler, "Bonobos Modify Communication Signals According to Recipient Familiarity," *Scientific Reports*, vol. 5, no. 16442 (2016).

61. Brian Skyrms, "Response," in *Why We Cooperate*, ed. Micheal Tomasello (Cambridge, MA: MIT Press, 2009), 145.

62. Cameron Buckner, "Morgan's Canon, Meet Hume's Dictum: Avoiding Anthropofabulation in Cross-Species Comparisons," *Biology and Philosophy*, vol. 28 (2013).

63. Ibid.

64. Donald Griffin, *The Question of Animal Awareness: Evolutionary Continuity of Mental Experience.* (New York, NY: Kaufmann, 1981), 11–12.

65. Boesch and Boesch-Achermann, *The Chimpanzees of the Taï Forest*; Jill Daphne Pruetz, "Targeted Helping by a Wild Adolescent Male Chimpanzee (Pan

Troglodytes Verus): Evidence for Empathy?" *Journal of Ethology*, vol. 29, no. 2 (2010): 365–68.

66. Elizabeth Bates, Luigia Camaioni, and Virginia Volterra, "The Acquisition of Performatives Prior to Speech," *Merrill-Palmer Quarterly*, vol. 21 (1975): 205–26.

67. See Timothy Racine, "Cognitivism, Adaptationism and Pointing," in *Current Developments in Primate Gesture Research*, ed. Katja Liebal (Amsterdam: Benjamins, 2011).

68. Ibid.

69. Stephanie Preston and Frans de Waal, "Empathy: Its Ultimate and Proximate Bases," *Behavioral Brain Science*, vol. 25 (2002).

70. See, for example, Sanae Okamoto-Barth and Masaki Tomonaga, "Development of Joint Attention in Infant Chimpanzees," in *Cognitive Development in Chimpanzees*, ed. Tetsuro Matsuzawa et al. (Dordrecht: Springer, 2006).

71. Lori Gruen, *Ethics and Animals* (Cambridge: Cambridge University Press, 2011), 9–12.

BIBLIOGRAPHY

Andrews, Kristin. *Do Apes Read Minds?* Cambridge, MA: MIT Press, 2012.

Andrews, Kristin. *The Animal Mind*. New York, NY: Routledge Press, 2015.

Andrews, Kristin, and Brian Huss. "Anthropomorphism, Anthropectomy, and the Null Hypothesis." *Biology and Philosophy*, vol. 29, no. 5 (2014): 711–29.

Barrett, Louise. *Beyond the Brain: How Body and Environment Shape Animal and Human Minds*. Princeton, NJ: Princeton University Press, 2011.

Bates, Elizabeth, Luigia Camaioni, and Virginia Volterra Capagrossi. "The Acquisition of Performatives Prior to Speech." *Merrill-Palmer Quarterly*, vol. 21 (1975): 205–26.

Bekoff, Marc, and Jessica Pierce. *Wild Justice: The Moral Lives of Animals*. Chicago, IL: Chicago University Press, 2009.

Boesch, Christophe, and Hedwige Boesch-Achermann. *The Chimpanzees of the Taï Forest: Behavioural Ecology and Evolution*. Oxford: Oxford University Press, 2000.

Buckner, Cameron. "Morgan's Canon, meet Hume's Dictum: Avoiding Anthropofabulation in Cross-Species Comparisons." *Biology and Philosophy*, vol. 28 (2013): 853–71.

Buttelmann, David, Frances Buttelmann, Malinda Carpenter, Josep Call, and Michael Tomasello. "Great Apes Distinguish True from False Beliefs in an Interactive Helping Task." *PLos One*, vol. 12, no. 4 (2017): e0173793.

Call, Josep, and Michael Tomasello. "Does the Chimpanzee Have a Theory of Mind? 30 Years Later." *Trends in Cognitive Sciences*, vol. 12 (2008): 187–92.

Carpenter, Melinda, and Josep Call. "How Joint is the Joint Attention of Apes and Human Infants?" In *Agency and Joint Attention*, edited by Janet Metcalfe and Herbert S. Terrace, 49–61. New York, NY: Oxford University Press, 2013.

Dennett, Daniel. "Beliefs about Beliefs." *Behavioral and Brain Sciences*, vol. 4 (1978): 568–70.

De Waal, Frans. "Are We in Anthropodenial?" *Discover*, vol. 18, no. 7 (1997): 50–53.

Fitzpatrick, Simon. "Doing away with Morgan's Canon." *Mind and Language*, vol. 23 (2008): 224–46.

Fletcher, Logan, and Peter Carruthers. "Behavior-Reading versus Mentalizing in Animals." In *Agency and Joint Attention*, edited by Janet Metcalfe and Herbert S. Terrace, 82–99. New York, NY: Oxford University Press, 2009.

Genty, Emilie, Christof Neumann, and Klaus Zuberbühler. "Bonobos Modify Communication Signals According to Recipient Familiarity." *Scientific Reports*, vol. 5, no. 16442 (2016): 16442.

Griffin, Donald. *The Question of Animal Awareness: Evolutionary Continuity of Mental Experience*. New York, NY: Kaufmann, 1981.

Gruen, Lori. *Ethics and Animals*. Cambridge: Cambridge University Press, 2011.

Hare, Brian, Josep Call, Bryan Agnetta, and Michael Tomasello. "Chimpanzees Know what Conspecifics Do and Do Not See." *Animal Behavior*, vol. 59 (2000): 771–85.

Hare, Brian, Josep Call, and Michael Tomasello. "Do Chimpanzees Know what Conspecifics Know?" *Animal Behavior*, vol. 61 (2001): 139–51.

Heyes, Cecilia. "Theory of Mind in Nonhuman Primates." *Behavioral and Brain Sciences*, vol. 21 (1998): 101–48.

Heyes, Cecilia. "Simple Minds: A Qualified Defense of Associative Learning." *Philosophical Transactions of the Royal Society B: Biological Sciences*, vol. 367 (2012): 2695–703.

Heyes, Cecilia. "Animal Mindreading: What's the Problem?" *Psychonomic Bulletin & Review*, vol. 2 (2015): 313–27.

Krupenye, Christopher, Fumihiro Kano, Satoshi Hirata, Josep Call, and Michael Tomasello. "A Test of the Submentalizing Hypothesis: Apes' Performance in a False Belief Task Inanimate Control." *Communicative & Integrative Biology*, vol. 10, no. 4 (2017). doi:10.1080/19420889.2017.1343771.

Lakatos, Imre. "Science and Pseudoscience." In *Philosophy in the Open*, edited by Godfrey Vesey. New York, NY: Open University Press, 1974.

Laudan, Larry. *Progress and Its Problems: Towards a Theory of Scientific Growth*. London: Routledge, 1977.

Lurz, Robert, Sharisse Kanet, and Carla Krachun. "Animal Mindreading: A Defense of Agnostic Optimism." *Mind and Language*, vol. 29, no. 4 (2014): 428–54.

Lurz, Robert. "Belief Attribution in Animals: On How to Move Forward Conceptually and Empirically." *Review of Philosophy and Psychology*, vol. 2 (2011): 19–59.

Meketa, Irina. "A Critique of the Principle of Cognitive Simplicity in Comparative Cognition." *Biology and Philosophy*, vol. 29, no. 5 (2014): 731–45.

Morgan, Conwy L. *An Introduction to Comparative Psychology*. London: W. Scott, 1894.

Okamoto-Barth, Sanae, and Masaki Tomonaga. "Development of Joint Attention in Infant Chimpanzees." In *Cognitive Development in Chimpanzees*, edited by

Tetsuro Matsuzawa, Masaki Tomonaga, and Masayuri Tanaka, 155–71. Dordrecht: Springer, 2006.

Penn, Derek, and Daniel J. Povinelli. "The Comparative Delusion: Beyond Behavioristic and Mentalistic Explanations for Nonhuman Social Cognition." In *Agency and Joint Attention*, edited by Janet Metcalfe and Herbert S. Terrace, 62–81. New York, NY: Oxford University Press, 2013.

Povinelli, Daniel J., and Timothy J. Eddy. "What Young Chimpanzees Know About Seeing." *Monographs of the Society for Research in Child Development*, vol. 61 (1996): 1–152.

Premack, David, and Guy Woodruff. "Does the Chimpanzee Have a Theory of Mind?" *Behavioral and Brain Sciences*, vol. 4 (1978): 515–26.

Preston, Stephanie, and Frans de Waal. "Empathy: Its Ultimate and Proximate Bases." *Behavioral Brain Science*, vol. 25 (2002): 1–72.

Pruetz, Jill Daphne. "Targeted Helping by a Wild Adolescent Male Chimpanzee (Pan Troglodytes Verus): Evidence for Empathy?" *Journal of Ethology*, vol. 29, no. 2 (2010): 365–68.

Racine, Timothy. "Cognitivism, Adaptationism and Pointing." In *Current Developments in Primate Gesture Research*, edited by Katja Liebal and Simone Pika, 165–80. Amsterdam: Benjamins, 2011.

Rollin, Bernard. "Animal Mind: Science, Philosophy, and Ethics." In *Animal Minds and Animal Ethics*, edited by Klaus Petrus and Markus Wild, 15–37. Bielefeld: Transcript Press, 2013.

Shettleworth, Sara J. "Modularity, Comparative Cognition and Human Uniqueness." *Philosophical Transactions of the Royal Society B: Biological Sciences*, vol. 367 (2012): 2794–802.

Skyrms, Brian. "Response." In *Why We Cooperate*, edited by Micheal Tomasello, 137–48. Cambridge, MA: MIT Press, 2009.

Sober, Elliott. "Comparative Psychology Meets Evolutionary Biology: Morgan's Canon and Cladistic Parsimony." In *Thinking with Animals: New Perspectives on Anthropomorphism*, edited by Lorraine Daston and Gregg Mitman, 85–99. New York, NY: Columbia University Press, 2005.

Spaulding, Shannon. "Embodied Cognition and Mindreading." *Mind & Language*, vol. 25, no. 1 (2010): 119–40.

Tomasello, Michael. *The Origins of Human Communication*. Cambridge, MA: MIT Press, 2008.

Vonk, Jennifer, and Daniel J. Povinelli. "Similarity and Difference in the Conceptual Systems of Primates: The Unobservability Hypothesis." In *Comparative Cognition: Experimental Exploration of Animal Intelligence*, edited by Edward A. Wasserman and Thomas R. Zentall, 363–87. New York, NY: Oxford University Press, 2004.

Whewell, William. *The Philosophy of the Inductive Sciences, Founded Upon Their History*. London: John W. Parker, 1840.

Chapter 5

Suffering Animals

Creaturely Fellowship and Its Denial

Craig Taylor

No one in the developed world with any access to mass media could be unaware of the conditions under which animals are treated in being raised for slaughter for meat on an industrial scale. That all this involves enormous suffering on the part of the animals concerned can hardly be denied; the facts here are not at all in dispute. That so many of us seem impervious to these facts, are so unmoved by them, is surely puzzling. Puzzling in part of course because some among us are struck, struck dumb even, in horror at the sheer magnitude of the unending yet everyday cruelty perpetrated by human beings on other animals; the kind of horror, for instance, that both wounds and isolates the writer Elizabeth Costello in John Coetzee's *The Life of Animals.*[1] How can these facts amount for so many other people to so little? In this chapter, I offer an explanation why. We clearly miss something concerning our moral relations with animals, but I suggest it is not a fact, specifically not the fact that they suffer. We might begin to understand this, I argue, when we consider that *our moral relations with each other* are not founded on the *fact* that *we* suffer.

MORAL INDIVIDUALISM

Of course, for Jeremy Bentham and other utilitarians it is precisely the fact that animals suffer that is of moral significance and the ground of our moral relations with them. More recently, various philosophers have expanded the number of facts that might be considered morally relevant there. So Jeff McMahan, James Rachels, and others have defended a view that has been called "moral individualism."[2] According to this view, our treatment of individuals—and by individuals these thinkers certainly do not mean just human beings—what matters morally, what justifies our treatment or renders it morally wrong, is simply the particular characteristics possessed by that individual. Along with suffering, other characteristics that may be considered morally relevant here are having interests, or being rational. The crucial point, as Rachels has put it, is that "if we think it is wrong to treat a human being in a certain way, because the human being has certain characteristics, and a particular non-human animal also has those characteristics, then consistency requires that we also object to treating the non-human in that way."[3]

This point bears some similarity with arguments advanced by, among others, the modern day utilitarian Peter Singer, according to which we have a certain prejudice in favor of our own species. As far as speciesism is concerned the comparison with other "isms" is problematic for reasons that Bernard Williams has made plain. As Williams says, "Oppressed human groups come of age in the search for emancipation when they speak for themselves, and no longer through reforming members of the oppressive group, but animals will never come of age; human beings will always act as their trustees. . . . in our relation to them the only moral question for us is how we should *treat* them."[4]

What one might also note is that if one puts the point the way Williams does, then the very idea that we stand in *moral* relations with other animals can seem slightly odd; at least, there can be in the relevant moral sense no *mutual* recognition here, only enlightened benefactors (us) and dumb beneficiaries (them). I would think that almost anyone who has lived with other animals, say as with pets or working animals like sheep dogs and the like, might wonder about that claim; that they might reply that there is all the same some sense in which we *share* a life with animals. It is in relation to such queries, I wish to suggest, that we can begin to see what is missing in the idea simply that the capacities of other animals provide our moral relevant facts in connection to how we should treat them.

PRIMITIVE RESPONSES

As I noted earlier, a place to begin here is to consider our relations, including our moral relations, with other human beings. And here I want to draw attention to how such relations, and in particular our sense of fellowship with other humans, are grounded ultimately in a certain natural responsiveness to others that is not mediated by reflection on any morally relevant facts, including facts about relevant capacities, concerning other human beings. This is a point I have considered at length in other places,[5] and of particular relevance to those considerations are certain ideas in the later work of Ludwig

Wittgenstein, and most notably certain remarks from his *Philosophical Investigations*.[6] In particular, this:

> I tell someone I am in pain. His attitude to me will then be one of belief; disbelief, suspicion; and so on.
>
> Let us assume he says: "It is not so bad."—Doesn't that prove that he believes in something behind the outward expression of pain?—His attitude is a proof of his attitude. Imagine not merely the words "I am in pain" but also the answer "It's not so bad" replaced by instinctive noises and gestures.[7]

What is important here is Wittgenstein characterizing belief as an attitude. To which one might reply: isn't belief here belief in *something*, that something being the pain as distinct from the expression of pain? After all, the expression could be an exaggeration, even a feigning, of being in pain. Hence, for example, Wittgenstein's remark "it is not too bad," that follows. Surely, as Wittgenstein's interlocutor goes on, this proves that there is something behind the expression of pain, the thing that we believe is present. To which Wittgenstein replies that it proves no such thing, that there is no*thing* behind this attitude of belief that provides its ground. How can that be? Well, suggests Wittgenstein, imagine this exchange replaced by instinctive noises and gestures, for you *can* imagine this; the expression of pain and belief, doubt or suspicion about that pain can be perfectly well conveyed in this way. But, it is important to note, insofar as our responses to another in such cases are *instinctive*, so immediate, unthinking, pre-reflective, we are not here conveying or expressing some thought about some inner thing, something behind their expression of pain. All of this is of a piece, and an expansion of Wittgenstein's earlier suggestion in PI that "if we construe the grammar of the expression of sensation on the model of 'object and designation' the object drops out of consideration as irrelevant."[8] A thorough treatment of these sections of the PI, what has been called his private language argument, is not possible here. What I do want to note though is that the point of the last sentence of § 310 is to remind us of how the meaning of our verbal expression of pain and our belief, disbelief, and so on in another's pain is connected to certain instinctive noises and gestures, noises and gestures which can, in certain cases, replace those verbal expressions. As Peter Winch has said in his insightful discussion of these points:

> His [Wittgenstein's] point, I take it, is that if we want to be clear what the belief (for instance) that someone is in pain comes to, we should not allow ourselves to be hypnotized by its verbal expression ("He is in pain"), but should look at the whole range of behaviour, demeanour, facial expression, etc. in which such verbal expressions are embedded, and with which they are continuous, which

give the words their particular sense and by some of which indeed the words can be replaced. The purpose of such an enquiry is not to show that what we are dealing with here is not "really" a case of belief at all, but something else. That would quite misleadingly imply that we have a secure paradigm of what it is to believe something, which does not draw its sustenance from the expressive behaviour in which it is embedded.[9]

What Wittgenstein is drawing our attention to in talking of belief as an attitude is the way in which our relations to each other, including our particular beliefs about each other, are founded on natural, immediate—I have elsewhere called them primitive[10]—ways of responding to each other which are not at all the result on any reflections we have about other human beings, about their pain, or even that they have an inner life at all. This is further elucidated by Wittgenstein in part II of the PI with the following remark:

"I believe that he is suffering"—Do I also believe that he isn't an automaton?
It would go against the grain to use the word in both connexions.
(Or is it like this: I believe that he is suffering, but I am certain he is not an automaton? Nonsense!)
Suppose I say of a friend: "He isn't an automaton." What information is conveyed by this, and to whom would it be informative? To a human being who meets him in ordinary circumstances? What information could it give him? (At the very most that this man always behaves like a human being, and not occasionally like a machine.)
"I believe he is not an automaton," just like that, so far makes no sense.[11]

Our particular beliefs about other human beings—that they are in pain, that they are exaggerating this, that they are pretending and so on—get their sense against the background of our natural responsiveness to other human beings that is *not* the subject of reflection or doubt in the ways these particular beliefs certainly can be on specific occasions. As Wittgenstein says, "'I believe he is not an automaton,' just like that, makes no sense."

But how, one might ask, are these reflections relevant to my suggestion that what is missing in our relations to other animals is not the fact, say, that they suffer? What exactly then is missing here? Well, consider first our primitive responsiveness to other human beings, and in particular the *kind of* expression that this sometimes involves. One primitive response I suggest is sympathy, sympathy understood as an immediate response to another's suffering; consider, for example, how automatic it can be to aid someone who has tripped and fallen in the street.[12] This is not to deny that helping another does often involve a good deal of reflection, but to note that at other times it does not.

Or consider the similar response of pity discussed by Wittgenstein: "How does it come out what the object of my pity is? Pity, one might say is a form of conviction that someone is in pain."[13] So, certain instances of pity are not *based* on a belief that another being is in pain, or indeed in any reflection on them at all; rather, pity is itself a form of recognition of pain. Responses such as this ground our conception of pain.

I have suggested, following Wittgenstein, that our beliefs about other human beings—but what I would now more generally want to call our conception of other human beings—are grounded in our primitive responses to them. But if that is so, then we need to consider what particular responses such as sympathy or pity contribute to that conception; what kind of conception of a human being do they help to ground and partially constitute? One way to approach this question is to imagine a case where our expression of pain and our range of expressive responses to pain are absent. Wittgenstein considers a situation like this in *Zettel*:

> Imagine that the people of a tribe were brought up from early youth to give no expression of feeling *of any kind.* They find it childish, something to be got rid of. . . . "Pain" is not spoken of . . . If anyone complains he is ridiculed or punished.
>
> . . . here life would run on differently.—What interests us would not interest them.
>
> "These men would have nothing human about them." Why?—we could not possibly make ourselves understood to them . . . We could not find our feet with them.[14]

We can imagine that life might go like this, but it would not be what we call human life, it is not our kind of life. There could be as Wittgenstein says no understanding between us, and by understanding here we could not be referring merely to the facts, such as that human beings have pains; we, them and us, all know *that*, only with them it is something to be "got rid of." What this tribe lacks is our particular and shared conception of what pain amounts to, what for us it is, and more generally, and connected to this, what it is for us to be a human being. At the same time, however, we know that the responsiveness to others that helps secure this conception of humanity can at certain times go missing in some people with respect to some other people— in different ways we see this, though I cannot go into details here, with the Holocaust and the extremes of slavery of the kind that existed in the southern states of the United States. And here too one might ask: how can the facts of human suffering on such a scale count for so little?[15]

OTHER ANIMALS AS FELLOW CREATURES

So what of our relations to other animals? As Raimond Gaita has suggested, "there is every reason to believe that [Wittgestein's point about the responses of human beings to each other] applies to the responses of human beings to animals and (to a limited degree) to their responses to us."[16] This is perhaps most obvious in our relations with those animals that we have, as one might say, developed together with; dogs, cats, and various farm and working animals, as I have already noted, such as sheep dogs. While these animals are not wholly part of the life we share with other human beings, it seems fair all the same to say that we share a life with them. As Gaita notes "dogs respond to our moods" and, as he continues, it is natural for us to see intentions in other animals such as for example when "a dog chases a cat."[17] To this I would add that certain animals, certainly dogs, can respond to our *suffering* in ways that indicate their concern for us just as we are moved on occasion to sympathy or pity by the suffering of animals. It is in virtue of such shared responsiveness that it makes sense to say they are indeed moral relations, in the sense of mutual recognition, between human beings and animals. But of course, in terms of our lives with animals one must add that there are distinctive obstacles to, as well as contradictions in, our relations with other animals.[18]

In terms of the contradictions, there is of course the way in which we treat our pets, as companions, as members of the family even, while at the same time buying meat in little plastic packets when we know full well the suffering that has been involved in the farming and slaughtering of the animals we are consuming. We are, as Cora Diamond notes, brought up with and into these contradictions.[19] Diamond notes the poem by Jane Legge, *Learning to be a Dutiful Carnivore*, which includes these lines: "Eat the creatures killed for sale/but never pull the pussy's tail."[20] Now one might argue at this point that the antidote for such confusion is, as someone such as Singer or McMahan would have it, to remind us that concerning those capacities that provide us with reasons for moral consideration of any individual, the animals slaughtered for meat have the same level of such capacities as our pets do. However, such a reply does not I think go to the heart of our confusions; for we do not just, or even necessarily at all, recognize our pets as moral individuals in the Rachel's/McMahan's sense. Rather we see these animals, as I noted, as companions; as creatures with which we share our life in a way that is much more substantive than them being just, to put it crudely, around our feet. As I have put it elsewhere, we see these animals not just as creatures of a certain sort (of course with certain capacities), but as *fellow* creatures (what that fellowship might entail, I will consider shortly).[21] The deepest puzzle or question about our relations with animals then is why we do not see those other creatures, the countless millions of them, that are reared and slaughtered in conditions of horrific cruelty as fellow creatures in the same way.

Here I need to turn to what I called the obstacles to seeing certain animals, as I would now want to put it, as fellow creatures. To begin, it is useful to consider Williams's remark above that "in our relation to [other animals] the only moral question for us is how we should *treat* them."[22] Leaving aside the issue of whether the following is a moral question, it can all the same certainly matter a great deal how some other animals (our pets, animals we work with) treat *us*. Note here that the mutual recognition between such animals and us humans, which is at least part of our shared life, and that sense of fellowship that there is between us, can break down; either of us can fail to live up to the demands of this fellowship. Of course, the pet dog will not ask: ought I to have acted in this way to my owner? Nevertheless, in our relations with pets and working animals, in the many immediate, unreflective, again as I say primitive, ways in which we respond to each other there are nevertheless on both sides expressions of, for example, anger, hurt and contrition, expressions that give sustenance to what I would suggest is a morally inflected conception of such relations. To be clear, I am not suggesting there is anything wrong or confused about Williams's remark earlier. My point is just that such a question can obscure the ways in which our relations with and concern for other animals can go so much deeper than that question.

Williams is right, obviously enough, that animals are never going to rise up and ask us to justify our treatment of them, our cruelties toward them, and so on. And neither can we ask them to explain themselves for their transgressions. (Or if we do, say when the pet dog steals the steak thawing out on the kitchen bench, we know, as per Wittgenstein's remark, that it is the noises and gestures that accompany our verbal expression that are conveying our thoughts to the dog.) Importantly here, our shared life with such animals, the fellowship that it involves, is again sustained by those primitive forms of responsiveness that I indicated before concerning our relations with other human beings. But unlike our relations with other human beings, what we share with animals does not involve reflections on those natural forms of responsiveness which are part of our sense of human fellowship; with animals there can be shared sympathy but nothing like a shared sense of justice.[23] To put the point another way, which also gives us I think the clearest sense of the kind of fellowship we share with other animals, the life we share with animals is one of bodily existence.

ANIMAL VULNERABILITY AND ITS DENIAL

To explain what I mean by a bodily existence, consider Diamond's discussion of the character Elizabeth Costello in John Coetzee's *The Lives of Animals*, originally his Tanner Lectures. Costello is haunted by the reality of the cruelty involved in our industrial scale slaughter of animals for food. Diamond sees Costello's experience as one of what she calls, using a phrase of John Updike's, "the difficulty of reality":

> The difficulty . . . in the apparent resistance by reality to one's ordinary mode of life, including one's ordinary modes of thinking: to appreciate the difficulty is to feel oneself being shouldered out of how one thinks, how one is apparently supposed to think, or to have a sense of the inability of thought to encompass what it is attempting to reach.[24]

Faced with the reality of our treatment of animals, Diamond says, "[W]e see [Costello] as wounded by this knowledge, by this horror, and by the knowledge of how un-haunted others are."[25] The central concern of Diamond's discussion of Costello is then to contrast, on the one hand, the sense in which Costello presents as a woman wounded by her experience of the horror of our treatment of animals and her knowledge that it is not so experienced by others—a woundedness that isolates her from those around her—with, on the other hand, the way in which the various commentators on these lectures, including notably Peter Singer, treat the lecturers, which is to see them as presenting in fictionalized form a range of ideas and arguments relevant for the resolution of ethical issues related to our treatment of animals. But in intellectualizing the experience of Costello, as Coetzee portrays it to us, as a philosophical argument about our treatment of animals, as an answer to a philosophical problem, these commentators deflect from the reality, from the truth, that Costello so struggles to encompass in her thought. The term "deflection" Diamond takes here from Stanley Cavell and his discussion of a comparable difficulty of reality, that difficulty of reality given in our feeling of separateness from other human beings, a feeling the appreciation of which is then deflected into philosophical skepticism. As Diamond puts Cavell's point:

> We may be filled with a sense of the facts, the ineluctable facts of our capacity to miss the suffering of others and the possibility of our own suffering being unknown and uncared about; we may be filled with a sense of these facts, of our distance from each other, and our appreciation be deflected, the problem itself be deflected, into one or another of the forms given in philosophical scepticism.[26]

To get clear about what such a deflection amounts to in relation to the question of our treatment of animals, consider Diamond's treatment of another idea of Cavell's presented in the same discussion, that of exposure. One aspect of that idea, so Diamond suggests, is given in a remark by Costello in the first of Coetzee's lectures. To quote Diamond:

Costello in Coetzee's first lecture speaks of her knowledge of her own death. . . .
"For an instant in time," she says, "I know what it is to be a corpse. The knowledge repels me. It fills me with terror; I shy away from it, refuse to entertain
it." She goes [Costello] on to say that we all have such moment, and that the
knowledge we then have is not abstract but embodied.[27]

As Costello says of such knowledge and as Diamond quotes: "I know what
a corpse cannot know: that it is extinct, that it knows nothing and will never
know anything anymore. For an instant before my whole structure of knowledge collapses in panic, I am alive inside that contradiction, dead and alive
at the same time."[28]

The particular awareness that is at issue here, Diamond suggests, is "awareness we each have of being a living body . . . [which] carries with it exposure
to the bodily sense of vulnerability to death, sheer animal vulnerability, the
vulnerability we share with [other animals]."[29] The problem with moral individualism and arguments against speciesism is that they turn suffering into a
fact that is relevant for moral consideration in the way we treat other animals.
But here the facts stand in the way of our facing what we share in common with
animals, which is a "sheer animal vulnerability"; our appreciation of *this* reality is deflected here too into a philosophical argument, in this case about our
treatment of animals. But it is precisely this reality—Costello's sense of our
shared bodily existence and the sense of sheer animal vulnerability that comes
with that—that overthrows Costello. It is this reality that she cannot encompass
in her thought or communicate adequately to others who see no such horror.

The question I began with was how the facts about the treatment animals in
factory farming that so haunts some of us, like it haunts Costello, can matter
so little to so many others. My answer has been that it is not the fact at all
that makes the difference here, but being struck, being wounded as Costello
is, by the reality of this horror, a reality that is founded in our sheer animal
vulnerability and which is otherwise deflected for many into a kind of abstract
problem. What are the properties relevant to moral concern? To what extent
do animals possess these properties too? And so on. The facts I would further
suggest are also a kind of protection from our sense of our bodily existence
and all that entails. My point here is to draw attention to a need for such a
protection from, or denial of, this sense of bodily vulnerability. I am not suggesting such a need will be experienced by everyone. One possibility is that
a person may, without evasion or deceit, accept the reality of this shared animal vulnerability, perhaps as part of the struggle just to survive; surely many
people at many times had neither our options, nor the possibility of distancing that factory farming provides.[30] But for many of us, facts and abstraction
create a kind of distance between us and other animals, a comfortable (for
us) distance in which their lives and suffering are an object for our reflection

within that other kind of life that is uniquely ours; a life in which the facts, our knowledge not just of animals but of all of the natural world, allow us to bracket our animal existence within this world at the same time as it promises us mastery of it, our question being not merely how should we treat other animals but how should we treat, alter, and manipulate the natural world itself.

That last point brings me to how on occasion this deflection from our animal vulnerability, from our fellowship in this with other animals, can be breached. For the sense of mastery of the natural world I have alluded to above and our intellectualizing deflections from our bodily existence within that world are themselves vulnerable to the possibility that the difficulty of reality I have been discussing will force itself on us. As I write, my country is on fire, from up and down the east coast states from Queensland, New South Wales, and then Victoria to Tasmania, South Australia, and Western Australia. So far, we are only half-way through summer, 15.6 million acres have burnt and 23 people and 1 billion animals have perished. The populations of entire towns surrounded by fires have been trapped on the beach under red skies, their eyes stinging, and their lungs choked, while the fires are so large they create their own weather systems, so massive that we cannot put them out; they will go out only if there is significant rain (which at present there is not) or if they run out of fuel. Some have called it a vision of hell, but it is at least a vision of sheer animal vulnerability, shared animal vulnerability with other creatures. In one photograph from the frontline of this catastrophe we see on the road a firefighter and a koala side by side staring dumbstruck at a wall of flame in front of them. In various other photographs, we see families with their animals, dogs, cats, rabbits, birds, even horses (in one news report from the Adelaide hills, we hear of Annie Whicker who walked her horse Silvah from the fires to safety) huddled together on beaches. In the face of such photographs and stories, it is difficult to keep our sense of shared vulnerability with other animals, sheer animal vulnerability, at bay. What one can see, indeed at times cannot help but see, in this situation is that all our intellectualized deflections, our comforting distancing of ourselves from our bodily nature and vulnerability, stripped away; nothing but bodies, animal bodies, and nothing but fear, helplessness, and incomprehension in the face of the sheer vulnerability that entails. There is no significance now to the capacities we do and do not have in common with other animals; at the same time, there is no place now for urbane reflection on the obvious differences between racism and speciesism. Here is Gus Goswell's report from the seaside town on Mallacoota as it was ringed by fire:

> We had been so anxious for the dawn to arrive, but when it finally did arrive, the dawn brought us no comfort, only new fear and danger. The long, mostly sleepless, night huddled together on the ground next to the Mallacoota foreshore

had been uncomfortable, but what the dawn brought to the thousands of us trapped by fire was terrifying. The dawn itself was only temporary. Almost as soon as the sky began to lighten the light was extinguished. The new day disappeared in darkness and we knew then we were in danger. As the bush to the south-west of us exploded in flame and the fire picked up speed as it raced towards us, the smoke turned day into night in minutes. Burnt leaves had been falling on Mallacoota through the night, now live embers were falling. Masks and shirts tied across faces brought little relief from the choking smoke and ash. Our eyes were full of it, our clothes smothered in it. The water was no longer our comfort—suddenly it seemed like our only hope of survival. My family—including our two-year-old daughter—and hundreds of other families, moved to the water's edge. We turned our backs to shield ourselves from the terrible wind whipping the fire towards us. . . . The sense of helplessness as we waited for the fire to hit us was unlike anything I have experienced. I never lost faith in the incredible firefighters out defending us and whatever else they could of Mallacoota, but we were hearing that the fire was a freight train and it was heading straight for us. And then we saw the sky turn from black to a terrifying red, and we felt heat on our backs and our faces when we turned and we heard the fire was in the town, and for the first time I really struggled to stay optimistic. As calmly as possible, we talked as a family about our plan for getting in the water, who would hold our daughter, who would have the dog, the shallowest paths across the water that would take us as far from the fire as possible, the importance of only getting into the water when we really had to. And we waited for that moment.[31]

Fortunately for Gus and his family that moment never arrived; the fire changed directions and they were saved. There are many reports such as this one, many variations on "unlike anything I have experienced"; "I cannot describe to you"; "impossible to wrap my head around"; and so on. But many will have seen the photographs from such places and all that a body waiting in fear can express—both human and other animals.

Our avoidance of the reality of the routine monstrous horror of our treatment of other animals is, I am suggesting, of a kind with our avoidance of our own nature as embodied creatures, of a kind with our avoidance, of the kind of life we share with animals and within which we can perhaps recognize that avoidance for what it is and the terrible wrong we inflict on our fellow creatures.

NOTES

1. John Coetzee, *The Lives of Animals* (Princeton, NJ: Princeton University Press, 1999).

2. See Jeff McMahan, "Our Fellow Creatures," *The Journal of Ethics* 9 (2005): 353–80; James Rachels, *Created From Animals: The Moral Implications of Darwinism* (Oxford: Oxford University Press, 1990).

3. Rachels, *Created From Animals*, 175.

4. Bernard Williams, "The Human Prejudice," in *Philosophy as a Humanistic Discipline*, ed. A. W. More (Princeton, NJ: Princeton University Press, 2006), 141.

5. See Craig Taylor, "Our Fellow Creatures," in *Ethics in the Wake of Wittgenstein*, ed. Benjamin De Mesel and Oskari Kuusela (Abingdon: Routledge, 2010); Craig Taylor, *Sympathy: A Philosophical Analysis* (Basingstoke: Palgrave MacMillan, 2002).

6. Ludwig Wittgenstein, *Philosophical Investigations* (Oxford: Basil Blackwell, 1958). *Philosophical Investigations* will be referred to as PI.

7. Ibid., § 310.

8. Ibid., § 293.

9. Peter Winch, "*Eine Einstellung zur Seele*," in *Trying to Make Sense* (Oxford: Basil Blackwell, 1987), 142.

10. Taylor, *Sympathy*.

11. Wittgenstein, *Philosophical Investigations*, II. iv.

12. Of course, it may be an equally primitive response to turn away in shock or embarrassment. But even such responses involve a recognition of our fellowship in suffering with others; why otherwise shock or embarrassment? Such responses are unlike our response to, say, a ladder, a mere object that has fallen across our path. For a more detail discussion and defense of these points, see Taylor, *Sympathy*.

13. Wittgenstein, *Philosophical Investigations*, § 287.

14. Ludwig Wittgenstein, *Zettel*, tr. G. E. M. Anscombe, ed. G. E. M. Anscombe and Georg Henrik von Wright (Oxford: Basil Blackwell, 1967), §§ 383–90.

15. Of particular relevance here is Stanley Cavell's discussion of "soul blindness" in his *The Claim of Reason* (Oxford: Oxford University Press, 1979).

16. Raimond Gaita, *The Philosopher's Dog* (Melbourne: Text Publishing, 2002), 60.

17. Ibid., 60.

18. Clearly the kind of responsiveness at issue here does not extend to a great many farm animals and one might then ask: "Should it?" It need not; we can certainly imagine human life being like that. I have touched on this question in another place (see Craig Taylor, "Our Fellow Creatures," in *Ethics in the Wake of Wittgenstein*, ed. Benjamin De Mesel and Oskari Kuusela (Abingdon: Routledge, 2019)) where I have suggested to answer that question we need to compare what the kind of shared life of creaturely fellowship I have indicated has, as opposed to what this other life has, internally to recommend it. Crudely put, do we want to live in the world with the kind of fellowship I am suggesting or one in which vast numbers of animals are raw materials in the production of meat?

19. Cora Diamond, "Eating Meat and Eating People," in *The Realistic Spirit: Wittgenstein, Philosophy and the Mind* (Cambridge, MA: Massachusetts Institute of Technology Press, 1995).

20. Ibid., 327.

21. See Taylor, "Our Fellow Creatures."

22. Williams, "The Human Prejudice,"141.

23. Here someone might raise the following query. Cora Diamond quotes the animal trainer Vicki Hearne's discussion of the story of a dog Fritz that Hearne thinks gave himself the moral law. The story is of Fritz, who is a police dog, attacking his policemen master when he, seemingly for fun, starts clubbing a black woman who was jaywalking. Diamond does not think that there in the story Hearne relates any place for the Kantian idea of Fritz placing himself *"under* a law he himself makes" (see Diamond Cora, "The Dog that Gave Himself the Moral Law," *Midwest Studies in Philosophy* 13 (1988): 177). At the same time, Diamond does think that there is room for the idea that Fritz is here putting his world back in order; that in his world, the world his trainers have brought him into, people are not beaten up for no good reason. Does that suggest that Fritz has a sense of justice? Not what we call justice at any rate, which of course involves reflection on what justice is.

24. Diamond Cora, "The Difficulty of Reality and the Difficulty of Philosophy," in *Philosophy and Animal Life*, ed. Stanley Cavell et al. (New York, NY: Columbia University Press, 2008), 58.

25. Ibid., 46.

26. Ibid., 68.

27. Ibid., 73.

28. Coetzee, *The Lives of Animals*, 32.

29. Diamond, "The Difficulty of Reality," 74.

30. Someone might want to say of course that many people in our society will not recognize out treatment of animals in factory farming as a kind of horror. That too is possible, but I am not sure how many people who might say so could truly walk through a factory scale abattoir without experiencing the kind of primitive responsiveness to our fellow creatures that concerns me. All the same there will be people for whom suffering, or at least some suffering, simply does not matter or matter much.

31. Gus Goswell, "What It was Like as the Mallacoota Bushfire Moved Towards Us on the Foreshore," *ABC News Australia*, last updated January 2020, https://www.abc.net.au/news/2020-01-01/mallacoota-bushfire-first-hand-account/11836264.

BIBLIOGRAPHY

Cavell, Stanley. *The Claim of Reason*. Oxford: Oxford University Press, 1979.

Coetzee, John. *The Lives of Animals*. Princeton, NJ: Princeton University Press, 1999.

Cora, Diamond. "The Dog that Gave Himself the Moral Law." *Midwest Studies in Philosophy* 13 (1988): 161–79.

Cora, Diamond. "Eating Meat and Eating People." In *The Realistic Spirit: Wittgenstein, Philosophy and the Mind*. Cambridge, MA: Massachusetts Institute of Technology Press, 1995.

Cora, Diamond. "The Difficulty of Reality and the Difficulty of Philosophy." In *Philosophy and Animal Life*. Edited by Stanley Cavell, Cora Diamond, John

McDowell, Ian Hacking, and Cary Wolfe. New York, NY: Columbia University Press, 2008.

Gaita, Raimond. *The Philosopher's Dog*. Melbourne: Text Publishing, 2002.

Goswell, Gus. "What It was Like as the Mallacoota Bushfire Moved Towards Us on the Foreshore." *ABC News Australia*. Last updated January 2020. https://www.abc.net.au/news/2020-01-01/mallacoota-bushfire-first-hand-account/11836264.

McMahan, Jeff. "Our Fellow Creatures." *The Journal of Ethics* 9 (2005): 353–80.

Rachells, James. *Created From Animals: The Moral Implications of Darwinism*. Oxford: Oxford University Press, 1990.

Taylor, Craig. *Sympathy: A Philosophical Analysis*. Basingstoke: Palgrave MacMillan, 2002.

Taylor, Craig. "Our Fellow Creatures." In *Ethics in the Wake of Wittgenstein*. Edited by Benjamin De Mesel and Oskari Kuusela. Abingdon: Routledge, 2019.

Williams, Bernard. "The Human Prejudice." In *Philosophy as a Humanistic Discipline*. Edited by A. W. More. Princeton, NJ: Princeton University Press, 2006.

Winch, Peter. *"Eine Einstellung zur Seele."* In *Trying to Make Sense*. Oxford: Basil Blackwell, 1987.

Wittgenstein, Ludwig. *Philosophical Investigations*. Translated by G. E. M. Anscombe. Oxford: Basil Blackwell, 1958.

Wittgenstein, Ludwig. *Zettel*. Translated by G. E. M. Anscombe. Edited by G. E. M. Anscombe and Georg Henrik von Wright. Oxford: Basil Blackwell, 1967.

Chapter 6

Brave New Salmon

From Enlightened Denial to Enlivened Practices

Martin Lee Mueller and Katja Maria Hydle

ENLIGHTENED DENIAL

The Norwegian salmon feedlot industry is a telling example of the ways in which the Enlightenment paradigm continues to make itself felt in human–animal relations. Meanwhile, Enlightenment thinking and practice are increasingly criticized as being conceptually outdated, morally calamitous, and practically impossible to sustain on a finite planet.

Our argumentation builds on a critique first developed by Horkheimer and Adorno, whose *Dialectic of Enlightenment* opens with a programmatic assertion: "Enlightenment, understood in the widest sense as the advance of thought, has always aimed at liberating human beings from fear and installing them as masters. Yet the wholly enlightened earth is radiant with triumphant calamity."[1] Reason, they argue, inherently focuses on dominating nature through an exclusive concern on instrumental knowing. Consequently, instrumental reason itself increasingly degrades into irrationality. In parallel with Horkheimer and Adorno's argument concerning how instrumental rationality assimilates culture, we here argue that that same rationality also assimilates *animals* into industrial frameworks, in the process homogenizing both culture and nature. In our case, this logic is immanent in the full-scope application of scientific, instrumental rationality to the industrial framing of Being salmon. Early Enlightenment thinkers forged the ideal of a detached, reductionist, disembodied objectivity. Rational human subjects reduced everything *other* than the human mind to radically mechanistic objects, determinate apparatuses principally devoid of inwardness, agency, subjectivity. If need be, spontaneous feelings of empathy with, or love for, other animals had to be actively denied.[2] This epistemological austerity insisted that only external quanta could be elevated to a status of true knowing. We consider this a root denial. It leads to the kind of "triumphant calamity" foreshadowed by Horkheimer and Adorno, namely, in our case, the rampant irrationality of a techno-scientific framework built by instrumental reason seeking near-total domination. We show how the animals drawn into its gravitational sphere suffer the entangled consequences of that root denial.

The case of Norwegian salmon farming demonstrates how this root denial still generates, gathers, and channels tremendous political and economic energies. Conceptually and practically, salmon become commodity, atomized and alienated units of flesh; the land and seas become resources; the growth imperative remains unchallenged; wealth is defined as the accumulation of profit; operations are modeled on competition and privatization; and humans are deemed separate and superior. We argue that it is necessary to interpret contemporary feedlot practices in the light of this centuries-old tradition of "enlightened denial." It is in this larger context that dynamics of denial can be exposed more clearly, and that we can begin to imagine more truthful, humane, morally just, successful, and indeed beautiful human–animal relations. To move through and beyond the critique of Enlightenment irrationality, we lean into the work of biologist-philosopher Andreas Weber, who documents the emergence of a new paradigm, what he calls Enlivenment: An era where humans are recognized as being materially and symbolically entangled with the biotic community; wealth is reconceptualized as distributed, shared, and decentralized commonwealth; successful housekeeping becomes disentangled from the growth-imperative and is realigned with steady-state economics; and inwardness is no exclusive possession of humans but an embodied quality inherent to all living beings.[3] We frame the discussion by asking a seemingly simple question: Who—or what—are salmon allowed to be inside industrial feedlot practices?

We critically examine empirical material gathered from 2010 to 2017 in Norway using open-ended and inductive research design. The material includes: (1) observations of salmon industrial sites at sea and on shore; (2) document studies; (3) multiple visits to and participant observations at fish farming sites, fish processing factories, and control rooms for several pens; (4) a thorough study of a three-day Hardanger Fjord Seminar, a periodic gathering of fish farming practitioners, researchers, and politicians; (5) interviews with local politicians and bureaucrats in a small municipality where both salmon fishing and salmon farm industry is threatened by sea pollution due to mining; (6) semistructured interviews with different managers within the fish farming industry, representing different companies; (7) factories and suppliers; (8) participant observation at one of Europe's best salmon fishing rivers with 80 percent genetically changed and also virus-contaminated salmon; and (9) a thorough study of the streaming of a two-day Norwegian national salmon seminar in 2016, with speakers from the national political level, the salmon industrial level as well as salmon fishing and tourist industry. All interviews were transcribed; participant observations and site visits were partly filmed and photographed. Our analysis of the material elaborates and extends the work both of Horkheimer and Adorno and of Weber, by identifying some of the covert dynamics of denial at play in contemporary human–animal encounters. Our central claim is that an industry modeled on an outmoded ontology of life—more precisely, what Hans Jonas calls the overwhelming factuality of an ontology of death[4]—leads to a structural, anticipated, and comprehensive denial of aliveness.

FROM A DENIAL OF FUNDAMENTAL CATEGORIES TO FINE-GRAINED, MINUTE DENIALS

Enlightenment thinking cemented a conceptual and perceptual rift between the rich inner worlds of humans and the rich inner worlds of all other living forms. The historically contingent divorce reinforces itself to this day through social structures such as mainstream law, politics, or economy, as well as through academic institutions still largely organized dualistically alongside the Enlightenment split, with the so-called "humanities" looking to worlds of (human) meaning-making and the so-called "natural sciences" looking to worlds of externally measurable quanta. From within that paradigm, salmon science and salmon politics reenact the largely unquestioned assumption that a host of "objective data" and analytical measurements alone can create successful, lasting human–salmon economies.

The following empirical material shows that Enlightenment objectivity has no clearly articulated notion of epistemological boundaries, or knowledge horizons that ought to be respected and upheld. This finds expression in the ostensibly "common sense" notion that living beings can be truthfully encountered as "biomass"—the perceived norm that "life" can be equated with "mass-produced life." Within that reference frame, fluctuations in production become a problem to be solved; a uniform and predictable turnover becomes a goal to strive for; and increased efficiency becomes a reliable marker of truth. While such logic may apply to machines in the proper sense, it leads to problematic practices when it circumscribes the lives of sentient beings. Enlightenment thinking, in Andreas Weber's words, "is an ideology that focuses on dead matter. Its premises have no way of comprehending the reality of lived experience . . . the Enlightenment project has no use for notions of life, sentience, experience, subjectivity, corporeal embodiment and agency. These concepts are in effect excluded from the Enlightenment view of the world."[5] Relevantly, this is an ontological positioning toward the world as being, not alive but dead, the Cartesian machine. It is from that fundamental ontological orientation that Horkheimer and Adorno's observation still rings with potency: "What human beings seek to learn from nature is how to use it to dominate wholly both it and human beings. Nothing else counts."[6]

We claim that once the salmon's aliveness is denied conceptually, there is potentially no limit to what structural–practical–moral boundaries can—and will—be breached. Whether or not the imperative to maximize biomass entails any moral dilemmas—say, the routine mass suffering of millions of sentient beings—becomes not only irrelevant practically and invisible structurally but also redundant conceptually. Questions of well-being or agency cannot, in principle, be admitted into any sustained critique of contemporary practices. They remain outside the scope of what can be thought at all. We argue that once the denial is instituted at the level of fundamental categories, of that primordial ontological orientation, floodgates open for any number of more fine-grained, detailed moments of denial.

Control

A thread that runs through Horkheimer and Adorno's *Dialectic* is the Enlightenment's consistent—or, more accurately speaking, insistent—focus on dominating nature. It brings to near-perfection the even older dream to "dominate nature boundlessly, to turn the cosmos into an endless hunting ground."[7] This, they argue, "was the purpose of reason, on which man prided himself."[8] Our findings corroborate this philosophical claim with empirical substance, pointing to the overarching importance of control in feedlot operations. We observe a drive toward controlling such external parameters as variations in weather, temperature, light, wind, and water. These become defined as problems that need to be solved through innovation. One informant says:

> You've got them out in the water. And the currents really are a problem—all those natural conditions become problems. You can tell that our fish are stressed, say, after a seal has come by. All those uncontrollable conditions—algae, diseases, storms—storms really are huge problems—all the instability with natural weather. Everyone talks about how difficult nature is.

We can distinguish between two larger phases in the lives of salmon, the juvenile or freshwater phase, and the post-smolt or saltwater phase. Most recent innovations toward fully contained saltwater systems address the saltwater phase. The industry has already largely succeeded in recreating an idealized outer nature for the salmon's juvenile phase. These much smaller fish are kept indoors, in halls where they recreate entire seasons and even, in principle, the length of the average day. Juvenile fish still respond to seasonal clues as they mature, but the technological lifeworld around them gives these clues independent from what is happening outside the halls. One informant speaks of the juvenile phase:

> You control the temperature one hundred percent. And you control the light one hundred percent. So when customers who have invested hundreds of millions of Norwegian kroners in new recycling hatcheries . . . there they control the temperature one hundred percent. So they know that if they put into a fertilized roe, the fry will weigh 80 grams nine months later . . . regardless whether it is Christmas Eve or New Year's Eve or midsummer. It doesn't matter. The environmental conditions are standardized in there. And they expect roe all year round. And they'd have zero understanding if we couldn't deliver roe all year round.

This quote, and the next, show that the wish to control outer nature is also affected by a market to whom seasonal fluctuations are a nuisance:

> Light and temperature signal to salmon when to mature sexually. If the customer says he wants roe delivered on 20 October at 12 o'clock, that's not so easy when . . . you rely on health, sea temperature, light, water temperature on land, etc. So, we think the fact that we produce roe that way . . . We must simply do some more of that . . . I won't say scientific, but controlled.

And another: "We now . . . produce smolt in recirculation systems on land. We produce much larger smolts. And the fish are under completely optimal conditions at 14 degrees Celsius."

Next to there being no principle boundary to what aspects of salmon's outer nature can, and will, be controlled, there is also no principle boundary to what aspects of the fishes' inner nature can, and will, be controlled. One informant speaks of the recent turn toward patenting salmons' genetic memory, a trade that has grown from early phenotypic selection programs in the 1970s:

> Each year we create 360 different families, all of them based on a single genotype, back from just under two decades ago. We're now constructing a breeding center where we've got 45 times 80 tanks lined up in long rows. In each tank you've got one family. You need to keep them separate until they're so big that you . . . can mix them. And then you test them against all sorts of diseases, and you can do tests out in the open sea concerning growth, fat, color, feed conversion, etc. By the time you make your choices about what fish to use in your future breeding programs, and in commercial roe production, you can lean on

enormous amounts of data. And then there's this true novelty in addition to the family breeding program—everything that's got to do with genetic selection. That's where we can zoom in from families and down to individuals. What gene markers impact different traits? Which individuals are most resistant to lice? . . . Our breeding program has just become infinitely more advanced and complex, in comparison with the family information we've had since 2000. We've got individual information about thousands of fish.

The Norwegian Institute of Marine Research has experimented with editing salmon genes such that typical color development is "turned off," resulting in yellow salmon; and the genes responsible for initiating sexual maturation are "turned off." Such fish produce no sex hormones and never mature sexually. Forced sterility is considered a desirable outcome, in part, because it will help counteract cross-breeding of escapees with wild populations, and in part because, as one researcher says: "research into sterile fish can lead to better overall welfare." Another prominent case comes from North America. In November 2015, the US Federal Drug Administration (FDA) approved AquAdvantage Salmon for human consumption, making salmon the first genetically modified animal ever to be approved for sale and consumption on the open market, anywhere in the world. The decision marked the preliminary climax of a legal battle that had spanned more than two decades. Half a year later, Canadian authorities followed suit. In a legal and rhetorical tug-of-war, AquaBounty Technologies—the company that has created AquAdvantage Salmon—had long pursued a strategy that defined their genetically modified Atlantic salmon (*Salmon salar*) as being "substantially equivalent" to nonmodified Atlantic salmon. In essence, the FDA's approval meant that they followed the company's argumentation: There was no material difference between nonmodified salmon and AquAdvantage Salmon—despite the fact that GM salmon have been modified with a growth hormone gene from one of their Pacific cousins, Chinook salmon (*Oncorhynchus tshawytscha*), and a promoter from an eel-shaped Atlantic fish called ocean pout (*Zoarces americanus*). That promoter functions essentially like an on–off switch to the growth hormone, with a twist: In AquAdvantage Salmon, the switch is perpetually turned "on": the fish ceaselessly produce growth hormones, reaching adult size in just 18 months, or nearly twice as fast as conventionally farmed Atlantic salmon. Critics nickname the fish *Frankenfish*, alluding to Shelley's famous nineteenth-century meditation on Enlightenment ideals unchecked by moral concerns.

Whether the control-imperative concerns weather patterns, water temperature, food composition, growth speed, or the fishes' genetic memory—every aspect of the lives of salmon becomes redefined as something that ought to be improved, perfected. Our findings are consistent with what Arne Johan

Vetlesen calls "the wholesale automization of culture vis-à-vis nature under-stood—and treated—as its radical other."[9] The guiding principle is to stream-line salmon increasingly with the logic of a growth-oriented, technological lifeworld. Until a better, more ideal nature emerges. Relevantly, these specific moments of denial are not incidental as much as they are inevitable aspects of an enlightened, instrumental reason that attempts, as Horkheimer and Adorno point out, to redefine nature increasingly through aspects of calculability and usefulness.

Growth

The inherent focus on calculability and instrumentality, which we now understand to be immanent to Enlightenment rationality, goes hand in hand with a denial of any boundary or limitation that is outside the scope of instrumental reason. Half a century ago, the Club of Rome popularized the profound ecological insight that to live on a spherical planet *must* mean to acknowledge, adjust to, and integrate into the political and economic imagination certain *limits to growth*. More recently, Rockström et al. have suggested that there are certain nonnegotiable "planetary boundaries" that cannot be breached, lest the biosphere tip out of its former dynamic disequi-librium—a complex, planetary system that has maintained relative stability across the span of at least ten millennia—and transition into a period of unprecedented instability, a geostorical event now often spoken of as the Anthropocene.[10] But reorienting human cultures toward being able to live indefinitely on a finite planet turns out to be exceedingly difficult within the reference frames of a rationality narrowly focused on instrumental concerns. Unbridled growth, from an enlightened point of view, *makes sense* in the narrow understanding of serving instrumental rationality. If, as Horkheimer and Adorno argue, instrumental reason takes it as a given that nature can be adequately understood only through quanta, and if the pursuit of rational-ity is a project of domination, then there principally exists an imperative to maximize the quantifiable—the economic maxim of boundless growth becomes articulation, mirror, and concrete enactment of instrumental reason itself.

The year 2011 became a record year for Norway. For the first time, Norway produced more than a million tons of salmon. This translates to roughly 14 million salmon meals every day. Or, to use another metaphor: stacking all the salmon fish boxes exported from Norway on top of each other, annually, you would stand before a tower over 360 km high—reaching the altitude of the International Space Station, or forty times the height of Mount Everest. In a white paper on the future of the fish farming industry, the Norwegian gov-ernment envisions to increase this present biomass output fivefold in the next human generation.[11] Other countries are following suit. The growth paradigm is intrinsic to feedlot practices.

To that end, maximizing biomass output is assigned overarching importance. Two strategies designed to achieve that end are consolidating surveillance and centralizing operations. "Feeding is the most important thing we're doing really," one informant says. We are shown a space known as the "control room." It consists of several rows of screens, each of which broadcasts live footage of salmon in their pens. There is one row with very large screens on the wall, and in front of it another with many smaller screens. Several controllers occupy the room at any given time, overseeing the frenzy on the screens. At its maximum capacity, the control room can oversee seventeen individual salmon farms, scattered across several Norwegian fjords and bays. Each of these farms consists of ten to twelve individual pens, adding up to a total of 176 pens. Taking a conservative estimate of 150,000 post-smolt salmon per pen, this room rounds up the two-dimensional representations of 26,000,000 individual lives. An informant specified:

> Now our personnel are supposed to control around 16 to 17 locations at any time. They sit and have cameras down in the pens and up at the surface. And so they . . . watch real-time footage, and they follow the fishes' activity and make sure the fish eat. And that's how you take control of the most important input factor we've got. Which is feeding. It is definitely the most important one both in relation to costs and revenues. And the thing is, you end up with dedicated people who are specialists in what they do. And we see major improvements regarding our feed conversion ratio, and regarding our ability to control.

The salmon's agency to eat has become usurped by human's agency to feed, which in turn has been mechanized, automated, and centralized in the control room. One seasoned informant cannot help but be impressed with the growth rates he has witnessed: "The first year we produced 150 tons, in total. Today we're finished with 150 tons at the factory at eleven a.m. in one day." Another informant puts the size of operations in relation to other livestock farming in Norway:

> Last year we slaughtered roughly four times the amount of Northern Norway's entire meat production, to give you a comparison. All the land animals, and all the birds. So, this is quite extensive. We have a very simple philosophy. We want to have fun and make money. We don't want to earn so much money that we forget about having fun, and we don't want to have so much fun that we forget about making money. Very simple supermarket-philosophy, but it works. And that's really what it's about. And it's about being able to look forward to going to work. Having people who are motivated is incredibly important. That's

why we work with the entire value chain, and with everything that could influence us, we try to take control of.

Across the industry, the aforementioned feed conversion ratio is a central measure of success or failure. Another informant elaborates:

> Feeding is what makes the fish grow, and if you get a feed conversion ratio of 1.3 . . . you give the fish 1.3 kg fodder and it grows 1 kg, but it is, in aquaculture . . . this is a bad ratio . . . You should preferably get down to 1.1 or even lower. Obviously, the little difference between 1.1 and 1.3 corresponds to several tons of feed in a big company. So, if you manage to get your FCR down, but still have a high growth—if you've got fast-growing fish that use little fodder in order to grow so fast—you earn that much more money.

Another informant confirms the increasing focus maximizing the feed conversion ratio:

> [Earlier], we used to arrive at the plant, begin the feeding, and then we were out and did other things. And then we were inside and checked if everything went ok. Now we've got someone who sits there and is just *there* . . . and that's how you reduce the feed conversion ratio by ten percent. Suddenly you've produced two hundred tons more fish on the same site. Two hundred tons, net gain, for free. Only through reducing feed costs. It's amazing.

One increasingly pressing hindrance to further maximizing growth has been the availability of food for the salmon. With fisheries across the globe facing serious concerns of overfishing, other nonconventional foods are increasingly tested as alternatives. One informant explains:

> If we had unlimited access to fish with fish oil, things would have been very easy, because clearly it's what salmon naturally eat. But now . . . these salmon are increasingly becoming vegetarian. That's the quantitative side of it. Then there's the qualitative, the functional side of it—which is about developing fodder and components in the feed that actually boost the performance of the fish. These could be components that prevent disease, or that heal diseases, or they could make the fish grow faster, what we call the food conversion ratio.

The current ratio of vegetable feed to animal feed is 70:30, with vegetable ingredients stemming from soy, maize, sunflower, rape, fava beans, and wheat. Researchers from the Norwegian Aquaculture Protein Center have also experimented with mixing South American lupines into the diet, as well as yeast grown on leftovers from the forestry industry, as well as bacteria fed on North Sea Gas.[12]

An additional way to optimize the ratio is to test what density of fish in the pens will result in the highest biomass output. Welfare, in this sense, can be defined as the optimum density necessary to achieve that goal. As one informant says:

> Biological measures typically have a positive effect on the economy. Get the fish to survive, and you make money from them instead of having to pay money for them. It's that simple. The ones who die, you've got to pay for. Lots of work. While the other ones, those you get paid for. If they grow better, you earn more money. So all benefit: the fish and the economy.

Despite such efforts to maximize biomass output, Norway's production has largely stalled around roughly 1.2 million tons since 2011.[13] Several well-documented major factors have limited further growth, including sea lice (*Lepeophtheirus salmonis*), escapees, access to fodder, and an increasing shortage of suitable open-water sites. These problems are not exclusive to Norway but constitute major challenges across the industry. In response, the industry is now pushing hard toward radical technological innovation, in the hopes to contain, circumvent, and control the accumulating problems, and to generate a renewed growth momentum.

Alienation

All the empirical findings we document here point to articulations of alienation. In this section, we speak primarily about ways in which salmon, when drawn into the gravitational sphere of instrumental reason, become alienated from their lifeworld as a direct consequence of their ongoing commodification. We argue that this too, like the maxim of growth, is an *inevitable* consequence of the project to dominate nature under the auspices of instrumental reason. Instrumental reason requires an epistemological reduction or simplification of the world into measurable "quanta" or discrete "units of information." Coupled with the totalizing assumption that *all* of nature is principally knowable through instrumental reason, this epistemological reduction will also result in practical, technological reduction. If the assumption is that salmon are principally knowable in the fullness of their Being as quantifiable units, then isolating or alienating them from their lifeworld is principally unproblematic. Like the maxim of growth, it too makes sense within the narrow confines of instrumental reason. The circularity between assumption, evidence, and practical application renders the act of alienating animal from lifeworld invisible, nonexistent, unproblematic. It cannot be grasped within the reference frames of instrumental reason. It is in this invisibility, we suggest, that the act of denial lies.

We can distinguish between two larger innovation trends. The *first* is a push toward fully contained ocean-based raising units. Here Norwegian actors stand out. Such floating closed-containment solutions would isolate the fish from sea lice, prevent mass escapes, and make sites far more independent from local conditions and therefore more universally applicable. A Norwegian company—one of the industry's worldwide leaders—recently developed its so-called Marine Egg-concept: huge, fully contained enclosures that might resemble giant igloos from above the surface, or egg-shaped icebergs from below, each able, in principle, to hold a thousand tons of salmon. The company also experiments with other fully closed ocean-based systems, one resembling giant donuts and another being large converted vessels that carry salmon within their metal hulks. Another Norwegian company envisions the construction of what they call the Salmon Stadium—floating concrete tanks that resemble football stadiums, each holding 2,000 tons of salmon, and able, in theory, to float in the ocean for a full century without needing replacing. This company leans on Norway's existing offshore technology from the petroleum sector and envisions supertanker structures, each 430 m long and 54 m wide, able to hold 10,000 tons of salmon or 2 million individual fish. The superstructures will have a fodder silo of 1,000 tons, cranes on a rail system, a quay for service boats, and a dead-fish station able to take out the deceased fish every day. They will be equipped with mini submarines that allow for maintenance and subsurface control rounds.

The *second* trend, a push toward fully land-based farms, is receiving innovation impulses from across the globe. This is not surprising, as Norway's geography has historically given other countries a competitive disadvantage. A Danish company is envisioning to build salmon farms in the Gobi Desert in north-western China. Using water from 100-m deep holes, the water recirculation site is envisioned initially to produce 1,000 tons of salmon every year, but with growth potential in coming years—positioning the producers strategically in relation to the huge Chinese market. In 2016, a Gibraltar-based company announced that it would build the world's largest on-land farm in Zamora, Spain. The director said, "There's no other on-land salmon farm in the world able to produce three thousand tons."[14] Since then, several others have claimed entitlement to the world record. That same year, another Norwegian company received approval for what they claim will become the world's largest land-based farm near a small town in Western Norway. The facility will produce 20 million 1-kg post-smolts, or 20,000 tons of salmon flesh. In a press release, Fletcher writes: "The facility . . . intends to utilize the latest in water recirculating technology and treatment. The technology choice means full control of water quality and ensures optimal fish health and welfare."[15] In 2017, another Danish company had begun building a land-based salmon farm in Miami Florida.

Using underwater wells that provide saline water, the closed containment, recirculating site will initially produce 10,000 tons of salmon every year, or five times the total current US production. In the future, the company envisions to increase the annual output to 90,000 tons.[16] Beside the speed of technological innovation, we observe that all developments share two basic premises: (1) a key to future success is considered to lie in increasingly alienating salmon from their natural surroundings and (2) alienation is taken to be a vector to more control over the production process, and over the full life cycle of living animals.

As a growing number of factors determining their lives become mechanized, the fish are being alienated from ecological entanglements and drawn more and more deeply into a technological lifeworld. One informant says:

> The point is that we've come quite far by now. The next thing will be that we'll start utilizing the sensor technology even better. So we've got sensors that feel at sorts of possible things. We've already got many sensors monitoring environmental conditions. Temperature, salinity, oxygen, and stuff like that. And being able to process here [inside the control room] can simplify operations, because you don't necessarily have to sit and watch the fish. Gradually, machines are taking over. So your computer will register, oh, there went a pellet past the fish. Oops, and here comes a warning. Now you need to go in and check. Also then you can go in and check. In the next generation again, you'll see, oh, a pellet went past the fish, so the machine will say to itself: let's reduce the feeding. So that's the way it's going.

Techno-standardization and mechanization go hand in hand with moments of conceptual alienation, such as fish as "raw material." As one informant said: "The choice of roe and smolt has very much to say . . . it's the raw material." Conceptualizing the living creature as a "product" is also commonplace in recent attempts to "improve" the genetic makeup of the fish:

> Well we go in and look at the gene stock. The breeding stock. And then we analyze it. And once we find a trait there that we can actually do anything with, we'll pick out the fish... And then we launch that product.

Another informant says:

> I'll say that breeding companies have largely behaved very seriously and properly and not come with a whole lot of goofy things. When we've come up with something, we've really documented it well, and it's worked. And in the first—call it "genomic product"—we brought out, we selected them down to individuals.

And another: "Then you've got to utilize the information for finding x products against lice and Pancreas Disease and whatever else there might be."

There is also the concept of salmon as "commodity": "If we are to work with health, then so that we can optimize our commodity. Our commodity is salmon, and it is its health. Will you be able to keep it at a hundred percent at all levels?" This next citation illustrates the short way from the speech act to the near-total commodification of the living creature:

> Our customers like to see where the fish come from. We ask them a little about what they appreciate and what they are looking for and things like that. So that we can do something to satisfy their needs, obviously. It's interesting to try and adapt the fish to those who want to buy them. We'll ask if they're satisfied with the quality, specific things they are looking for. Depends on what requirements they've got. They've got different things they look for when they're out. Could be the shape of the fish, could be the meat quality, anyway, that's what it used to be. Color is something that some of them measure. Some measure fat.

"Biomass" is that other prominent concept we have already alluded to:

> We have three . . . parameters for doing business in farming. One is clearly your slaughter quality. That you get a high quality on that which comes to shore. Then you measure your food conversion ratio. And then you've got a low mortality rate. That one's an important parameter too. You don't want so many to die along the way. You want to maximize your allowed biomass capacity. You want to keep that at top level at all times. There are important criteria to achieve that. And so you've got to keep the fish in full steam until they lie on the slaughter bank.

Another says:

> Well you've got a certain number of tons you're allowed to have at one site. The way things are here now, we're only allowed to have 2,340 tons at any one time. And then, come September when you set out your fish, they'll be so and so big. And then in October there'll be a few more that are a little smaller. That not all the fish grow equally at the same pace. Because then you could quickly end up with 2,340 tons of fish that may only be 3 kilograms on average, and then you'd have to begin slaughtering them when they're technically a bit too small still, but you have to because you're not allowed to go over those 2,340. But over the course of a few months it'll be ready for slaughter. So now they take the largest first, and it's been taken out, and then you've got your biomass, as it's called, those 2,340 tons will be less if you include those first fish, and so we'll fatten up the others so that they'll grow and become that big.

There is a notable hesitation in this last quote, a moment's distance between the concept "biomass"—"as they call it"—and the conceptual-technological alienation. In its simplicity, the moment's hesitation bears testament to the close intertwinement of various salmon farming practices, including basic saying and material arrangements. It illustrates what we document here at length: The mechanization, standardization, and centralization of farming practices enter into a feedback loop with alienating language. Each creates further distance between "us" and "them"; each contributes to making the other more plausible; each makes the denial of the fish as living agent seem more "matter-of-factly" and "commonsensical"; each obscures and conceals the other as something that might need to be questioned in the first place. The practical alienation finds itself mirrored in the conceptual and vice versa, in a self-amplifying loop. The particular style or mode of technological innovation we document here makes it possible to actually produce "biomass"—to actually mass-produce life. Concepts such as "biomass," "product," "raw material," or "commodity" nudge the engineering imagination toward looking for practical solutions for what is now defined as a set of problems or challenges: the fish must be improved, perfected, enhanced. Concepts contribute to creating incentives to overcome "imperfections." The maximization of mass-produced life, in this logic, becomes framed, first and foremost, as a technical problem that has *not yet* been solved. The "not yet" of these complementary aspects creates a nearly irresistible imperative to actively deny both the fishes' inner life and to deny their entanglement in ecological processes. Success, in this, is framed as whatever technical solutions will help produce even greater masses of life at a certain speed at a certain time.

Enter now fully grown farmed salmon, about to be slaughtered. The next two informants emphasize how quickly salmon today can be brought in from their waiting pens, slaughtered, frozen down, and be processed for shipment:

> Today, the situation is like this. At seven in the morning they can decide. Oh, now we've got a few seven-to-eight-kilogram fish too many today. So we'll throw them into the freezer. So they start the freezer and they move the fish in there. And at noon, the truck goes out with the fish. Fully frozen.

The other says:

> The fish go in [to the slaughterhouse], then 240 minutes pass, then they're bathed in a glazing substance, and then they're packed right away. So then you can ask, how long will it take to pack up a whole car? Well maybe it'll take two hours until the car is full. In all, the entire process is over in just five hours. If you start the day at seven, your car can leave at twelve.

Another informant says that it would take about forty-seven hours, in total, for their fish to move from the waiting pens to the slaughterhouse, trucks, airport, and finally arrive at their designated market in Asia.

One informant launches into a detailed description of the importance of ensuring high-quality routines across all aspects of a domesticated salmon's life and death, including the conditions in the cages, the density of fish, their health, food safety, quality, and customer satisfaction. Then he asks rhetorically: "How are the fish doing in the transport boxes? This has something to say for the end-product." He goes on: "Slaughter is welfare. And welfare and stress levels during slaughter have something to do with the quality. The handling underway. The product quality then goes all the way. The slaughterhouse and the hygiene."

For our analysis of such self-amplifying practices of denial, it seems less relevant to ask which of them came first than to document, first and foremost, that such self-amplifying dynamics of denial emerge in the first place. Instrumental reason organizes action and action organizes instrumental reason, creating a technological lifeworld whose principal quality is that it is *just there*. The closed loop between instrumental reason and the technological lifeworld becomes the proverbial serpent biting its own tail, a self-amplifying, entangled dynamic where the drive to make nature more calculable creates the techno-worlds we see, and the techno-worlds we see reflect back to reason the reassurance that its narrow focus on instrumentality does in fact work. What is overseen, what is outside the loop, what is invisible to reason—what is therefore actively denied and increasingly rendered nonexistent—is the living creature *as* expression of aliveness. Denial becomes the normal course of things. It infuses thought and action alike. Consequently, it conceals the possibility of entirely other styles of thought or action.

PRINCIPLES OF ENLIVENMENT

From an enlivened point of view, the critical point is still the Enlightenment paradigm's active denial of the inner lives of fish. Weber asks, "What is life?" and argues that non-reductionist answers must begin with the acknowledgment that to be alive is always already to be embodied. To be an embodied subject is to actively demark boundaries. It is to experience an inner drive toward a dynamic equilibrium, felt from within as wellbeing. When that dynamic equilibrium is compromised or upset, the fish will experience suffering. The inner experience of suffering is a subjective expression that a boundary has been crossed that should not have been crossed. From an enlivened perspective, such experiences must be considered objectively real. Weber speaks of the "'empirical subjectivity' of living beings, and . . . the 'poetic objectivity' of meaningful experiences."[17] It is from that point of view that we argue, still, that reducing fish to external quanta—"biomass," "products," "functions of growth speed," "efficiency-driven life cycles"—while structurally denying their inner lives is not incidental to business-as-usual as much as it is programmatic to the Enlightenment paradigm. The denial is in the organization of knowledge, in what constitutes "true" ways of knowing the world and what does not. We argue that approaching salmon through the lens of instrumental rationality alone cannot, in principle, encounter the salmon in the empirical subjectivity and poetic objectivity of their lives, because it already denies the first-person experience of being a living fish. To make this claim is not "just" to tread along familiar tracks of animal rights discourse. It is, more primordially, an ontological and epistemological recalibration toward inhabiting organic reality through a body.

The Unbearable Heaviness of Being Feedlot Salmon

Other beings share our capacity for world-making, Weber writes. Living nature, in that view, must be seen "as an unfolding process of ever-growing freedom and creativity paradoxically linked to material and embodied processes."[18] To be alive is to be existentially invested in meaning-making. The meaning-making of wild fish is embodied, and it is participative. Salmon, the feeling subject, arises between her cold-blooded flesh and the cold water world she inhabits. Smelling the faint signature of home in an ocean of smells might irradiate her sensing flesh with a mixture of excitement, recognition, resolve, a rich blend she transforms into the decision to keep voyaging until she has found her way back. Leaping up roaring winter cascades might feel like an acutely focused will to her, an irresistible determination. Spilling eggs from her wounded body and into the holes she has dug might release qualities of ecstasy, completion, bliss. Her inwardness is inseparable from being a feeling body, and importantly, being a feeling body is inseparable from being immersed inside the multiple agencies that co-constitute the biosphere. Wildness is not so much background but existential context of her intelligence, the irreducible medium inside which her inwardness blooms into the subtle fragrances endemic to being salmon. Her inwardness is not confined to her body but is *in* the ocean and *in* the river. For the sake of argument, let us understand this literally. She actively composes a topography of meaning through her body's fluid participation with autumn floods, Arctic summers, droning humpbacks, or sun-speckled red willow roots. Salmon's experience of "inner" coherence is inseparable from calibrating herself constantly in relation to a coherent "outer" world: ocean tides, subsurface earthquakes, moon phases, nocturnal luminescent algae, hunting packs of killer whales, blue-green icebergs, magnetic fields, the trickly caress of bubbling whitewater falls: all add nuance, grain, touch, texture, quality to the felt coherence of being salmon. They are no "environment" as much as they are the concrete spatial–temporal coordinates of her inwardness. She comes to her senses *between* the animate flesh of her body and the animate flesh of the Earth body.[19]

This enlivened perspective on inwardness is relevant for the question of denial in feedlot practices. Participative inwardness is the template for all salmon, free-roaming and captive. However, whether salmon can emerge into their participatory aquatic intelligence is structurally insignificant from the standpoint of Enlightened denial. As we have seen, feedlot salmon increasingly live out their lives in fully contained techno-worlds. Inside concrete halls or steel tanks, temperatures, the sun's pace, the very seasons can be manipulated to tailor-fit rapidly growing biomass to meet market demands. Vacuous tanks offer no temporal–spatial guidance, no felt texture that would allow feedlot salmon to compose a coherent topography of inwardness. Food presents itself to her, not as elusive enigma that must be stalked, pondered, known. There is no more prey whose will to live would demand of salmon that she sharpen her senses, hone her alertness, gather a richer and more fluid inwardness. Food comes as repetitive, uniform overabundance, offering that much less friction against which a coherent agent can emerge. How might salmon experience the sum of such frustrations if she is denied, as a matter of routine, the chance to transform embodied participation into meaningful action? Weber, in discussing laboratory deprivation experiments with other animals, writes: "The sensory world that these miserable figures have created around them from only their restricted experiences is a spooky caricature of reality."[20]

In addition to such sensory incoherence, feedlot salmon also suffer from physical deformity. Several studies document the prevalence of functional blindness in farmed Atlantic salmon, linking cataract development to intolerable water temperature fluctuations, rapid growth rates, rushed changes in water salinity, or the increase of vegetable ingredients in fish feed.[21] Rapid growth rates have also been suggested as a cause for permanent deafness to up to half of all farmed salmon worldwide.[22] Caged salmon have been documented to portray behavior consistent with severe mammal depression, such as reduced activity and a reduced appetite, symptoms that have been successfully treated with antidepressants.[23] Their loss of appetite is a remarkable finding when we consider that captive salmon are bred to be hungry. We observe that within the dominant paradigm, suffering fish are an inconvenience, (in)calculable expenditure, an externality to an Enlightenment paradigm that principally knows no epistemological boundaries. The routine suffering of millions of captive fish must be structurally denied because it does not fit conceptually into the paradigm of a fully mechanizable, fully controllable nature perceived as radical other. What matters is to uphold the paradigm, not to integrate the evidence that salmon's boundaries—those of living subjects whose sentient bodies yearn to actively compose a topography of meaning inside a coherent lifeworld—cannot be persistently breached through measures of increasing control, mechanization, and alienation. Their suffering is objectively real. And yet it cannot be allowed into a comprehensive accounting because that would mean to question foundational thought and power structures. If need be, a brave new machine world designed in denial of sentient animals' inner worlds will even go to such lengths as applying antidepressants, medication which by the very nature of its existence *acknowledges* the inner lives of living subjects. We see here: Denial takes form as structural violence. We also see: From an enlivened point of view, antidepressants are a pressure point, a moment where the Enlightenment paradigm collapses momentarily, a thorn pinching through the delicate veil of denial we document here.

The acknowledgment that living beings can no longer be conceptualized in denial of their embodied, meaning-making inwardness is a hallmark of enlivened thinking. Hildegard Kurt and Weber observe that "natural science, which by applying its rule of empirical objectivity, finds it opposite—meaningful subjectivity—in the depths of the unfoldings of the biosphere."[24] In this thinking, life can be thought of a creative and indeed poetic meshwork of mutual entanglement, interpenetration, and dynamic interactions.

Commonwealth: Enlivenment Housekeeping

From an enlightened point of view, wealth is measured in terms of technological efficiency, growth, and profit. To achieve such ends, one must actively deny the oft-observed paradox of assuming infinite growth curves on a finite planet. One must further assume ever greater technological control at the expense of ecological entanglements. Enlightened thinking implies methodological reduction and practical isolation. It implies centralization of production and power, implying a necessity to deny the erosion of place-based, small-scale local economies. It also entails a necessity to deny a loss of meaning as salmon slip from the imagination, ritual, story, collective memory. It further implies a necessity to deny salmon's indiscriminate generosity, an abundance that comes for free, having the ontic quality of a gift. We have exposed the necessity to deny salmon's privation of poetic-subjective-embodied meaningfulness inside feedlots. These are various aspects which, from an enlivened point of view, enable us to argue that the business-as-usual model is not mass-producing wealth in a truer sense. It is mass-producing scarcity. Weber and Kurt write: "A policy of life searches for alternatives to the dogma of growth and addition to consumerism. It does not seek technological control but pursues the creative negotiation between equal participants in an ecosystem that all need to preserve. It strives to promote the experience of aliveness. It creates economic productivity through ecological stability and meaningful actions."[25]

The living world—that self-composing meshwork of expressive, meaning-making entanglements and embodied agents—does not come about through isolating agents from one another. Nor does it flourish when wealth becomes monopolized in the hands of a few at the expense of many. Life blooms in richly composed ecological communities of shared aliveness. Salmon are aptly recognized as keystone species; their very lives are practically and conceptually inseparable from the lives of hundreds of other species from every kingdom of life. Salmon keystone entanglements include carbon sequestration cycles, nurturing wolf mothers, old-growth temperate rainforests, Californian vineyards, or human gift economies modeled on the life cycles of salmon, to name just a few. Such entanglements are a sustained lesson in what Weber thinks of as "commons" economies. The notion of commons economies suggests a different notion of wealth. Weber argues that wealth is a measure of the relative depth of connections between every agent of socio-ecological communities, including human meaning-making but also including large-scale nutrient cycles, self-organizing predator–prey relationships, or the uncontained migration habits of aquatic, avian, or terrestrial travelers. Weber suggests some relevant aspects of such an enlivened perspective on wealth.[26] (1) *Sharing.* From an enlivened perspective, monopolization, centralization, and privatization are recognized as privations of possibilities for socio-ecological communities to emerge into deeper relationship. Salmon, as keystone species, share the gift of their flesh indiscriminately with all. Their life cycle is the concrete embodiment of the Enlivenment metaphor of wealth as commonwealth. (2) *Open access.* Commonwealth necessitates that resources not be withheld from participative flows, whether through conceptual or physical dams, fences, walls. Air, water, nutrients, or meaningful relationships enrich living beings precisely because they can be accessed freely. As they are received, they create new possibilities for being gifted forward. Enlivenment thinking is commensurate with gift economies.[27] (3) *Steady state.* "The biosphere does not grow," writes Weber. "The quantity of biomass does not increase. The throughput of matter does not expand; nature is running a steady-state economy . . . The only dimension that really grows is the diversity of experiences: ways of feeling, modes of expression, variations of appearance, novelties of patterns and forms. Therefore, nature does not gain mass or weight, but rather depth."[28] Depth expresses itself through increasingly rich cascades of relationship, expression, voice, mutuality, inwardness, freedom, or autonomy. (4) *Richness and depth of experience (human and more-than-human).* Human–salmon economies modeled on

Enlivenment principles have existed for millennia, many of them indigenous. They tend to be culturally robust, ecologically resilient, and model their specific place-based socio-poetic sphere in close participation with salmon. Rich and deeply alive ecological relationships tend to enter into mutually reinforcing feedback cycles with rich and deeply alive cultural expressions: binding together human and more-than-human worlds, allowing both to coexist over time, allowing members a sense of well-being, belonging, relationship, meaningfulness.

We now recognize wealth conceived as concentrated power and profit as a denial of aliveness. It views nature as dead matter composed of isolatable building blocks. But aliveness, in a truer sense, brings forth a commonwealth of relationships which expresses itself not only biologically, ecologically, or geologically, but also symbolically and poetically. In Enlivenment thinking, those are no opposites. They are mutually reinforcing aspects of the irreducible expression of life, here on this water planet.

LEAPING UPSTREAM AND BEYOND DENIAL

How far is the Enlightenment paradigm going to go before it gives way? What is the threshold? The possible total eradication of wild salmon seems no viable threshold. The unraveling of ecological entanglements seems no viable threshold. The routine mass suffering of millions of fish seems no viable threshold. The impoverishment of the cultural imagination seems no viable threshold. We have argued here that the denial of boundaries—inherent limitations of living bodies who strive to unfold in fluid networks of shared aliveness—is immanent to the Enlightenment paradigm. We developed this argumentation through the lens of the empirical case of contemporary salmon economics. This has allowed us to elaborate and critically reflect on Weber's concept of Enlivenment, and on potential implications of his thinking for future human–salmon encounters.

What, then, would it take to acknowledge such boundaries as the inner lives of fish, limits to material growth, or ecological flows, at the level of a comprehensive culture of aliveness? Weber and Kurt write:

> A policy of life strives for a civilization in which principles, institutions, and economic practices follow the maxim that life *shall be* . . . A policy of life searches for alternatives to the dogma of growth . . . It does not seek technological control but pursues the creative negotiation between equal participants in an ecosystem that all need to preserve. It strives to promote the experience of aliveness. It creates economic productivity *through* ecological stability and meaningful actions . . . [A policy of life strives for an] economy that does not

support the "use" of resources in a "market" built on "objectivity" and separation but enlarges the possibilities to participate in a shared planetary metabolism of commons economy and is guided by an understanding of economic exchange as the shared household of the biosphere.[29]

Such enlivened practices will boldly leap upstream and beyond the multiple contemporary expressions of the denial of aliveness. They will be co-created and emerge as we begin to integrate the true character of shared aliveness into our academic institutions, our moral landscape, our technological imagination, our ways of speaking.

NOTES

1. Max Horkheimer and Theodor W. Adorno, *Dialectic of Enlightenment. Philosophical Fragments*, tr. Edmund Jephcott (Stanford, CA: Stanford University Press, 2002), 1.

2. Martin Lee Mueller, *Being Salmon, Being Human: Discovering the Wild in Us and Us in the Wild* (White River Junction, VT: Chelsea Green Publishing, 2017).

3. Andreas Weber, *The Biology of Wonder. Aliveness, Feeling, and the Metamorphosis of Science* (Gabriola Island: New Society Publishers, 2016).

4. Hans Jonas, *Organismus und Freiheit: Ansätze zu einer Philosophischen Biologie* (Göttingen: Vandenhoeck und Ruprecht, 1973).

5. Andreas Weber, *Enlivenment. Towards a Fundamental Shift in the Concepts of Nature, Culture and Politics* (Berlin: Heinrich Böll Stiftung, 2013), 11–15.

6. Horkheimer and Adorno, *Dialectic of Enlightenment*, 2.

7. Ibid., 206.

8. Ibid.

9. Arne Johan Vetlesen, *The Denial of Nature. Environmental Philosophy in the Era of Global Capitalism* (London: Routledge, 2015), 4.

10. Bruno Latour, *Facing Gaia. Eight Lectures on the New Climatic Regime* (Medford, OR: Polity Press, 2017); Johan Rockström et al., "Planetary Boundaries: Exploring the Safe Operating Space for Humanity," *Ecology & Society* 14, no. 2 (2009): 32, http://www.ecologyandsociety.org/vol14/iss2/art32/.

11. The Norwegian Government, *Meld. St. 16 (2014–2015). Forutsigbar og miljømessig bærekraftig vekst i norsk lakse- og ørretoppdrett* (Oslo: Det Kongelige Nærings- og Fiskeridepartementet, 2015).

12. Bård Amundsen, "Laks på plantefôr," *Norges forskningsråd*, March 19, 2011, https://forskning.no/fisk-oppdrett-mat/2011/03/laks-pa-plantefor.

13. Emiko Terazono, "Norway Turns to Radical Salmon Farming Methods," *Financial Times*, March 13, 2017, https://www.ft.com/content/a801ef02-07ba-11e7-ac5a-903b21361b43.

14. Cliff White, "Atlantic Sapphire Building USD 350 Million Land-Based Salmon Farm in Miami," *Seafood Source*, March 19, 2017, https://www.seafoods

ource.com/news/aquaculture/atlantic-sapphire-building-usd-350-million-land-based
-salmon-farm-in-miami.

15. Rob Fletcher, "Licence for World's Largest Land-Based Salmon Farm," *Fishfarming Expert*, June 30, 2016, https://www.fishfarmingexpert.com/news/world-largest-land-based-salmon-farm-is-granted-license/.

16. White, "Atlantic Sapphire."

17. Weber, *Enlivenment*, 11.

18. Ibid., 22.

19. David Abram, *Becoming Animal. An Earthly Cosmology* (New York, NY: Vintage, 2010).

20. Weber, *The Biology of Wonder*, 182.

21. Sofie Charlotte et al., "Lens Metabolomic Profiling as a Tool to Understand Cataractogenesis in Atlantic Salmon and Rainbow Trout Reared at Optimum and High Temperature," *PLoS One* 12, no. 4 (2017): e0175491, doi:10.1371/journal.pone.0175491.

22. Tormey Reimer et al., "Rapid Growth Causes Abnormal Vaterite Formation in Farmed Fish Otoliths," *The Journal of Experimental Biology* 220, no. 16 (2017): 2965, doi:10.1242/jeb.148056.

23. Marco A. Vindas et al., "Brain Serotonergic Activation in Growth-Stunted Farmed Salmon: Adaption Versus Pathology," *Royal Society Open Science* 3, no. 160030 (2016), doi:10.1098/rsos.160030; Marco A. Vindas et al., "Depression-Like State Behavioural Outputs May Confer Beneficial Outcomes in Risky Environments," *Scientific Reports* 9, no. 3792 (2019), doi:10.1038/s41598-019-40390-3.

24. Andreas Weber and Hildegard Kurt, "Towards Cultures of Aliveness. Politics and Poetics in a Postdualistic Age. An Anthropocene Manifesto," *The Solutions Journal* 9–10, no. 15 (2015): 61, https://cultures-of-enlivenment.org/sites/cultures-of-enlivenment.org/files/manifesto_solutions_weber_kurt_dec_2015.pdf.

25. Weber and Kurt, "Towards Cultures," 63.

26. See Weber, *Enlivenment*.

27. Robin Wall Kimmerer, *Braiding Sweetgrass. Indigenous Wisdom, Scientific Knowledge and the Teaching of Plants* (Minneapolis, MN: Milkweed Editions, 2015); Andreas Weber, *Matter and Desire. An Erotic Ecology* (White River Junction, VT: Chelsea Green Publishing, 2017).

28. Weber, *Enlivenment*, 27.

29. Weber and Kurt, "Towards Cultures," 63–64.

BIBLIOGRAPHY

Abram, David. *Becoming Animal. An Earthly Cosmology*. New York, NY: Vintage, 2010.

Amundsen, Bård. "Laks på plantefôr." *Norges forskningsråd*, March 19, 2011. https://forskning.no/fisk-oppdrett-mat/2011/03/laks-pa-plantefor.

Fletcher, Rob. "Licence for World's Largest Land-Based Salmon Farm." *Fishfarming Expert*, June 30, 2016. https://www.fishfarmingexpert.com/news/world-largest-la nd-based-salmon-farm-is-granted-license/.

Horkheimer, Max, and Theodor W. Adorno. *Dialectic of Enlightenment. Philosophical Fragments*. Translated by Edmund Jephcott. Stanford, CA: Stanford University Press, 2002.

Jonas, Hans. *Organismus und Freiheit: Ansätze zu einer Philosophischen Biologie*. Göttingen: Vandenhoeck und Ruprecht, 1973.

Kimmerer, Robin Wall. *Braiding Sweetgrass. Indigenous Wisdom, Scientific Knowledge and the Teaching of Plants*. Minneapolis, MN: Milkweed Editions, 2015.

Latour, Bruno. *Facing Gaia. Eight Lectures on the New Climatic Regime*. Medford, OR: Polity Press, 2017.

Mueller, Martin Lee. *Being Salmon, Being Human: Encountering the Wild in Us and Us in the Wild*. White River Junction, VT: Chelsea Green Publishing, 2017.

The Norwegian Government. *Meld. St. 16 (2014–2015). Forutsigbar og miljømessig bærekraftig vekst i norsk lakse- og ørretoppdrett*. Oslo: Det Kongelige Nærings- og Fiskeridepartementet, 2015.

Reimer, Tormey, Tim Dempster, Anna Wargelius, Per Gunnar Fjelldal, Tom Hansen, Kevin A. Glover, Monica F. Solberg, and Stephen E. Swearer. "Rapid Growth Causes Abnormal Vaterite Formation in Farmed Fish Otoliths." *The Journal of Experimental Biology* 220, no. 16 (2017): 2965. doi:10.1242/jeb.148056.

Remø, Sofie Charlotte, Ernst Morten Hevrøy, Olav Breck, Pål Asgeir Olsvik, and Rune Waagbø. "Lens Metabolomic Profiling as a Tool to Understand Cataractogenesis in Atlantic Salmon and Rainbow Trout Reared at Optimum and High Temperature." *PLoS One* 12, no. 4 (2017): e0175491. doi:10.1371/journal.pone.0175491.

Rockström, Johan, Will Steffen, Kevin Noone, Åsa Persson, F. Stuart III Chapin, Eric Lambin, Timothy M. Lenton et al. "Planetary Boundaries: Exploring the Safe Operating Space for Humanity." *Ecology & Society* 14, no. 2 (2009): 32. http://www.ecologyandsociety.org/vol14/iss2/art32/.

Terazono, Emiko. "Norway Turns to Radical Salmon Farming Methods." *Financial Times*, March 13, 2017. https://www.ft.com/content/a801ef02-07ba-11e7-ac5a-9 03b21361b43.

Vetlesen, Arne Johan. *The Denial of Nature. Environmental Philosophy in the Era of Global Capitalism*. London: Routledge, 2015.

Vindas, Marco A., Siri H. Helland-Riise, Göran E. Nilsson, and Øyvind Øverli. "Depression-Like State Behavioural Outputs May Confer Beneficial Outcomes in Risky Environments." *Scientific Reports* 9, no. 3792 (2019). doi:10.1038/s41598-019-40390-3.

Vindas, Marco A., Ida B. Johansen, Ole Folkedal, Erik Höglund, Marnix Gorissen, Gert Flik, Tore S. Kristiansen, and Øyvind Øverli. "Brain Serotonergic Activation in Growth-Stunted Farmed Salmon: Adaption Versus Pathology." *Royal Society Open Science* 3, no. 160030 (2016). doi:10.1098/rsos.160030.

Weber, Andreas. *Enlivenment. Towards a Fundamental Shift in the Concepts of Nature, Culture and Politics*. Berlin: Heinrich Böll Stiftung, 2013. https://www

.boell.de/en/2013/02/01/enlivenment-towards-fundamental-shift-concepts-nature-c
ulture-and-politics.

Weber, Andreas. *The Biology of Wonder. Aliveness, Feeling, and the Metamorphosis
of Science*. Gabriola Island: New Society Publishers, 2016.

Weber, Andreas. *Matter and Desire. An Erotic Ecology*. White River Junction, VT:
Chelsea Green Publishing, 2017.

Weber, Andreas, and Hildegard Kurt. "Towards Cultures of Aliveness. Politics
and Poetics in a Postdualistic Age. An Anthropocene Manifesto." *The Solutions
Journal* 9–10, no. 15 (2015): 58–65. https://cultures-of-enlivenment.org/sites/cul
tures-of enlivenment.org/files/manifesto_solutions_weber_kurt_dec_2015.pdf.

White, Cliff. "Atlantic Sapphire Building USD 350 Million Land-Based Salmon
Farm in Miami." *Seafood Source*, March 19, 2017. https://www.seafoodsource
.com/news/aquaculture/atlantic-sapphire-building-usd-350-million-land-based
-salmon-farm-in-miami.

Chapter 7

The Animal That Therefore Was Removed from View

The Presentation of Meat in Norway, 1950–2015

Karen Lykke Syse and Kristian Bjørkdahl

Between 1916 and 1926, an idyllic garden suburb materialized on the outskirts of Oslo, Norway. Built in the style of British country vernacular, an entire neighborhood of low red brick houses emerged in green surroundings centered on *Damplassen*, a market square with a pond at its core. The suburb, Ullevål Hageby, was designed for the laboring and lower middle classes,[1] and would provide its inhabitants with everything they needed for a wholesome, modern life: sound housing, a small allotment garden, and a market with a food store, a baker, a butcher, a charcuterie, a dairy, a post office, and a police station.

The history of this suburb's market square is a microcosm of how ordinary people's meeting with meat has changed throughout the last 100 years or so. Precisely because it was designed as a self-contained suburban universe, it can exemplify the development that Norway, and indeed many other parts of the world, has been through. From its inception, the square housed a butcher, which is a telling sign that this was indeed where most people bought their meat at the time. A historical photograph from the Damplassen butcher depicts sausages hanging in a neat row, draping a line of more mixed produce, such as joints, hams, halved carcasses, and bellies of pork (see figure 7.1). On the counter stands a plate of pigs' trotters, and behind it, two pigs' heads. At specialty stores like this one, butchers in full view of the consumer would dismember animal carcasses and divide them into pieces of meat, bone, and offal according to the customer's needs. The connection between animal and meat was apparent for all to see, and consumers were reminded

Figure 7.1 Damplassen Cooperative Butcher, ca. 1926. Photo: Unknown. Owned by and used with permission by Oslo Havebyselskap.

of the work that went into making meat of animals every time they met the butcher, a skilled professional.

Across the square from the Damplassen butcher was a grocery store, a bakery, a dairy, and a charcuterie (see figure 7.2). In the latter, consumers could go to buy sausages, patés, terrines, and cured cold cuts of meat, which would be sliced up or divided into suitable pieces by the ladies behind the delicatessen counter. Here too, the presentation of meat was explicit, and again, tied to skill and professionalism: However, the division of labor between the butcher and the charcuterie was clear; each required separate stores, a different—not to mention differently gendered—staff, and distinct skills.

In 1966, the charcuterie and the grocery shop merged, which meant that processed meats from then on would be sold alongside all sorts of other groceries.[2] This change reflected a general shift that had set in all across Norway, toward self-service stores that would come to be called "supermarkets." In the new supermarket on Damplassen, goods were no longer distributed over the counter, but stacked on shelves in an open floor plan. Here, customers would forage on their own, filling their shopping trolleys or baskets at will. Where the old butcher and charcuterie had highlighted the origin of meat, as well as the expertise that went into transforming animals into meat, the new supermarket made meat a grocery like any other, in a jungle of goods that the customer had to traverse on her own (see figure 7.3). While some supermarkets did retain a separate meat counter, these too would disappear with time. When that happened, any reminder of the work and the skills needed to

Figure 7.2 Damplassen—Dairy and Charcuterie Counter around 1926. Photo: Ingimundur Eyjolfson. Used with Permission from Arbeiderbevegelsens arkiv og bibliotek.

transform big chunks of animal into consumable pieces of meat disappeared along with them.

The supermarket was such a success that the Damplassen butcher went out of business in the early 1980s, and the local residents were left with merely a supermarket and a bakery. The inhabitants of this idyllic garden suburb were thus placed in the same, paradoxical situation in which we all find ourselves today: While we eat more meat than ever, we no longer encounter any reminder of the animal origin of meat, or of the work and skill that goes into making animals edible. Without these reminders, we have grown increasingly distanced from the animal origin of meat—and the result, we argue, is *denial*.

As we have suggested elsewhere, one way to understand contemporary consumers' denial of the animal origin of meat is to see it as the product of a process of alienation along three separate, but intertwined, axes: the spatial, the social, and the cultural.[3] First, throughout the twentieth century, ordinary consumers–citizens grew increasingly alien to the places and sites where animals are kept, reared, killed, and partitioned. This development was partly due to urbanization, that is, people living at an increasing distance to the sites of meat production, and partly due to a concentration within agriculture, which saw more animals reared and killed on an increasingly small

Figure 7.3   The New Supermarket Made Meat a Grocery Like Any Other. Owned by Byhistorisk samling, Oslo Museum.

number of farms and slaughterhouses. This spatial alienation was closely related to a social and occupational corollary, namely that a dwindling number of people had knowledge about animal rearing and slaughter, not to mention the skills to perform such work. For most people, the work and knowledge required to make meat of animals rescinded even further into the distance. Over time, these first two forms of alienation removed many of the resources we previously used to justify and make sense of animal killing and consumption. While, as John Berger once pointed out, the old time "peasant becomes fond of his pig and is glad to salt away its pork," we moderns experience doubts that the parts of that sentence can be plausibly connected by an "and."[4] As recent research on the so-called "meat paradox" indicates, reminders of the animal origin of meat cause cognitive dissonance, since we no longer have any way to justify respect for animals, on the one hand,

and consuming their meat, on the other.[5] Rather than making sense of this animal killing, we deny it. We forget, neglect, ignore, overlook, cover up, and marginalize that fact that the meat we are eating stems from a sentient creature.[6]

Drawing on an ongoing study into the cultural history of meat production and consumption in Norway, we aim, in this chapter, to put some historical meat on the bones of this admittedly rather crude thesis. We focus on how the presentation of meat as a commodity in grocery stores has changed over time, to understand what role the provision, processing, and presentation of meat has had in enabling the denial documented by psychologists. How has consumers' meeting with meat—at the point of purchase—changed over time, and how has this changed those consumers' relation to meat?

MEAT OVER THE COUNTER

To understand how the presentation of meat has changed in recent decades, we can stop first at a shift that had its origins in the post–World War II years. Before the war, Norwegian consumers had bought meat and other food items in a variety of specialized stores, as we saw in the case of Damplassen. After the war, however, grocerers began considering the prospect of self-service stores, which had become a growing trend abroad. How could this new idea be introduced to Norway—and how could storeowners be brought to embrace such a shift? They had ample reason not to: Most existing stores had been designed as narrow rooms that ran along a long counter which separated customers from store attendants, and refitting them for self-service was bound to be both cumbersome and expensive.

In addition, according to widespread advice at the time, a self-service store ought to be rather large, at least 100–150 m². This size would allow for both a comfortable display of food and easy navigation and movement for the customers.[7] This need for more space increased rents, however, and thus required a higher turnover. Nevertheless, the benefits were obvious: Fewer employees could serve more customers, and customers would be free to browse and shop without forgetting anything. Not least, in open floor self-service stores, customers would be tempted to pick up things they did not really need, as they now had a variety of interesting goods within easy reach.

While the call for profit within self-service shopping was hovering above, the structural changes within the whole supply chain that were needed to beef up the yields were still largely wishful thinking. Not only did the stores have to change, the shelving, technology, and groceries themselves had to be adjusted. In fact, it did not take long before grocers started realizing that the goods on sale would have to change almost as much as the store itself for the

self-service idea to work. For instance, a director of Norway's retail cooperative stated at the time that "I believe self-service stores for food will become
popular (. . .) but the full benefits will only be harvested when foods are
delivered pre-packaged in standardized packages."[8] This call was echoed the
following year: "We need pre-packaged goods," wrote another representative
of the cooperative, while explaining the benefits of plastics, which would
become a key technology in the display of goods in self-service stores. With
the novel product *transofilm*—a see-through cellophane-like material that
was suitable for prepackaging and displaying meats and sausages—customers could easily see and reach tidy meat packages. Self-service meat required
more than packaging, though, and store owners were given strict advice to
invest a particular cooling counter to display foods such as meats and sausages, dairy, and vegetables. Although less technical solutions could be used
for vegetables and dairy, they were told that it was a requirement rather than
a suggestion for meat stuffs.[9]

The requirement for coolers went hand in hand with one of the most important technical innovations of the twentieth century: electricity. In the present
context, this technology was pivotal in the sense that it allowed fundamental
changes in meat consumption habits. While Norwegian meat traditionally
had been eaten cured, dried, and sometimes smoked, now, thanks to electri-
cal coolers, fresh meat became readily available to both the rural and the
growing urban market. By the 1950s the electric fridge was an obtainable,
if not quite yet a widespread, feature in Norwegian households. Its obvious
usefulness caused its popularity to grow wildly, and by 1967, 74 percent of
all Norwegian households had an electric fridge.[10]

Electric refrigeration had repercussions not just for private households,
however, but also for large-scale, commercial uses. Largely thanks to
refrigeration, grocery store refittings like the ones contemplated in the late
1940s and early 1950s were now becoming economically viable, and many
stores shifted to self-service interiors, where a key component were cooling
counters displaying meat and other perishables. These counters meant that
a greater number of meat products could be moved out of the butcher's and
into the grocery store. In the 1960s, a new Norwegian word even followed in
the wake of this: *ferskvare*. This literally translates as "fresh goods," but in
Norwegian, the word had a more specific meaning: meat or fish sold fresh.[11]
Although butchers and fish mongers were already using ice blocks to sell
fresh meat and fish, it was the electrically chilled presence of fresh produce
among the other groceries that engendered the new terminology.

New terminologies were also invented—or imported—for the packages in which the food was displayed. "*Foodtainers*—the latest in the
field" announced the retail co-op's magazine in 1961 and explained
that these were ideal for packaging meats.[12] Foodtainers were made of

cardboard and had been saturated with wax to partly absorb and partly contain any meat juices, while protecting the meat on display to the customer. The same article instructs store workers on how to use food-tainers and emphasizes the importance of professionalism when dealing with meat. The hygiene requirements, the characteristics of the packaging material, and the packaging technique all required strict adherence to rules of conduct rather than mere intuition. Meat was a foodstuff that had to be handled with care, and the stores were ready to take over this part of the caretaking.[13]

With time, however, the emergence of self-service stores would have notable repercussions for both of these groups, in the first instance for those professionals who, up to this point, had done a significant part of the preparation of meat for consumption, namely the housewives. While a butchers' knife and a meat mincer would still be found in any respectable housewife's kitchen, these tools were now increasingly left unused. "Even the most talented housewife can find it difficult to follow the accelerating changes within housework. But the co-operative will make this easy for you," was the message directed to housewives trying to find their footing in 1963.[14] With a greater selection of ready-minced and prepared pieces of meat, the housewife could let both the meat mincer and the butchers' knife rust away, unused in the kitchens' bottom drawer. Many domestic tasks that used to be carried out by the housewife were now largely taken over by other actors, most notably the meat industry, which increasingly began to heed the call for "pre-packaged [meat] in standardized packages." And as their skills grew increasingly less useful, housewives became food consumers rather than food producers.[15]

THE BEAST LEAVES THE BUILDING

In 1972, the Norwegian people voted against joining the EEC, but there was nevertheless a growing feeling that Norway would have to adapt to its European surroundings. This was certainly true in agricultural circles. In the meat co-op, by far Norway's biggest actor in the meat market, many felt that the No vote amounted to nothing more than a "reprieve," and that "a society in line with the ideals of the common market would emerge regardless."[16]

While Norway's agricultural sector had always been heavily regulated, giving ample room to cooperatives as "market regulators," the 1970s saw a renewed optimism about "what could be gained through political governance."[17] Consequently, in 1973, the Norwegian government enacted a set of "consumer subsidies" to make (particularly red) meat more affordable. This caused an immediate and quite dramatic hike in Norwegians' meat consumption. At the same time, the co-op took steps to centralize its operations, while it also had a boost in creating the so-called "regulation facilities," essentially storage facilities that could buffer market demand.

In this period of growth, several things happened at once, which would radically change the way meat was presented to Norwegian consumers. First, and perhaps the most significant, was the coming of effective plastic (vacuum) packaging techniques, which was a vast improvement on the aforementioned cellophane. This was important, since it facilitated presenting meat to consumers in such a way that there was no longer any obvious trace of the animal. Even squidgy or irregular pieces of meat could be neatly encased and displayed. More concretely, this technology incentivized the meat co-op to take control over a larger part of the meat-cutting market. Representatives of the co-op had been on "study trips" to the United States in 1975 and had grown quite adamant that there should be a "rationalization of meat sales at the point of retail," which in practice meant making sure that there was no "integration from the retailers into production and packaging."[18] Calculations had revealed that control of cutting and packaging of meat was a source of substantial profits, and the meat co-op's sustained effort to gain such control had several consequences.

From cutting 42 percent in 1974, their share of this market grew to 50 percent in 1985, and further to 75 percent in 2004.[19] The incentive for meat producers to gain a large share of the market in cutting in effect boosted a development that had already been underway since the late 1960s, namely a transition from independent butchers to meat counters in the supermarket. "One of the [meat co-op's] most important aims throughout the 1970s," write historians of the co-op, "was to transfer as much of this activity as possible to their own slaughterhouses, and rather sell 20–30 kilo Gilde-branded multi-packages of ready-cut, standardized pieces to the stores."[20]

Meanwhile, the retail co-op's own meat brand, "Goman," was aggressive in their campaign to take over the butchers' role—though they conveniently did not mention the word "butcher": "Don't cross the road for your cold cuts" read the headline for a 1977 ad. "You pay so much for your cold cuts of meat today, that you can demand high quality—whether you purchase it in a package or by weight."[21] Another two-page ad read:

> Don't cross the road for meat. Domus/S-laget has all the meat worth eating. Whether you shop for a weekday dinner, a good old fashioned Sunday's dinner or a special stew for a Saturday night—you don't have to leave the grocery store to get the meat you need.[22]

The meat co-op's increasing control over cutting was only a first step. Over time, this move lead to another shift, this time within the supermarkets themselves: From the staffed meat counter, where meat was displayed in ani-mal-like pieces and cut in a backroom, to meat increasingly being displayed as boneless, ready-cut, and plastic-wrapped in refrigerators and freezers around the supermarket. So, while the meat co-op established itself in the supermar-kets' meat counters early in the 1970s, later in the decade it would take further steps to blend in with all the other ingredients in the supermarket jungle.[23]

As the industries were increasingly doing work that previously had been divided between in-store butcher professionals and the shopping housewives, the role of the consumer changed accordingly. "The ready for the pan meat is all over the stores' cooling units, lying pretty packed in neat rows," wrote the editor of Norway's only food magazine in 1979.[24] Her writing carried a fair amount of nostalgia of the good old days, when the housewife was given qualified advice by a specialist, the butcher. He would ask the housewife, "What do you plan to cook with it?" and procure a piece of meat that was perfect for this particular use. The editor questions the point of all the ready-spiced bits of meat labeled with silly names such as "Mexican Steak" or "Stewing Meat," as these names do not say anything at all to the consumer about what kind of meat this is. Herself firmly in possession of the skills and knowledge required to transform animal parts into food, she argues that the vital thing to know about a piece of meat is what cut it is. Covering a random piece of meat with spices and labeling it as Mexican is a form of seduction, luring the customer to buy without knowing what they buy. She claimed that one of the most important tasks at hand for the magazine she represented was to provide consumers with knowledge, as only this would allow consumers to eat both economically and well.[25]

The lack of direct knowledge or preparatory cooking skills that the maga-zine editor referred was also a concern for *Opplysningskontoret for Kjøtt* [The information office for meat], a meat propaganda agency financed by meat farmers' organizations. Its agenda was to increase Norwegian meat consump-tion, and they believed that the dwindling of meat-processing skills among consumers could be resisted if they filled the educational gap themselves. An army of "meat hostesses," dressed in brown checked pinafores and armed with suitcases containing a portable gas stove, knives, and brochures, entered the Norwegian stores. Their task was to show Norwegian housewives how to cook different meat cuts and hand out tasty tidbits demonstrating what it was possible to cook, and how to carry out the process at home. Leaflets, bro-chures, cooking thermometers, and inspiration of all kinds were distributed to whoever wanted to read or listen.[26] The Meat Hostess Instructions, from 1972 to 1974, explain the role of the meat hostess thus:

> Being a meat hostess requires in-depth knowledge about meat, and that you can transfer this knowledge to each and every customer, whether this concerns

purchase, cooking or storing it. (. . .) the meat hostess should be placed by the store's meat section, preferably before the customer arrives at the meat counter.[27]

A huge effort to increase meat sales by information and customer education was carried out, and this effort was especially directed toward the "difficult" joints, tougher cuts of meat that required more time, skills, and attention from the cook. Norway's only food magazine, *Alt om mat*, which was published between 1975 and 1983, emphasized three factors for busy homemakers: price, time, and ease of preparation. The meat industry was very much aware of these factors, and in addition to re-professionalizing the housewife they saw a way of increasing meat consumption by transforming the undesirable or tough cuts of meat into mincemeat. The leaflets that were handed out from the propaganda office contained new uses for minced meat, and traditional Norwegian mince recipes that required time and cooking skills such as meat loaf and meat cakes were given company. A bastardized international crossover cuisine entered the scene; that of spaghetti bolognese, pre-prepped international freeze-dried bases like "Mexican Hot-Pot" or "Hunters Stew" ("just add mince"), even pizza topped with mincemeat. Mincemeat was fairly inexpensive, fast, and easy to cook, and filled all three requirements of price, time, and ease of preparation.

These incentives, which emerged as the role of the housewife gradually faded away, meant that consumers were growing less knowledgeable about meat, not to mention less skilled in treating it. As a corollary, another figure emerged, namely "the critical consumer." If we understand new technology and the economic incentives that came along with them as pull factors of the changes in how meat was presented, a significant push factor was that consumers were growing increasingly *demanding*, probably because of their dwindling knowledge of meat. The co-op's sales division noted this development in 1973, when it stated that the so-called "consumerism" which had begun to emerge,

> entails that certain consumers or representatives of consumers, like the Consumer Council, self-professed 'consumer apostles' evaluate each product with a critical eye. With better education, increasing distance between consumer and producer, and less materialistic attitudes, we can expect consumers to grow ever more critical to what he eats, what influence he is put under by advertising, how the products are presented, and so on.[28]

The co-op's response to this perceived development would turn out to work together with the economic incentives already mentioned. In short, the co-op shifted from the traditional meat classification scheme, which was regulated by law, toward increasing use of branding. Consumers would no longer buy meat-piece-so-and-so-classification-this-or-that, they would buy Gilde Salami, or Gilde Pork Chops, and so on. This was also the time when the co-op began using declaration of contents. The plastic packaging that was increasingly becoming the standard way of presenting meat to consumers was a help even to this shift, since the plastic wrapping made branding far easier; all they had to do was to print stickers with the co-op's logo, and a list of contents, and stick it onto the plastic. The name Gilde was taken from a line of traditional local products, but would increasingly be used as a national brand, and over time began to fill the role that the classification scheme had in the past. The brand, which the co-op advertised heavily by attaching it, on the one hand, to national tradition, and on the other, to the farmers themselves (since the co-op was owned by farmers), now became what consumers used to satisfy any doubts they might have about the safety or quality or nutritional soundness of the product. As historians of this co-op note, "Traditional products . . . could be standardized and be redefined as brands."[29]

THE SUPERMARKET REVOLUTION

While the technological, economic, and advertising shifts of the 1970s were certainly significant, the real shift arguably took place somewhat later, in the late 1980s and early 1990s, with the coming of the supermarket chains to Norway—a shift that affected the Norwegian retail market more heavily than in almost every other country. While the number of grocery stores went dramatically down from the late 1970s to the early 2000s, the supermarket chains' share of the market in groceries expanded more or less absolutely. While in late 1980s, their share had been 42 percent, and this had grown to as much as 80 percent in 1990. The truly amazing development came thereafter, however, as the chains' command of the market grew to 99.6 percent in 2000.[30]

The amazing growth of the chains was in fact made possible, in part, by the meat co-op's success with taking over the market in meat cutting, which lead to the removal of meat counters from the stores, as well as by the corresponding plastic wrapping and branding of meat. Both of these developments had made the job of retailing meat easier and less knowledge-intensive: While an in-store meat counter required skilled professionals, the task of stocking a refrigerator with plastic-wrapped pieces of ready-cut meat—which even paraded all relevant information about the product on a sticker attached—did not. Having left the job of quality control and consumer information to producers and processers, all that was left for the supermarkets to do was to keep its shelves full of merchandise. To put it crudely, their only job was to pass products through their stores; they were—and were also initially criticized for being—little more than temporary storage facilities for food.

At this point, beginning in the early 2000s, the distancing from the animal origin of meat had reached a temporary end point. Meat was now sold as any other ingredient and did not often carry a reminder of the process that had made meat of a sentient creature.[31] Knowledge of that process had also been extracted from the point of retail, when the meat counters disappeared. The only technology left by which consumers could try to close the gap between production and consumption was the sticker on the plastic wrapping, informing the consumer about the "contents." The sociologist Nick Fiddes sums up the process concisely when he writes that, "Nowadays, the consumer need never encounter animal flesh in its vulgar undressed state," and adding that we, as a result, "prefer not to think too directly about where our meat has come from, [as] unwelcome reminders can be distinctly off-putting."[32]

THE FROZEN PIGLET INCIDENT

In October 2014, a controversy arose in the Norwegian public sphere, as the Facebook page of the TV host and publisher, Arve Juritzen, became an illustration of just how far removed Norwegian consumers had become from the animal origin of meat. While shopping in his local supermarket, Juritzen had come across a whole suckling pig, encased in translucent plastic and placed alongside other frozen goods. Juritzen must have felt a need to test his own reaction of disbelief with his virtual friends, as he posted the following on Facebook: "I went food shopping. In a plain freezing unit in an ordinary store I found this!! Is this possible!!?? I'm going vegetarian!" (see figure 7.4). Juritzen's update was shared 900 times, as his feed turned into a veritable flood of comments. The reactions, in short, amounted to a stream of shock, disgust, aversion, and disbelief at seeing a whole animal where they had come to expect meat as a disembodied ingredient.

Some comments were short but descriptive: "Ouch!"; "Omg"; "Nasty"; "Yuck"; "Horrible!"; "Cruel!"; "Disgusting!"; "Ouch, macabre!!"; "How horrible!"; "Totally grotesque!"; "My God horrible!" Other commenters mirrored Juritzen's expression of disbelief: "Is this possible?!"; "Poor little thing"; "OMG agree, is this possible?"; "Ouch. This doesn't really give me an appetite. Think I'm going vegetarian"; "A disagreeable surprise in the freezer, it doesn't make me want to eat or buy anything." Another category of response displayed empathy with the animal and disgust at seeing it presented in this manner: "Shock and horror!"; "One thing is to let adults see this, but what about children?"; "Ohhhh it hurts to see this"; "Disgusting"; "Yuck, I can't stand seeing any kind of pork after this picture." Finally, some even doubted this was legal in Norway: "Jee, is this legal?" one person asked outright, while others questioned whether the picture really did stem from his own neck of the

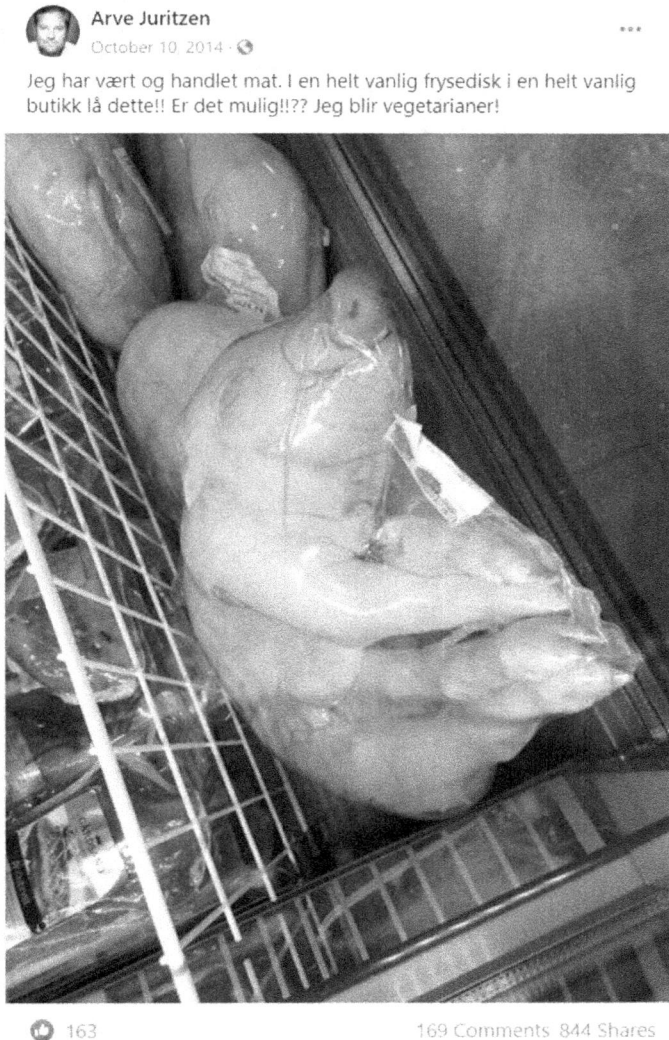

Arve Juritzen
October 10, 2014 · 🌐

Jeg har vært og handlet mat. I en helt vanlig frysedisk i en helt vanlig butikk lå dette!! Er det mulig!!?? Jeg blir vegetarianer!

🤍 163   169 Comments 844 Shares

Figure 7.4   Screenshot of Arve Juritzen's Facebook page. Used with permission from the author.

woods: "Nooooo. Here in Norway?" Some expressed disappointment or anger by learning that it was indeed from Norway: "This is sad, can't understand that it's happening"; "Sickest thing I've seen! Makes me really mad."

The interesting aspect of this flood of shocked comments, we argue, is not simply the disgust itself, but the fact that it appeared to come from an internalized failure to make the connection between animals and meat. The dead piglet seemed genuinely to surprise many people, who were now forced to think: *Is* this *what I eat*? Admittedly, among the more than 900 comments were also a few that displayed neither disgust nor ignorance. "It shouldn't come as a surprise that the meat we eat comes from animals," said one person, while another wrote, "Before it is jointed, meat is an animal." But objections like these were neither numerous nor effective enough to shift the balance of Juritzen's feed, and a response to the latter comment displays just how deep-seated the failure to connect animals and meat has become: "Sure, we know that animals are animals before they are parted. But [for the most part] we don't have to look at grim photos like this one, which is enough to rob anyone of their appetite."

This incident illustrates the process we have called cultural alienation from the animal origin of meat, that is, that we have been left without any work-able frame into which we can place our own consumption of meat. Unlike what certain scholars seem to suggest,[33] this process of alienation was not purposively designed as such. Rather, as we have seen in the Norwegian case, multiple contingent factors—including the economic ambitions of the cooperatives, the liberation of women and corresponding "death of the house-wife" and, not least, the coming of the huge supermarket chains—all contrib-uted to removing consumers from the animal origin of meat. This coincides roughly with the story told by historian Roger Horowitz, in his 2006 book *Putting Meat on the American Table*, in which he shows that the growth in Americans' meat consumption in the course of the twentieth century was due to a combination of supply and demand. Horowitz focuses on the dynamic interplay between forces of production and forces of consumption, and finds that meat, especially after World War II, was increasingly organized accord-ing to a "logic of convenience."[34] The implicit goal sought by both produc-ers and consumers of meat, he argues, was, "Building convenience into the meat purchased by consumers."[35] This was also a notable effect of how meat was sold in Norway, but here as elsewhere this convenience has come with a price.

For while display, purchase, preparation, and consumption of meat has become ever more convenient, the thought that we must kill sentient creatures to eat them has become steadily less so. While the use of denial to avoid relat-ing to inconvenient circumstances has been well known ever since Stanley Cohen's famous *States of Denial* from 2001, scholars have more recently begun to look into how this phenomenon arises in human–animal relations. In recent years, a growing literature has identified what is now called the "meat paradox,"[36] which refers to the psychological trouble—the cognitive disso-nance—that ensues when one realizes that one is eating a sentient creature that one also happens to care about.

One seemingly straightforward way out of this type of cognitive dissonance is to respond with one of the "four Ns," and claim that meat is natural, normal, necessary, and nice.[37] For those who are not capable of this type of response, however, the remaining options are what Darst and Dawson (adapting Hirschman) describe as exit, voice, or denial: We can *voice* our protests against how we treat animals, but such protests have tended to be fragmented, conflicting, and confused.[38] To the extent protesting is not sufficient, many could in principle be lead toward two different forms of *exit*—either substitution and abstention—but they are both felt by most to be overly demanding. That leaves only *loyalty*, which in this context means continued meat consumption. And given what we know, Darst and Dawson argue, this amounts to "socially organized denial of the evidence and its implications."[39]

While we believe denial of human treatment of animals to be a widespread phenomenon in contemporary society, it is important to point out that this is primarily a social, not an individual, phenomenon. As we have seen in the historical sketch we provided earlier, a variety of factors have contributed to distancing ordinary consumers from the animal origin of meat and from the work involved in transforming animals into meat. To the extent we, as a social collective, can know anything at all, we have to conclude that we know both the evidence and its implications. For any particular individual, however, the increased spatial, social, and cultural alienation from the process that turns animals into meat means that one does in fact not know—or at least, that one's knowledge is strongly curtailed.

The implication of this, we believe, is that one cannot expect to deal with denial of the animal origin of meat as an individual, moral question. Rather we have to attack the problem at its socioeconomic root. Not only has the animal been removed from view, but the process that turns the animal into meat, has been removed from view too.

NOTES

1. Anne Fogt, Siri Meyer, and Anne Ullmann, *Ullevål Hageby gjennom 90 år: Fra bolignød til Kardemommeby* (Oslo: Unipax, 2007), 11.

2. See Anne Hals, "Damplassen før og nå," *Årsskrift for Sogn og Tåsen historielag*, 2015.

3. Kristian Bjørkdahl and Karen Lykke Syse, "Kjøtt, fremmedgjøring og fornektelse," *Nytt norsk tidsskrift* 36, no. 3 (2019): 255–67.

4. John Berger, "Why Look at Animals?" in *About Looking* (New York, NY: Pantheon Books, 1980), 7.

5. There is a growing literature on this paradox, see, for example, Steve Loughnan, Brock Bastian, and Nick Haslam, "The Psychology of Eating Animals," *Current Directions in Psychological Science* 23, no. 2 (2014): 104–8.

6. For an argument that runs roughly in the same direction, see Robert Magneson Chiles, "Hidden in Plain Sight: How Industry, Mass Media, and Consumers' Everyday Habits Suppress Food Controversies," *Sociologia Ruralis* 57, no. 1 (2016): 791–815.

7. Peder Fremstad, "Vi må få selvbetjeningsbutikker: Forsøk og erfaring i Oslo," *Forbrukeren* 7 (1949): 146–8.

8. Ibid.

9. Ivar Stovner, "Vi må få ferdigpakkede varer," *Forbrukeren* 4 (1950): 80.

10. "Percentage of Households with Different Types of Equipment," *NOS Survey of Housing Conditions 1988*, Accessed February 11, 2020, http://www.ssb.no/a/hists tat/tabeller/13-13-4t.txt.

11. Annechen Bahr Bugge, *Fattigmenn, tilslørte bondepiker og rike riddere: Mat og spisevaner i Norge fra 1500-tallet til vår tid* (Oslo: Cappelen Damm Akademisk, 2019), 333.

12. Ivar Stovner, "Ferdigpakking av kjøttvarer: Foodtainere, det siste på området," *Forbrukeren* 7 (1961): 142.

13. Ibid.

14. NKL Norges Kooperative Landsforenings kjøttforedlingskomite, "Samvirkelaget innbyr til husmoraften," *Forbrukeren* 2 (1963): 44.

15. Bugge, *Fattigmenn*, 300.

16. Sverre A. Christensen and Yngve Nilsen, *Langs gilde veier: Gilde Norsk Kjøtt 1931–2006* (Oslo: Dinamo forlag, 2006), 123.

17. Ibid., 124.

18. Ibid., 143.

19. Ibid., 180.

20. Ibid., 141–2. "Gilde" has been, and still is, the main brand name used by the meat co-op.

21. Ad from *Alt om mat* 10 (1979): 90–91.

22. Ad from *Alt om mat* 8 (1977): 72–73.

23. See Christensen and Nilsen, *Langs gilde veier*, 144.

24. Karin Aubert Stenholm, "Du tjener på å vite," *Alt om mat* 10 (1979): 5.

25. Stenholm, "Du tjener," 5.

26. Opplysningskontoret for Kjøtt, archive.

27. Ibid.

28. Christensen and Nilsen, *Langs gilde veier*, 136–7.

29. Ibid., 144.

30. Ibid., 187.

31. See Bjørkdahl and Syse, "Kjøtt, fremmedgjøring og fornektelse."

32. Nick Fiddes, *Meat: A Natural Symbol* (London: Routledge, 1991), 95.

33. In our view, Fiddes in *Meat* seems occasionally to go too far in attributing intentionality to this process. He refers, for instance, to "a deliberate process of disguising the source of animal foods" (p. 95), and while certain actors, not least the meat industry, have taken many deliberate steps to avoid an association between animal and meat, the process, as we believe we have shown, is more complex.

34. Roger Horowitz, *Putting Meat on the American Table: Taste, Technology, Transformation* (Baltimore, MD: The Johns Hopkins University Press, 2006), xii.
35. Ibid., 135.
36. Loughnan, Bastian, and Haslam, "The Psychology of Eating Animals."
37. Jared Piazza et al., "Rationalizing Meat Consumption: The 4 Ns," *Appetite* 91, no. 1 (2015): 114–28.
38. Robert G. Darst and Jane I. Dawson, "Exit, Voice, and Denial: Confronting the Factory Farm in the United States," *Society & Animals* 27, no. 1 (2019): 36–54.
39. Ibid., 38.

BIBLIOGRAPHY

Berger, John. "Why Look at Animals?" In *About Looking*, 3–30. New York, NY: Pantheon Books, 1980.
Bjørkdahl, Kristian, and Karen Lykke Syse. "Kjøtt, fremmedgjøring og fornektelse." *Nytt Norsk Tidsskrift* 36, no. 3 (2019): 255–67.
Bugge, Annechen Bahr. *Fattigmenn, tilslørte bondepiker og rike riddere: Mat og spisevaner i Norge fra 1500-tallet til vår tid.* Oslo: Cappelen Damm Akademisk, 2019.
Chiles, Robert Magneson. "Hidden in Plain Sight: How Industry, Mass Media, and Consumers' Everyday Habits Suppress Food Controversies." *Sociologia Ruralis* 57, no. 1 (2016): 791–815.
Christensen, Sverre A., and Yngve Nilsen. *Langs gilde veier: Gilde Norsk Kjøtt 1931–2006.* Oslo: Dinamo forlag, 2006.
Cohen, Stanley. *States of Denial: Knowing about Atrocities and Suffering.* Cambridge: Polity, 2001.
Darst, Robert G., and Jane I. Dawson. "Exit, Voice, and Denial: Confronting the Factory Farm in the United States." *Society & Animals* 27, no. 1 (2019): 36–54.
Fiddes, Nick. *Meat: A Natural Symbol.* London: Routledge, 1991.
Fogt, Anne, Siri Meyer, and Anne Ullmann. *Ullevål Hageby gjennom 90 år: Fra bolignød til Kardemommeby.* Oslo: Unipax, 2007.
Fremstad, Peder. "Selvbetjeningsbutikker: Forsøk og erfaring i Oslo." *Forbrukeren* 7 (1949): 146–8.
Hals, Anne. "Damplassen før og nå." *Årsskrift for Sogn og Tåsen historielag,* 2015.
Horowitz, Roger. *Putting Meat on the American Table: Taste, Technology, Transformation.* Baltimore, MD: The Johns Hopkins University Press, 2006.
Loughnan, Steve, Brock Bastian, and Nick Haslam. "The Psychology of Eating Animals." *Current Directions in Psychological Science* 23, no. 2 (2014): 104–8.
NKL Norges Kooperative Landsforenings Kjøttforedlingskomite. "Effektiv og rasjonelldrift på kjøttsektoren." *Forbrukeren* 7 (1962): 160.
NKL Norges Kooperative Landsforenings Kjøttforedlingskomite. "Samvirkelaget innbyr til husmoraften." *Forbrukeren* 2 (1963): 44.
"Percentage of Households with Different Types of Equipment." *NOS Survey of Housing Conditions 1988.* Accessed February 11, 2020. http://www.ssb.no/a/histstat/tabeller/13-13-4t.txt.

Piazza, Jared, Matthew B. Ruby, Steve Loughnan, Mischel Luong, Juliana Kulik, Hanne Watkins, and Mirra Seigerman. "Rationalizing Meat Consumption: The 4 Ns." *Appetite* 91, no. 1 (2015): 114–28.

Stenholm, Karin Aubert. "Du tjener på å vite." *Alt om mat* 10 (1979): 5.

Stovner, Ivar. "Vi må få ferdigpakkede varer." *Forbrukeren* 4 (1950): 77–80.

Stovner, Ivar. "Ferdigpakking av kjøttvarer: Foodtainere, det siste på området." *Forbrukeren* 7 (1961): 142.

Chapter 8

Political Economy of Denialism

Addressing the Case of Animal Agriculture

John Sorenson and Atsuko Matsuoka

Stanley Cohens[1] work is widely recognized as "exceptionally important . . . an immense contribution"[2] to the understanding of denialism. However, embedded within Cohen's book is a peculiar absence: despite his awareness of cruelties inflicted on animals, acknowledgment that there is no rational defense of such practices and recognition of the ethical case for vegetarianism, Cohen[3] admits his own "total denial" of animal rights issues. Those issues are significant. Keeping with use of animals for food alone, the scale of suffering and killing is immense: billions of land animals are killed each year. Including aquatic animals moves this into the trillions. In addition to those raised to be killed are huge numbers of pests and predators who are poisoned or shot, wildlife whose habitat is destroyed and bycatch, the incidental capture of nontarget species. Raising animals for food is a major contributor to biodiversity collapse, mass extinction, environmental degradation, pollution of air, soil and water and climate crisis, all of which have detrimental impacts on human populations. Such dangers are underscored by the devastating 2020 coronavirus pandemic, widely believed to have originated in a seafood market in China, only one of many zoonoses spread by using animals for food. While Cohen himself neglects these issues, his work nonetheless provides us with useful tools for understanding denialism about them.

Given the overwhelmingly negative consequences of animal agriculture, some attention is being given to why humans persist in meat consumption and deny the harms this creates. Psychologists focus on practices of denial, using the term "meat paradox" to examine dissonance that meat-eaters encounter as they claim to care about animals but consume billions of them, paying for them to be killed.[4] Joy[5] identifies key rationalizations employed to justify this which assert that consumption of animals is natural, necessary, and normal. Such studies are important and useful but they focus on individual psychological processes; analysis must also include materialist consideration of broader structural factors. Cohen[6] observed that the political economy of denial is yet to be written. Some important efforts have been made, noting how tobacco industry strategies (creating doubt and spreading misinformation supplied by scientists paid to produce studies serving corporate interests) have been adopted by alcohol, asbestos, chemical, lead, plastics industries and used in climate change denial.[7] This chapter contributes to the political economy of denialism by examining strategies of the animal industrial complex, using examples from the United States and the United Kingdom.

TECHNIQUES OF DENIAL

Understanding institutionalized denialism means identifying vested interests with direct financial stakes in perpetuating exploitation and commodification of nonhuman animals. Ideas about consuming animals are deliberately shaped by massive agribusiness interests that devote billions of dollars to advertising and marketing efforts to influence consumers' attitudes and understanding, as well as lobbying and political spending to ensure that their activities can continue unimpeded by exposure from animal and environmental activists. Industries and lobbyists present animals as objects to be purchased and consumed rather than as sentient individuals with their own inherent value who are owed ethical consideration and justice. They present exploitation of animals as morally acceptable and normalize violence against them. Indeed, they work to ensure that these exploitation and violence are not even recognized as a moral issue.

Institutionalized denialism from these massive industries operates not only discursively but also through initiatives to shape laws. Part of this denialism involves creating legislation to serve industry interests, such as exempting certain animals from cruelty legislation and Ag-Gag laws criminalizing exposure of conditions on factory farms and slaughterhouses. Another example concerns the so-called humane products. While exposure of ghastly conditions in which egg and poultry industries confine billions of birds convinced many people to become vegans, others opted for less ethically consistent responses by endorsing modifications in production, such as the so-called cage-free or humanely produced eggs, even though some modifications are minor.

To some extent, the so-called humane modifications were simply marketing strategies. However, some producers found even these adjustments too much of an interference with their extraction of maximum profit from animals at the cheapest possible cost. For example, after California passed Proposition 2 legislation that prohibited confining animals in cages too small to allow movement, Iowa poultry producers sought to maintain access to California markets without modifying their own practices and encouraged Iowa's governor to sue California government officials. After this failed, Iowa's state legislature passed a law requiring stores participating in federal food aid programs to sell conventional eggs.[8]

Nevertheless, denialism involves rhetorical techniques, drawing on intertwined ideologies of speciesism and capitalism in which animals are constructed as resources to be used by humans. Animals' suffering and death disappear as problems, becoming normal. Normalization is a key mechanism of denial,[9] a social process in which undesirable situations are made to appear unremarkable, part of the ordinary functioning of society. As a problem becomes socially accepted, it becomes culturally interpreted as inevitable.

Cohen identifies three variants of denial: literal (facts are not acknowledged), interpretive (facts are given different meanings), and implicatory (facts are recognized but their implications are denied).[10] These may occur in sequence but also simultaneously, even in the same message.[11] Among the rhetorical devices of denial, Cohen identifies the account, not simply as a response to defend oneself after committing some offence but as a story that exists before the act is committed, drawn from a collective repository and culturally transmitted.[12] It serves to excuse behavior by denying responsibility for actions or justifying them by denying negative interpretations. The animal industrial complex denies responsibility for killing animals by downplaying the violence or denying that this constitutes violence at all: endless killing is recast as part of a natural order, although industrialized animal agriculture is a recent invention, its violence unprecedented. Accounts allow development of groupthink, "a collective mind-set that protects illusions from uncomfortable truths."[13] Agribusiness industries do not directly coerce consumers to purchase their products but rather play on preexisting cultural attitudes and practices to create the idea that those products are not only natural, necessary, and normal but that they are supremely desirable, prized commodities imbued with near-magical powers. Speciesism is deeply rooted and industries mobilize such prejudices to serve their own ends as advertising messages construct fantasy worlds in which consumers are interpellated. Here, we consider how various forms of denialism operate in the context of institutionalized animal abuse.

Literal Denial: Groupthink and "Moms"

Industry lobby organizations work to literally deny scientific information about the negative impact of animal agriculture. They create a form of groupthink that denies ethical consideration of the rights of nonhuman animals. Groupthink is reinforced not only by corporations and industry groups acting directly to deny scientists' and activists' evidence but also through astroturfing, the creation of ostensible grassroots groups to promote industry objectives. For example, in 2010 the United Soybean Board, National Corn Growers Association and Osborn Barr public relations company (slogan: "We Create Belief") created Common Ground, a network of hundreds of women famers across the United States.[14] Using research from the industry-run Center for Food Integrity and the US Farmers and Ranchers Alliance showing that mothers consider other mothers as trusted sources, Common Ground (ND) assembled women farmers, ordinary "moms" who endorse the industrial agriculture agenda, and provided channels allowing them "to have conversations with moms," reassuring them of the safety of antibiotics, chemicals, genetically modified organisms (GMOs), hormones, and pesticides and seeking to convince them that animal welfare is the "top priority" of industries based on killing billions of them for profit.[15]

Similarly, self-described "Entrepreneur . . . Farm Girl . . . Mom" Michele Payn created CauseMatters ("Connecting with Moms") and AgChat to "empower farmers and ranchers," and train them in "agvocacy" to "tell agriculture's story from their point of view."[16] As well as literally rejecting scientific evidence about the negative impacts of industrialized animal agriculture, corporate-backed "moms" facilitate interpretive denial; for example Payn notes a key point by Ontario egg farmer Diane McComb: "Cages look cruel to the untrained eye. They are more of a luxury condo."[17]

Another "mom" promoting the industrial agenda is Amanda Radke, former National Beef Ambassador for American National CattleWomen, now editor and blogger for *Beef* newsletter and a regular paid speaker at industry events. On her website, Radke says that she seeks to "protect our freedoms to farm and our freedom of choice at the grocery store [and overcome] external challenges that aim to . . . eliminate our industry [and] loud voices of animal welfare activists, environmentalist zealots, biased media reporters, health care practitioners with plant-based agendas and celebrity influencers."[18]

Her childrens' book was "spearheaded" by the Georgia Beef Board and funded by the Beef Checkoff (see below), as was her participation in the Masters of Beef Advocacy program, an online training course that provides "communication skills and information to be confident in sharing beef stories."[19] In 2019, she identified her "number one topic" as denial of links between animal agriculture and climate change.[20]

Recruiting "mommy bloggers" who appear independent but serve industry interests is an astroturfing tactic widely used by corporations like Monsanto to promote its biotechnology and chemical products.[21] Astroturfing involves deployment of individuals who seemingly have no connection to industries but who post on social media, responding to any events or reports considered detrimental to those industries, exemplified by Monsanto's Let Nothing Go campaign.[22] Astroturfing often targets particular individuals; for example, Vani Hari,[23] who examines food additives and chemicals in her *Food Babe* blog, describes one such attack mobilized by Michelle Miller who started her own *Farm Babe* blog in *Ag Daily*, a publication supported by Bayer and Monsanto corporations. Miller promotes antibiotic use in farmed animals, GMOs, pesticides, and other chemicals, denies animal agriculture's impact on climate crisis, and champions mammoth agribusiness corporations such as Monsanto and Tyson. On her website, Miller sells herself as a social media influencer to promote individual farm operations and corporations, promising to "educate the masses" and "positively impact . . . your bottom line."[24]

A major rhetorical device these "moms" use is denial of the victims. The suffering and killing of individual animals is presented, not as a matter of injustice but as something else: tradition, pleasure, profit, freedom. They describe animals as being bred for slaughter as if that is their purpose; observation of brutal fact is presented as a law of nature, the inevitable unfolding of elemental rules. For example, hog farmer and Common Ground "mom" Wanda Patsche asks "Who Do You Want to Raise Your Bacon?"[25] making pigs disappear as sentient individuals to become only delivery mechanisms for bacon. As well as encouraging consumption of animals, industry representatives downplay and conceal their suffering, along with these industries' disastrous environmental impacts, their role in creating climate change and negative consequences for human health from both production and consumption.

"Moms" also deploy the rhetorical device Cohen identifies as condemning the condemners. This requires disparagement of animal advocates as effete, emotional urbanites interfering with normal hardworking people and as humorless extremists, zealots and violent terrorists.[26] It involves efforts to prevent them from exposing atrocities that are essential to industry operations. Industries depict themselves as under siege by activists, allegedly funded by powerful forces. For example, Animal Agriculture Alliance, a lobby group serving livestock, feed, biotechnology, and pharmaceutical corporations, was created in 1987 to monitor animal activists[27]; it rails against "extremists" who are "aggressively targeting" these industries, warning that "Anyone could be a target" and urging constant vigilance.[28] Purportedly providing insider information, the Alliance touts its Animal Rights Activist Web as a major resource, showing "how activist groups are connected through funding, project collaboration, and flow of staff and volunteers" and revealing their "agenda of ending animal agriculture," according to Alliance head Kay Johnson Smith.[29] In fact, it is simply a graphic that connects logos of US advocacy groups, without explanation or evidence of any connections. While presenting activists as violent extremists, the animal industrial complex creates an image of farmers and ranchers as "ordinary people," reliable "moms."

In fact, these "moms" are deployed by a gigantic industry. In the United States, the National Meat Institute[30] estimates that "red meat" alone accounts for US$80 billion in annual sales; with production, sale, and suppliers considered, meat and poultry industries contribute US$894 billion to the economy (although it is unclear if biotechnology, seed, feed, and pharmaceutical sales are included here). Economic significance means political influence. Individual farmers and ranchers and dairy, egg, livestock, and meat processing corporations all contribute millions annually to political parties. In 2016, livestock industry campaign contributions in the United States were over US$11 million[31] and the industry spent millions more lobbying to limit environmental protection and avoid rules concerning air pollution and disclosure of information concerning use of GMOs. Despite serious scientific concerns about negative human health impacts from giving antibiotics to animals, groups such as the American Farm Bureau, National Beef Packing Company, and National Pork Producers Council spent millions blocking any restrictions; pharmaceutical corporations Eli Lilly and Merck alone spent at least US$14 million in 2013 lobbying government on this. Political contributions and lobbying spending increase in direct response to scandals that regularly emerge when information is revealed about institutionalized animal suffering, climate change, outbreaks of epidemic diseases among farmed animals, environmental pollution, and harm to human health[32]; industries mobilize to deny the extent and significance of these issues, block government action, and convince consumers to continue purchasing their products. Enlisting "mommy bloggers" to serve as benign and trustworthy spokespersons promotes a collective mindset that denies cruel truths.

Interpretive Denial: Fighting Veganism

Industries and governments spend huge amounts not only literally denying negative impacts of meat production but also on campaigns of interpretive denial, especially to combat veganism as a rational attempt to avoid those negative impacts, especially exploitation of and cruelty to animals. Institutionalized denialism interprets veganism not as compassionate and sensible but as a malicious fringe movement and promotes meat as a healthy and environmental-friendly choice. Over three years, the EU spent tens of millions of euros on anti-vegan/vegetarian campaigns, countering health warnings and characterizing growing awareness about animal cruelty as "fake news."[33] Addressing the Worshipful Company of Butchers in London, Ian Wright, chief executive of the Food and Drink Association, urged industry executives to "fight" veganism with a well-resourced campaign to include pressuring government.[34] In fact, the industry is fully engaged to combat the threat of veganism. For example, in January 2020, three UK levy boards (similar to North American checkoff programs), namely the Agriculture and Horticulture Development Board (AHDB), Meat Promotion Wales, and Quality Meat Scotland (QMS), joined forces to "counter misinformation" and battle "Veganuary" campaigns that encourage people to change their diet and attitudes toward animals. Their strategy included coordinating "expert speakers," "social media influencers," and celebrity chefs to promote meat consumption and distribute commentary to national media to ensure that "messaging around red meat's positive nutritional role stayed present in public discourse." Additionally, "to combat negative press," the AHDB launched its own Food Advisory Board of diet and agriculture "experts . . . ready to provide commentary in response to cases of media exaggeration" about meat and to "write and contribute to proactively placed advertorials in national press."[35] Supported by a dozen meat-related organizations, QMS relaunched its 2019 "Meat With Integrity" campaign emphasizing animal welfare and environmental sustainability. Featuring farmers, a chef, and a butcher to serve as relatable "faces" of meat production, the campaign included "year-round activity in schools" including a voucher system to encourage "every secondary school in Scotland" to buy meat.[36]

Industry representatives also mobilized to deny negative information about environmental damage caused by meat production presented in Channel 4's television documentary, *Apocalypse Cow*, and to denounce it as unbalanced. The National Sheep Association complained that their industry was "denigrated."[37] The CEOs of the UK levy boards published an Open Letter to the BBC denouncing another documentary, *Meat: A Threat to Our Planet*, as "unbalanced . . . inaccurate . . . misleading [and] fail[ing] to show the positives." The three CEOs complained that meat was being used as a "scapegoat" in climate change discussions and reducing meat consumption was presented as a "simple" lifestyle change. *Meat Management* magazine ("directly serving the UK meat industry") published the letter and assembled numerous industry representatives to attack the BBC's "anti-meat bias."[38] Editor Pam Brook asserted that meat was being "demonized by unsubstantiated claims" and that the industry must respond to the "growing urban myth that meat is killing our planet."[39]

Claiming victory in forcing the BBC to reedit its #xmaslife trailer to remove all references to veganism, AIMS Head of Policy Norman Bagley characterized this as leading a challenge to the "creeping tide of vegan propaganda" and part of the industry's "huge response" to the BBC's "increasing biased [*sic*] against the meat industry"; AIMS also complained that Channel 4's documentary, *How to Steal Pigs and Influence People*, was biased in favor of animal activists and demanded that Mitsubishi withdraw its sponsorship of the program[40]; the National Pig Association threatened legal action against Channel 4 for showing "blatant criminal activity."[41]

Regardless of local differences in forms of production, the global meat industry is unified in its deployment of interpretive denial to allay consumers' concerns about animal suffering and environmental catastrophe. The industry is alarmed by the rapid rise of plant-based foods, especially the popularity of fast-food alternatives to meat burgers. For example, in the United States, the industry-funded Center for Consumer Freedom (CCF) designed an attack campaign advertising in major newspapers, suggesting that plant-based meat was dangerous to health, listing "chemical culprits hiding in your fake meat" and emphasizing the "processed" character of these foods.[42] The CCF's lobbying for alcohol, fast food, and tobacco industries indicates that consumers' health is less of a concern than threats posed to meat industry profits by these alternatives. The *Los Angeles Times* pointed out that the "chemical culprits" are found in most packaged foods, that the CCF obscures the "bigger point" about animal suffering and environmental catastrophe, and that the meat industry's real worry is that plant-based food can provide tastes consumers crave, with fewer harmful effects.[43]

Other industry campaigns focused on denial of meat's negative impact on human health. Although the World Health Organization[44] identified meat as a likely carcinogen and the American Cancer Council/World Cancer Research Fund, Cancer Research UK, Cancer Council (Australia), and other leading medical organizations warn of meat's links with various forms of cancer, a meat industry social media campaign forced cancer support charity Macmillan to stop its "Meat-Free March" initiative; farmers declared they would no longer donate to the charity and warned of "mental anguish" caused to farmers "already under attack from vegan extremists and environmental campaigners."[45]

Additional pressure comes from industry associations such as the American Meat Institute and political organizations such as Freedom Partners, funded by the Koch brothers to channel dark money to various right-wing groups.[46] In 2014, Freedom Partners spent US\$3.8 million putting Republican Joni Ernst into the Senate; Ernst's campaign analogized her farm background castrating pigs to her pledge to cut government spending, which meant opposing environmental protection and action on climate change.[47] In addition to funding politicians to serve their interests, industry organizations coordinate efforts to shape legislation, influence government nutrition guidelines, and deny scientific findings, recommending reduced consumption of animal-based products. Initiatives include attacking scientists' and health professionals' methodologies as well as funding journalists who supply more appropriate messages. For example, Nina Teicholz, whose popular book promotes consumption of butter, cheese, and meat, is funded by billionaires John and Laura Arnold who created the Nutrition Coalition to reform dietary guidelines in the United

States. Coalition members received funding from beef and dairy checkoff programs, National Dairy Council, Dairy Research Institute, Egg Nutrition Center, Global Dairy Platform, National Pork Board, Campbell Soup Co., and Kraft General Foods.[48]

Responding to specific animal rights and vegan messages is a fundamental aspect of institutionalized denial. For example, in 2020 the Ulster Farmers' Union (UFU) expressed outrage at Go Vegan World advertisements placed on public transport. Demanding their removal, the UFU said their "emotive language . . . perpetuate[d] a negative narrative about eating meat and dairy products." UFU president Ivor Ferguson stated: "We respect all personal decisions when it comes to diets but to demonize the livestock industry to promote another industry is wrong." Go Vegan World's director, Sandra Higgins, responded that it did not oppose farmers and was ready to help them transition to more ethical and sustainable livelihoods, noting: "We see this objection to our ads as an indication that people are uncomfortable about making a living from exploiting defenseless animals and consumers are uncomfortable about creating a demand for the violence of animal agriculture or any other form of animal exploitation."[49]

In addition to advertising particular brands, industries operate commodity checkoff programs that impose mandatory levies on all producers. Institutionalized interpretive denialist discourse is funded by such programs in North America. For example, the US Beef Checkoff program was created under the 1985 Farm Bill, mandating that all producers and importers pay US$1 per animal. The Cattlemen's Beef Board collects and spends the funds, overseen by the US department of Agriculture. The purpose is to increase profits by promoting sales and consumption through advertising, marketing partnerships, public relations, and development of new products "by keeping beef top-of-mind with consumers, restaurants, butchers and other food retailers."[50] While checkoff programs appear to be a tax on producers, costs ultimately are passed on to consumers who thus pay for both the commodities they purchase and the advertising that exhorts them to do so.

Checkoff programs collect hundreds of millions of dollars, creating a powerful marketing force to increase demand and promote the image of a particular industry.[51] Funds are used to market products, not specific brands. Checkoff programs funded influential marketing campaigns, creating such memorable slogans as "Got Milk?" "Pork: the other white meat," and "Beef: it's what's for dinner." Crafted at the cost of millions of dollars, involving recognizable actors, evocative music, and imagery of happy families, such commercials became embedded in consumers' consciousness. For example, in 2017, the National Cattlemen's Beef Association revived its "iconic" 25-year-old beef campaign to capitalize on nostalgic memories of the original advertisements and "quash 'misrepresentations' [from] people out there in public dialogue that have an agenda [to] make the case that people shouldn't be eating meat."[52]

Wielding huge resources, these programs deploy initiatives across North America. For example, in Canada, the Beef Cattle Checkoff funds the Beef Cattle Research Council that supports research to: "Enhance industry competitiveness . . . improve beef demand and quality . . . improve public confidence in Canadian beef."[53] It also funds Canada Beef that promotes consumption in association with the Canadian Cattlemen's Association that has its own advocacy programs. These campaigns and programs "empower the industry chain" stimulate greater consumption and generate more profits: "For every $1 spent in a research and promotion program the return on investment can range as high as $18."[54]

Explaining the necessity of checkoff programs, the Canadian Cattleman's Association describes a "huge challenge" of "increas[ing] public trust in the beef industry," requiring training of industry spokespersons to "tell the beef production story."[55] In 2019, the National Pork Board celebrated the 10,000th presentation under its Operation Mainstreet program.[56] The Board arranges speaking engagements with medical professionals, nutritionists, chefs, local government officials, and other influential groups and provides funding, training, prepared speeches, and PowerPoint presentations to approximately 1,500 speakers "to tell the pork industry's story" and create positive impressions of that industry.[57] The American Dairy Association North East's Dairy Food Advocacy Network provides training for young propagandists who are required to engage in social media engagements on "key topics" a minimum of five times a week.[58]

While Checkoff programs are ostensibly prevented from lobbying and political debate, the groups themselves acknowledge that they operate to deny their industries' negative impact in terms of animal suffering, environmental damage, and threats to human health. For example, the Beef Checkoff "has enlisted educated spokespersons armed with scientific facts to counter the misinformation shared by anti-beef activists."[59]

Among those enlisted is hog-farming "mom" Wanda Patsche who spins interpretive denial on her blog, rejecting the term "factory farm," saying opponents of efficient modern farming use it to evoke emotional responses against farmers who "care for animals."[60] Patsche demonstrated the extent of such care on her Facebook page, applauding the National Pork Producer Council and American Farm Bureau for opposing California's Proposition 12 legislation that required more space for breeding pigs, egg-laying hens, and calves raised for veal. Similarly, Miller rejects the term "factory farm," stating that 97 percent of farms in the United States are family-owned, a point she frequently repeats to neutralize negative connotations of industrialized agriculture and to substitute images of production characterized by "care and love."[61] But family and factory farms are not mutually exclusive. The term family farm simply designates those owned by their operators and relatives, specifying nothing about size or practices. Since the 1970s, the number of farms in North America declined significantly and remaining farms are concentrated into larger, more industrialized operations that supply most meat, egg, and dairy products. These mammoth industries operate within the logic of capitalism to maximize profit and minimize costs; consequences include not only suffering and death for animals but also negative impacts on humans as communities disintegrate. Environmental damage includes widespread contamination of water and soil with chemicals and waste, spreading disease, air pollution, and odors so overpowering that those living nearby must remain indoors as their property values plummet.

Echoing Patsche's denialism, Miller criticizes actress Natalie Portman for her "anti-meat movie" *Eating Animals* and for using the "offensive" term "factory farm."[62] Miller rejects as "myths" the fact that animals are treated cruelly, given antibiotics and hormones and kept in "agricultural facilities that increase production, while . . . keep[ing] the operation secret from the public."[63] In fact, cruelty inflicted on animals in factory farms has been documented extensively by activists and recognized in mainstream media, as have the agriculture lobby's efforts to criminalize exposure of the abuse through various "ag-gag" laws.[64] The World Health Organization reports that in various countries "80 percent of consumption of medically important antibiotics is in the animal sector" and that such misuse of antibiotics is contributing to the rise of antibiotic resistance.[65] Rejecting these documented facts as "myths" about factory farms, Miller instead prefers sheer fantasy, linking to California dairy farmer Jason Mast's claim to provide "the truth about factory farming." Echoing McComb's characterization of battery cages as "luxury condos," Mast insists, "this isn't a factory farm, it's an all inclusive bovine luxury resort" where farmers "build big barns and deliver food to them so the cows can relax and just make milk."[66] However, even mainstream media acknowledge the dairy industry's cruelty: lifelong confinement, repeated forced impregnation of cows, removal of babies so farmers can steal milk intended for them and sell it for profit, killing of unwanted male babies either immediately or after a few months if they are to be sold as veal, and use of drugs to force cows to produce unnatural amounts of milk until their bodies break down and they are slaughtered.[67]

Implicatory Denial

Implicatory denial employs forms of rationalization that release one from moral duties. Since the animal industrial complex is based on mass killing of animals and commonsense understandings urge us to be kind to animals, justifications are required to reconcile conflicting imperatives. One solution is to appeal to human exceptionalism and speciesist ideas of dominion. Animal Agriculture Alliance funded a serviceable resource, the book *What Would Jesus Really Eat? The Biblical Case for Eating Meat*, edited by Southern Baptist minister and professor of public relations Wes Jamison and theologian Paul Copan, both at Palm Beach Atlantic University, a private Christian institution. Their objective is to "refute" arguments that eating meat is morally wrong. Jamison says his main theme is that Christians have "freedom to eat meat without it being a question of conscience. In fact, not only can they do it, they are blessed when they do it and the source of the meat is not really an issue in the New Testament . . . We are allowed to eat meat from any type of animals . . . with joy."[68]

Industry sites such as *Ag Daily*, *Beef Magazine*, *National Hog Farmer*, and *Pork Business* enthusiastically promoted the book, as did right-wing Christian groups such as Cornwall Alliance. Here, dominionist and capitalist ideologies converge to justify animal exploitation.

The basic technique of implicatory denial is to invoke personal choice. Institutionalized denialist discourse presents calls for compassion and justice, entailing veganism, as assaults on freedom and choice. Industry-funded bloggers maintain that they have nothing against veganism, claiming that they respect personal choice while vegans impose their opinions on others. This claim that animal activists and vegans are limiting freedom and choice is a key theme in denialist discourse. For example, presenting the issue as "All About Choice," *Beef* writer Sara Spangler praises Guest Choice Network's fight to stop "'nannies' trying to take meat off Americans' plates."[69] The Network (later called CCF, then Center for Organizational Research and Education) is a lobby group funded by alcohol, fast food, meat, and tobacco industries. Animal Agriculture Alliance identifies "promot[ing] consumer choice" as one of its main objectives. When New York City announced plans to adopt "Meatless Mondays" in public schools, the North American Meat Institute wrote to Mayor Bill de Blassio denouncing this as a misguided infringement on personal choice, praising meat as healthy and nutritious, and denying environmental impacts of livestock production.[70]

Radke warns that animal activists threaten "our freedoms and liberties as property owners, livestock producers and meat eaters."[71] By presenting use of nonhuman animals as personal choice and consumer freedom, denialist discourse erases it as a matter of social justice. By presenting exploitation and violence as personal preferences, they reject judgment and accountability. Animals are made invisible as sentient individuals with rights to their own lives; justice toward them is displaced by assertion of human desires. These desires for temporary and trivial pleasures are presented as more significant than the entire lives of other beings who have interests in living and not suffering. Since a vegan diet is widely acknowledged as healthy and sustainable,[72] claims for necessity of a meat-based diet for survival are not relevant for most people. Those who consume meat deny the significance of nonhuman animals' lives, reducing them to the status of objects and commodities. Fundamental to industry denialism is this transformation of beings into objects and refusal to acknowledge them as victims of institutionalized violence conducted for profit.

ACKNOWLEDGMENT AND ACTIVISM

Denialism is frequently depicted as an individual response to psychological discomfort. While such analyses offer important insights, these responses occur within particular historical contexts. In this chapter, we have emphasized the political and economic aspects of denialism to show how denialism is structured to serve particular interests. In the case of animal agriculture, industry objectives are normalized by strategies such as using "mommy bloggers," producing unified groupthink that champions industrial agriculture in general but also defends particular corporations such as Monsanto, Smithfield, and Tyson, and promotes mass use of antibiotics on farmed animals, GMOs, pesticides, herbicides, and other chemicals such as glyphosate. Analysis of denial of the harms created by the meat industry clearly demonstrates how powerful industries manufacture consent.

However, such consent is neither seamless not inevitable. In the penultimate chapter of *States of Denial*, Cohen considers why some ordinary people do acknowledge the suffering of others and do something about it; he cites the significance of transforming encounters that lead to recognition of inclusivity. In terms of animal exploitation, while it is true that speciesist oppression is normalized, animal activists, scientists, and philosophers have produced powerful counter-discourses that recognize animal sentience, our ethical duties toward other animals, and present feasible alternatives to such oppression. In particular, activists' exposure of animal suffering and environmental destruction present opportunities for transformational encounters, which threaten profits. These economic threats explain industries' determined production of massively funded, professionally crafted forms of institutionalized denialism intended to undermine growing ethical concerns about the suffering of other beings and efforts to live without causing harm. Although Cohen himself failed to make this commitment, it is important to include animal rights in the imagining of "an alternative ethical landscape" shaped by "a sense of responsibility for the safety of others"[73] and a commitment to justice—regardless of species.[74]

NOTES

1. Stanley Cohen, *States of Denial: Knowing About Atrocities and Suffering* (Cambridge: Polity, 2001).

2. Jacqueline Tombs, "Book Review: States of Denial: Knowing About Atrocities and Suffering," *Punishment and Society* 5, no. 1 (2003): 113–5.

3. Cohen, *States of Denial*, 289.

4. See Brock Bastian and Steve Loughnan, "Morally Troublesome Behavior and Its Maintenance," *Personality and Social Psychology Review* 21, no. 3 (2017); Jonas R. Kunst and Sigrid M. Hohle, "Meat Eaters by Dissociation: How We Present, Prepare and Talk About Meat Increases Willingness to Eat Meat by Reducing Empathy and Disgust," *Appetite* 10, no.1 (2016); Steve Loughnan, Brock Bastian, and Nick Haslam, "The Psychology of Eating Animals," *Current Directions in Psychological Science* 23, no. 2 (2014); Steve Loughnan, Nick Haslam, and Brock Bastian, "The Role of Meat Consumption in the Denial of Moral Status and Mind to Meat Animals," *Appetite* 55, no. 1 (2010).

5. Melanie Joy, *Why We Love Dogs, Eat Pigs and Wear Cows: An Introduction to Carnism* (San Francisco, CA: Conari Press, 2010).

6. Cohen, *States of Denial*, xiv.

7. Jane Mayer, *Dark Money: The Hidden History of the Billionaires Behind the Rise of the Radical Right* (New York, NY: Doubleday, 2016); David Michaels, *Doubt is their Product: How Industry's Assault on Science Threatens Your Health* (New York, NY: Oxford University Press, 2008); David Michaels, *The Triumph of Doubt: Dark Money and the Science of Deception* (New York, NY: Oxford University Press, 2020); Naomi Oreskes and Erik M. Conway, *Merchants of Doubt: How a Handful of Scientists Obscured the Truth on Issues from Tobacco Smoke to Global Warming* (London: Bloomsbury, 2010).

8. Glenn Greenwald and Leighton Akio Woodhouse, "Consumers Are Revolting Against Animal Cruelty—So the Poultry Industry is Lobbying for Laws to Force Stores to Sell Their Eggs," *The Intercept*, March 2, 2018, https://theintercept.com/2018/03/02/consumers-are-revolting-against-animal-cruelty-so-the-poultry-industry-is-lobbying-for-laws-to-force-stores-to-sell-their-eggs/.

9. See Cohen, *States of Denial*.

10. Ibid., 7–9.

11. Ibid., 103.

12. Ibid., 58–59.

13. Ibid., 66.

14. Missy Morgan, "Farmers Seeking City Moms, Start with Coffee—CommonGround: Case in Point," *Medium*, November 22, 2017, https://medium.com/@Osborn.Barr/farmers-seeking-city-moms-start-with-coffee-8d5a44bd4663.

15. "Common Ground's Campaign," *AgriMarketing*, June 1, 2016, https://www.thefreelibrary.com/CommonGround%27s+campaign.-a0458159273.

16. Michele Payn, "Connecting With Moms," *Cause Matters*, May 18, 2020, https://causematters.com/agchat-archives/connecting-with-moms/.

17. Michele Payn, "Do You Know the Pecking Order of the Egg?" *Cause Matters*, January 28, 2020, https://causematters.com/advocacy/egg-pecking-order/.

18. Amanda Radke, "Speaking," *Amanda Radke*, accessed April 3, 2020, https://amandaradke.com/pages/speaking.

19. "Masters of Beef Advocacy," *Beef Checkoff*, accessed April 3, 2020, https://www.beefitswhatsfordinner.com/masters-of-beef-advocacy.

20. Amanda Radke, "It's not Cow Farts; Cattle and Climate Change Link Debunked, Again," *Beef*, December 4, 2019, https://www.beefmagazine.com/beef/its-not-cow-farts-cattle-and-climate-change-link-debunked-again.

21. Carey Gillam, *Whitewash: The Story of a Weed Killer, Cancer, and the Corruption of Science* (Washington, DC: Island Press, 2017), 128.

22. Ibid., 129.

23. Vana Hari, "How the Food Industry Tries to Silence Us (My Appearance on CNN)," *Food Babe*, accessed April 3, 2020, https://foodbabe.com/how-the-food-industry-tries-to-silence-us-my-appearance-on-cnn/.

24. Michelle Miller, "Influencer," *The Farm Babe*, accessed April 3, 2020, https://thefarmbabe.com/influencer/.

25. Wanda Patsche, "Who Do You Want to Raise Your Bacon?" *Minnesota Farm Living*, August 5, 2018, http://www.mnfarmliving.com/2018/08/who-do-you-want-to-raise-your-bacon-2.html.

26. John Sorenson, *Constructing Ecoterrorism: Capitalism, Speciesism and Animal Rights* (Black Point, CA: Fernwood, 2016).

27. Bob Larson, "Animal Agriculture Alliance, Pt. 1," *Ag Information Network of the West*, January 10, 2020, https://www.aginfo.net/report/44861/Washington-State-Farm-Bureau-Report/Animal-Agriculture-Alliance-Pt-1.

28. Hannah Thompson-Weeman, "Anyone Could Be a Target," *Hoard's Dairyman*, July 16, 2019, https://hoards.com/blog-25926-anyone-could-be-a-target.html.

29. *National Hog Farmer*, "Animal Agriculture Alliance Site to Offer More Farm Security Resources," January 8, 2020, https://www.nationalhogfarmer.com/livestock/animal-agriculture-alliance-site-offer-more-farm-security-resources.

30. National Meat Institute, *Fact Sheet, Studies of U.S. Red Meat Industry Structure: A Summary*, January 2015, https://www.meatinstitute.org/index.php?ht=a/GetDocumentAction/i/89479; National Meat Institute, *Fact Sheet, The Economic Impact of the Meat Industry in the U.S.*, January 2015, https://www.meatinstitute.org/index.php?ht=a/GetDocumentAction/i/93337.

31. Center for Responsive Politics, "Livestock: Long-Term Contribution Trends," *Open Secrets*, accessed April 3, 2020, https://www.opensecrets.org/industries/totals.php?cycle=2016&ind=A06.

32. Niv M. Sultan, "Where's the Beef? When Meat's in Trouble, Lobbying Expands," *Open Secrets*, March 30, 2017, https://www.opensecrets.org/news/2017/03/wheres-the-beef-meat-lobby/.

33. Daniel Boffey, "EU Spending Tens of Millions of Euros a Year to Promote Meat Eating," *The Guardian*, February 14, 2020, https://www.theguardian.com/environment/2020/feb/14/eu-spending-tens-of-millions-of-euros-a-year-to-promote-meat-eating.

34. *Meat Management*, "Meat Sector Urged to 'Stand Up' to Veganism," January 14, 2019, https://meatmanagement.com/meat-sector-urged-to-stand-up-to-veganism/.

35. *Meat Management*, "Levy Board Activity to Reassure People There's no Need to Cut out Red Meat in January," January 8, 2020, https://meatmanagement.com/levy-board-plan-activity-to-reassure-people-theres-no-need-to-cut-out-red-meat-in-january/.

36. *Cattle Site*, "Meat With Integrity Campaign Creatives Unveiled," July 25, 2019, http://www.thecattlesite.com/news/54279/meat-with-integrity-campaign-creatives-unveiled/.

37. *Meat Management*, "Criticism of Channel 4's 'Apocalypse Cow' Documentary," January 10, 2020, https://meatmanagement.com/criticism-of-channel-4s-apocalypse-cow-documentary/.

38. *Meat Management*, "Strong Industry Reaction to BBC Documentary Meat: A Threat to our Planet," November 29, 2019, https://meatmanagement.com/strong-industry-reaction-to-bbc-documentary-meat-a-threat-to-our-planet/.

39. Pam Brook, "Enough is Enough and It's Time to Fight Back," *Meat Management*, December 19, 2019, https://edition.pagesuiteprofessional.co.uk/html5/reader/production/default.aspx?pubname=&edid=afecd94e-25aa-480a-b6fc-387d5188411a.

40. *Meat Management*, "AIMS Calls on Mitsubishi to Remove Links to TV Programme," January 10, 2020, https://meatmanagement.com/aims-calls-on-mitsubishi-to-remove-links-to-tv-programme/.

41. Alistair Driver, "Channel 4 'How to Steal Pigs'—NPA Response," *Pigworld*, January 15, 2020, http://www.npa-uk.org.uk/Channel_4_How_to_Steal_Pigs_documentary-NPA_response.html.

42. *Center for Consumer Freedom*, "Ad: What Chemical Culprits Are Hiding in Your Fake Meat?" January 14, 2020, https://www.consumerfreedom.com/2020/01/ad-what-chemical-culprits-are-hiding-in-your-fake-meat/.

43. "Editorial: The Beef Industry is Freaking Out Over Plant-Based Meat? Too Bad," *Los Angeles Times*, January 7, 2020, https://www.latimes.com/opinion/story/2020-01-07/tasty-burger-without-a-supersized-side-of-guilt.

44. *World Health Organization*, "Stop Using Antibiotics in Healthy Animals to Prevent the Spread of Antibiotic Resistance," November 7, 2017, https://www.who.int/news-room/detail/07-11-2017-stop-using-antibiotics-in-healthy-animals-to-prevent-the-spread-of-antibiotic-resistance.

45. Philip Clarke, "Macmillan Agrees to Stop Promoting Meat-Free March," *Farmers Weekly*, January 31, 2020, https://www.fwi.co.uk/news/macmillan-agrees-to-stop-promoting-meat-free-march.

46. Nick Surgey, "Revealed: Extensive Koch Links to New Right-Wing $250 Million Mega Fund," *PR Watch*, September 16, 2013, https://www.prwatch.org/news/2013/09/12244/revealed-extensive-koch-links-new-right-wing-250-million-mega-fund.

47. Jason Noble, "Joni Ernst: I was 'Extremely Offended' by AWOL Attack," *Des Moines Register*, May 9, 2014, https://www.desmoinesregister.com/story/news/

politics/elections/2014/05/09/joni-ernst-us-senate-des-moines-register-editorial-boar
d/8901677/.

48. Jim O'Hara, "Coalition is Full of Baloney on Nutrition Guidelines," *The Hill*, November 20, 2015, https://thehill.com/blogs/congress-blog/healthcare/257353-co
alition-is-full-of-baloney-on-nutrition-guidelines.

49. "UFU Calls for Removal of Vegan Advertisements on Buses," *South Antrim Vox*, January 18, 2020, https://southantrimvox.co.uk/ufu-call-for-removal-of-ve
gan-advertisements-on-buses/?fbclid=IwAR0L_geRkg69yNizukZGB1gfpI5eMdnO
YYjVm1pPFA87K5uFiQ6zTvUIcwU.

50. *Beef Board*, "What is the Beef Checkoff?" accessed April 3, 2020, https://
www.beefboard.org/checkoff/.

51. Geoffrey S. Becker, "Federal Farm Promotion ('Check-off') Programs," *Congressional Research Service Report for Congress*, October 20, 2008, http://nat
ionalaglawcenter.org/wp-content/uploads/assets/crs/95-353.pdf.

52. Alexandra Bruell, "Beef is Back for Dinner as Marketers Woo Nostalgic Millennials," *Wall Street Journal*, October 5, 2017, https://www.wsj.com/articles/b
eef-industry-aims-to-herd-millennials-with-nostalgic-ad-1507201382.

53. *Beef Cattle Research Council*, "Research Priorities," accessed April 15, 2020, http://www.beefresearch.ca/for-researchers/research-priorities.cfm.

54. David R. Shipman, "Industry Insight: Checkoff Programs Empower Business," *U.S. Department of Agriculture*, February 21, 2017, https://www
.usda.gov/media/blog/2011/09/21/industry-insight-checkoff-programs-empower
-business.

55. Lorraine Stevenson, "Town Hall Speakers Talk About Where the Money Goes," *Manitoba Co-Operator*, December 14, 2017, https://www.manitobacoope
rator.ca/news-opinion/news/local/town-hall-speakers-talk-about-where-the-money
-goes/.

56. National Pork Board, "Pork Checkoff's Operation Main Street Marks 10,000th Presentation," *Pork Business*, October 25, 2019, https://www.porkbusi
ness.com/article/pork-checkoffs-operation-main-street-marks-10000th-present
ation.

57. *Pork Checkoff*, "Operation Main Street," accessed April 3, 2020, https://www
.pork.org/community/operation-main-street/.

58. *American Dairy Association North East*, "Dairy Food Advocacy Network," accessed April 3, 2020, https://www.americandairy.com/for-farmers/dairyfan.stml.

59. *Beef Board*, "Does the Beef Checkoff Do Anything About Anti-Beef Activists and Action Groups Who Constantly Criticize the Beef Industry?" accessed April 3, 2020, https://www.beefboard.org/checkoff/frequently-asked-questions/how-does
-the-checkoff-respond-to-anit-beef-activists/.

60. Wanda Patsche, "Let's Take the Factory Out of Factory Farm," *Minnesota Post*, June 3, 2014, https://www.minnpost.com/minnesota-blog-cabin/2014/06/let-s-
take-factory-out-factory-farms/.

61. Michelle Miller, "Don't Judge a Farm by its Cover," *AG Daily*, September 27, 2016, https://www.agdaily.com/livestock/farm-babe-dont-judge-farm-cover/.

62. Michelle Miller, "Hey Natalie Portman, Here's Why Your Term Factory Farm is so Offensive," *AG Daily*, July 3, 2018, https://www.agdaily.com/features/farm-ba be-hey-natalie-portman-heres-why-your-term-factory-farm-is-so-offensive/.

63. Michelle Miller, "In Defense of 'Factory' Farming and 'Industrial, Big Ag'," *AG Daily*, February 27, 2018, https://www.agdaily.com/insights/farm-babe-in-defe nse-of-factory-farming-and-industrial-big-ag/.

64. "Exposing Abuse on the Factory Farm," *New York Times*, August 9, 2015, https://www.nytimes.com/2015/08/09/opinion/sunday/exposing-abuse-on-the-fac tory-farm.html.

65. *World Health Organization*, "Stop Using Antibiotics."

66. Jason Mast, "The Truth About Factory Farming," *My Job Depends on Agriculture*, December 10, 2016, https://www.myjobdependsonag.com/the-truth-ab out-factory-farming/.

67. Chas Newkey-Burden, "Dairy is Scary: The Public are Waking Up to the Darkest Part of Farming," *The Guardian*, May 30, 2017, https://www.theguard ian.com/commentisfree/2017/mar/30/dairy-scary-public-farming-calves-pens-alterna tives.

68. Ann Hess, "Eating Meat Should Not Be a Question of Conscience," *National Hog Farmer*, July 19, 2019, https://www.nationalhogfarmer.com/business/eating-meat-should-not-be-question-conscience.

69. Sara Spangler, "All About Choice," *Beef*, August 1, 2000, https://www.bee fmagazine.com/mag/beef_choice.

70. "Letter to Mayor Bill de Blassio," *North American Meat Institute*, March 12, 2019, https://www.meatinstitute.org/index.php?ht=a/GetDocumentAction/i/ 154188.

71. Amanda Radke, "Lobbyists Working Hard to Steal Ranchers' Freedoms," *Beef*, November 25, 2019, https://www.beefmagazine.com/management/lobbyists-working-hard-steal-ranchers'-freedoms.

72. See, for example, Academy of Nutrition and Dietetics, "Position of the Academy of Nutrition and Dietetics: Vegetarian Diets," *Journal of the Academy of Nutrition and Dietetics* 116, no. 12 (2016): 1970–80.

73. Cohen, *States of Denial*, 276.

74. Atsuko Matsuoka and John Sorenson, eds., *Critical Animal Studies: Towards Trans-Species Social Justice* (London: Rowman and Littlefield, 2019); John Sorenson and Atsuko Matsuoka, *Dog's Best Friend?: Rethinking Canid–Human Relations* (Montreal: McGill-Queen's University Press, 2019).

BIBLIOGRAPHY

Academy of Nutrition and Dietetics. "Position of the Academy of Nutrition and Dietetics: Vegetarian Diets." *Journal of the Academy of Nutrition and Dietetics* 116, no. 12 (2016): 1970–80.

American Dairy Association North East. "Dairy Food Advocacy Network." Accessed April 15, 2020. https://www.americandairy.com/for-farmers/dairyfan.stml.

Bastian, Brock, and Steve Loughnan. "Morally Troublesome Behavior and Its Maintenance." *Personality and Social Psychology Review* 21, no. 3 (2017): 278–99.

Becker, Geoffrey S. "Federal Farm Promotion ('Check-off') Programs." *Congressional Research Service Report for Congress.* October 20, 2008. http://nationalaglaw center.org/wp-content/uploads/assets/crs/95-353.pdf.

Beef Board. "What is the Beef Checkoff?" Accessed April 15, 2020. https://www .beefboard.org/checkoff/.

Beef Board. "Does the Beef Checkoff Do Anything About Anti-Beef Activists and Action Groups that Constantly Criticize the Beef Industry?" Accessed April 15, 2020. https://www.beefboard.org/checkoff/frequently-asked-questions/how-does -the-checkoff-respond-to-anit-beef-activists/.

Beef Cattle Research Council. "Research Priorities." Accessed April 15, 2020. http:/ /www.beefresearch.ca/for-researchers/research-priorities.cfm.

Beef Checkoff. "Masters of Beef Advocacy." Accessed April 15, 2020. https://www .beefitswhatsfordinner.com/masters-of-beef-advocacy.

Boffey, Daniel. "EU Spending Tens of Millions of Euros a Year to Promote Meat Eating." *The Guardian.* February 14, 2020. https://www.theguardian.com/environ ment/2020/feb/14/eu-spending-tens-of-millions-of-euros-a-year-to-promote-meat -eating.

Brook, Pam. "Enough is Enough and It's Time to Fight Back." *Meat Management.* December 19, 2019. p. 3. https://edition.pagesuite-professional.co.uk/html5/reader /production/default.aspx?pubname=&edid=afecd94e-25aa-480a-b6fc-387d518841 1a.

Bruell, Alexandra. "Beef Is Back for Dinner as Marketers Woo Nostalgic Millennials." *Wall Street Journal.* October 5, 2017. https://www.wsj.com/articles/beef-industry -aims-to-herd-millennials-with-nostalgic-ad-1507201382.

Cattle Site. "Meat With Integrity Campaign Creatives Unveiled." July 25, 2019. http://www.thecattlesite.com/news/54279/meat-with-integrity-campaign-creatives -unveiled/.

Center for Consumer Freedom. "Ad: What Chemical Culprits Are Hiding in Your Fake Meat?" January 14, 2020. https://www.consumerfreedom.com/2020/01/ad -what-chemical-culprits-are-hiding-in-your-fake-meat/.

Center for Responsive Politics. "Livestock: Long-Term Contribution Trends." *Open Secrets.* Accessed April 15, 2020. https://www.opensecrets.org/industries/totals .php?cycle=2016&ind=A06.

Clarke, Philip. "Macmillan Agrees to Stop Promoting Meat-Free March." *Farmers Weekly.* January 31, 2020. https://www.fwi.co.uk/news/macmillan-agrees-to-stop -promoting-meat-free-march.

Cohen, Stanley. *States of Denial: Knowing About Atrocities and Suffering.* Cambridge: Polity, 2001.

"Common Ground's Campaign." *AgriMarketing.* June 1, 2016. https://www.thefreel ibrary.com/CommonGround%27s+campaign.-a0458159273.

Driver, Alistair. "Channel 4 'How to Steal Pigs'—NPA Response." *Pigworld.* January 15, 2020. http://www.npa-uk.org.uk/Channel_4_How_to_Steal_Pigs_do cumentary-NPA_response.html.

"Editorial: The Beef Industry is Freaking Out Over Plant-Based Meat? Too Bad." *Los Angeles Times.* January 7, 2020. https://www.latimes.com/opinion/story/2020-01 -07/tasty-burger-without-a-supersized-side-of-guilt.

"Exposing Abuse on the Factory Farm." *New York Times.* August 9, 2015. https://ww w.nytimes.com/2015/08/09/opinion/sunday/exposing-abuse-on-the-factory-farm. html.

Gillam, Carey. *Whitewash: The Story of a Weed Killer, Cancer, and the Corruption of Science.* Washington, DC: Island Press, 2017.

Greenwald, Glenn, and Leighton Akio Woodhouse. "Consumers Are Revolting Against Animal Cruelty—So the Poultry Industry is Lobbying for Laws to Force Stores to Sell Their Eggs." *The Intercept.* March 2, 2018. https://theintercept.com/ 2018/03/02/consumers-are-revolting-against-animal-cruelty-so-the-poultry-industr y-is-lobbying-for-laws-to-force-stores-to-sell-their-eggs/.

Hari, Vana. "How the Food Industry Tries to Silence Us (My Appearance on CNN)." *Food Babe.* Accessed April 15, 2020. https://foodbabe.com/how-the-food-industry -tries-to-silence-us-my-appearance-on-cnn/.

Hess, Ann. "Eating Meat Should Not Be a Question of Conscience." *National Hog Farmer.* July 19, 2019. https://www.nationalhogfarmer.com/business/eating-meat- should-not-be-question-conscience.

Joy, Melanie. *Why We Love Dogs, Eat Pigs and Wear Cows: An Introduction to Carnism.* San Francisco, CA: Conari Press, 2010.

Kunst, Jonas R., and Sigrid M. Hohle. "Meat Eaters by Dissociation: How We Present, Prepare and Talk About Meat Increases Willingness to Eat Meat by Reducing Empathy and Disgust." *Appetite* 10, no. 1 (2016): 758–74.

Larson, Bob. "Animal Agriculture Alliance, Pt. 1." *Ag Information Network of the West.* January 10, 2020. https://www.aginfo.net/report/44861/Washington-State-Fa rm-Bureau-Report/Animal-Agriculture-Alliance-Pt-1.

Loughnan, Steve, Brock Bastian, and Nick Haslam. "The Psychology of Eating Animals." *Current Directions in Psychological Science* 23, no. 2 (2014): 104–8.

Loughnan, Steve, Nick Haslam, and Brock Bastian. "The Role of Meat Consumption in the Denial of Moral Status and Mind to Meat Animals." *Appetite* 55, no. 1 (2010): 156–9.

Mast, Jason. "The Truth About Factory Farming." *My Job Depends on Agriculture.* December 10, 2016. https://www.myjobdependsonag.com/the-truth-about-factory -farming/.

Matsuoka, Atsuko, and John Sorenson, eds. *Critical Animal Studies: Towards Trans-Species Social Justice.* London: Rowman and Littlefield, 2019.

Mayer, Jane. *Dark Money: The Hidden History of the Billionaires Behind the Rise of the Radical Right.* New York, NY: Doubleday, 2016.

Meat Management. "Meat Sector Urged to 'Stand Up' to Veganism." January 14, 2019. https://meatmanagement.com/meat-sector-urged-to-stand-up-to-vegan ism/.

Meat Management. "Strong Industry Reaction to BBC Documentary Meat: A Threat to our Planet." November 29, 2019. https://meatmanagement.com/strong-industry -reaction-to-bbc-documentary-meat-a-threat-to-our-planet/.

Meat Management. "Levy Board Activity to Reassure People There's no Need to Cut out Red Meat in January." January 8, 2020. https://meatmanagement.com/levy-boa rd-plan-activity-to-reassure-people-theres-no-need-to-cut-out-red-meat-in-january/.

Meat Management. "Criticism of Channel 4's 'Apocalypse Cow' Documentary." January 10, 2020. https://meatmanagement.com/criticism-of-channel-4s-apocalyps e-cow-documentary/.

Meat Management. "AIMS Calls on Mitsubishi to Remove Links to TV Programme." January 10, 2020. https://meatmanagement.com/aims-calls-on-mitsubishi-to-remove-links-to-tv-programme/.

Michaels, David. *Doubt is their Product: How Industry's Assault on Science Threatens Your Health*. New York, NY: Oxford University Press, 2008.

Michaels, David. *The Triumph of Doubt: Dark Money and the Science of Deception*. New York, NY: Oxford University Press, 2020.

Miller, Michelle. "Don't Judge a Farm by its Cover." *AG Daily*. September 27, 2016. https://www.agdaily.com/livestock/farm-babe-dont-judge-farm-cover/.

Miller, Michelle. "In Defense of 'Factory' Farming and 'Industrial, Big Ag'." *AG Daily*. February 27, 2018. https://www.agdaily.com/insights/farm-babe-in-defense -of-factory-farming-and-industrial-big-ag/.

Miller, Michelle. "Hey Natalie Portman, Here's Why Your Term Factory Farm is so Offensive." *AG Daily*. July 3, 2018. https://www.agdaily.com/features/farm-babe -hey-natalie-portman-heres-why-your-term-factory-farm-is-so-offensive/.

Miller, Michelle. "Influencer." *The Farm Babe*. Accessed April 15, 2020. https:// thefarmbabe.com/influencer/.

Morgan, Missy. "Farmers Seeking City Moms, Start with Coffee—CommonGround: Case in Point." *Medium*. November 22, 2017. https://medium.com/@Osborn.Barr/ farmers-seeking-city-moms-start-with-coffee-8d5a44bd4663.

National Hog Farmer. "Animal Agriculture Alliance Site to Offer More Farm Security Resources." January 8, 2020. https://www.nationalhogfarmer.com/livest ock/animal-agriculture-alliance-site-offer-more-farm-security-resources.

National Meat Institute. *Fact Sheet. Studies of U.S. Red Meat Industry Structure: A Summary*. January 2015. https://www.meatinstitute.org/index.php?ht=a/GetDo cumentAction/i/89479.

National Meat Institute. *Fact Sheet. The Economic Impact of the Meat Industry in the U.S.* January 2015. https://www.meatinstitute.org/index.php?ht=a/GetDocumen tAction/i/93337.

National Pork Board. "Pork Checkoff's Operation Main Street Marks 10,000th Presentation." *Pork Business*. October 25, 2019. https://www.porkbusiness.com/a rticle/pork-checkoffs-operation-main-street-marks-10000th-presentation.

Newkey-Burden, Chas. "Dairy is Scary: The Public are Waking Up to the Darkest Part of Farming." *The Guardian*. May 30, 2017. https://www.theguardian.com/ commentisfree/2017/mar/30/dairy-scary-public-farming-calves-pens-alternatives.

Noble, Jason. "Joni Ernst: I was 'Extremely Offended' by AWOL Attack." *Des Moines Register*. May 9, 2014. https://www.desmoinesregister.com/story/news/ politics/elections/2014/05/09/joni-ernst-us-senate-des-moines-register-editorial -board/8901677/.

North American Meat Institute. *Letter to Mayor Bill de Blassio*. March 12, 2019. https
://www.meatinstitute.org/index.php?ht=a/GetDocumentAction/i/154188.

O'Hara, Jim. "Coalition is Full of Baloney on Nutrition Guidelines." *The Hill*.
November 20, 2015. https://thehill.com/blogs/congress-blog/healthcare/257353-co
alition-is-full-of-baloney-on-nutrition-guidelines.

Oreskes, Naomi, and Erik M. Conway. *Merchants of Doubt: How a Handful of
Scientists Obscured the Truth on Issues from Tobacco Smoke to Global Warming*.
London: Bloomsbury, 2010.

Patsche, Wanda. "Let's Take the Factory Out of Factory Farm." *Minnesota Post*.
June 3, 2014. https://www.minnpost.com/minnesota-blog-cabin/2014/06/let-s-
take-factory-out-factory-farms/.

Patsche, Wanda. "Who Do You Want to Raise Your Bacon?" *Minnesota Farm
Living*. August 5, 2018. http://www.mnfarmliving.com/2018/08/who-do-you-want
-to-raise-your-bacon-2.html.

Payn, Michele. "Connecting With 'Moms'." *Cause Matters*. May 18, 2010. https://ca
usematters.com/agchat-archives/connecting-with-moms/.

Payn, Michele. "Do You Know the Pecking Order of the Egg?" *Cause Matters*.
January 28, 2020. https://causematters.com/advocacy/egg-pecking-order/.

Pork Checkoff. "Operation Main Street." Accessed April 15, 2020. https://www.pork
.org/community/operation-main-street/.

Radke, Amanda. "Lobbyists Working Hard to Steal Ranchers' Freedoms." *Beef*.
November 25, 2019. https://www.beefmagazine.com/management/lobbyists-worki
ng-hard-steal-ranchers'-freedoms.

Radke, Amanda. "It's not Cow Farts; Cattle and Climate Change Link Debunked,
Again." *Beef*. December 4, 2019. https://www.beefmagazine.com/beef/its-not-cow
-farts-cattle-and-climate-change-link-debunked-again.

Radke, Amanda. "Speaking." *Amanda Radke*. Accessed April 3, 2020. https://aman-
daradke.com/pages/speaking.

Shipman, David R. "Industry Insight: Checkoff Programs Empower Business." *U.S.
Department of Agriculture*. February 21, 2017. https://www.usda.gov/media/blog
/2011/09/21/industry-insight-checkoff-programs-empower-business.

Sorenson, John. *Constructing Ecoterrorism: Capitalism, Speciesism and Animal
Rights*. Black Point, CA: Fernwood, 2016.

Sorenson, John, and Atsuko Matsuoka. *Dog's Best Friend?: Rethinking Canid–
Human Relations*. Montreal: McGill-Queen's University Press, 2019.

Spangler, Sara. "All About Choice." *Beef*. August 1, 2000. https://www.beefmaga
zine.com/mag/beef_choice.

Stevenson, Lorraine. "Town Hall Speakers Talk About Where the Money Goes."
Manitoba Co-Operator. December 14, 2017. https://www.manitobacooperator
.ca/news-opinion/news/local/town-hall-speakers-talk-about-where-the-money-g
oes/.

"Stop Using Antibiotics in Healthy Animals to Prevent the Spread of Antibiotic
Resistance." *World Health Organization*. November 7, 2017. https://www.who
.int/news-room/detail/07-11-2017-stop-using-antibiotics-in-healthy-animals-to-pr
event-the-spread-of-antibiotic-resistance.

Sultan, Niv M. "Where's the Beef? When Meat's in Trouble, Lobbying Expands." *Open Secrets*. March 30, 2017. https://www.opensecrets.org/news/2017/03/wheres-the-beef-meat-lobby/.

Surgey, Nick. "Revealed: Extensive Koch Links to New Right-Wing $250 Million Mega Fund." *PR Watch*. September 16, 2013. https://www.prwatch.org/news/2013/09/12244/revealed-extensive-koch-links-new-right-wing-250-million-mega-fund.

Thompson-Weeman, Hannah. "Anyone Could Be a Target." *Hoard's Dairyman*. July 16, 2019. https://hoards.com/blog-25926-anyone-could-be-a-target.html.

Tombs, Jacqueline. "Book Review: States of Denial: Knowing About Atrocities and Suffering." *Punishment and Society* 5 no. 1 (2003): 113–5.

"UFU Calls for Removal of Vegan Advertisements on Buses." *South Antrim Vox*. January 18, 2020. https://southantrimvox.co.uk/ufu-call-for-removal-of-vegan-advertisements-on-buses/?fbclid=IwAR0L_geRkg69yNizukZGB1gfpI5eMdnO YYjVm1pPFA87K5uFiQ6zTvUIcwU.

Chapter 9

Celebrate the Anthropocene?

Why "Techno-Eco-Optimism" Is a Strategy of Ultimate Denial

Helen Kopnina, Joe Gray, Haydn Washington, and John Piccolo

TECHNO-ECO-OPTIMISM

A growing discourse in conservation and sustainability claims that, despite the clear evidence of human-caused biodiversity loss,[1] and rapidly declining environmental indicators,[2] nature is, in fact, thriving. Conservation biologist Chris Thomas[3] has argued that both the effects of climate change and extinction are exaggerated. Thomas writes:

> We altered the world's habitats, and vast numbers of species have taken advantage of the new conditions. We changed the atmosphere, and hence climate and species have spread into new regions as a consequence. . . . These represent biological gains for animals, plants, fungi, microbes, viruses and any other kind of organism you wish to mention. Furthermore, the overall consequence of the arrival of new species into each region, be that a particular country or island, has been to raise the biological diversity of that part of our planet.[4]

Marris invited readers to celebrate the Anthropocene's "new ecosystems" and "dynamic ecologies"—seen as a "rambunctious garden" planted by humanity.[5] In a similar way, in *The World We Made*, Porritt happily narrates a story about how humanity got the planet back from the brink of collapse to inaugurate "genuine sustainability."[6] Praising technology breakthroughs, lifestyle revolutions, transformations, and human ingenuity, Porritt concludes that we are heading toward a very exciting future.

Louise Fresco typifies this eco-optimist stance. She has stated that agriculture can be further intensified to provide higher yields, and that currently "unused" areas (possibly including protected areas) can also be used for food production. Environmentalists, according to Fresco, are alarmist and pessimistic, presenting her audience with the choice between "fear and innovation."[7]

These views are widely known as eco-optimism, but we here term them as "techno-eco-optimism" because they rely on the belief that we will find technological solutions. As Rolston[8] and Batavia and Nelson[9] have noted, eco-optimistic scholars often ignore the arguments in support of values inherent in nonhuman nature. Pyron stated that "extinction does not carry moral significance, even when we have caused it."[10]

Since philosophical or ethical standing has powerful practical consequences, in our analysis of eco-optimism, we intentionally do not divorce the ethical and practical implications of eco-optimism. As "we have utterly changed our world; now we'll have to see if we can change our ways . . . creating a sustainable future for ourselves and the rest of the living world."[11] Discussing just how we might proceed is a key objective in this article. In particular, we focus on "the rest of the living world" and how techno-eco-optimism pays short shrift to the ethical implications of ecocide,[12] to the great peril not only to ourselves but also to a web of life with which we coexist on Earth. This article uses generalized "we" to designate humanity.

This chapter argues that there are many reasons to be skeptical of optimism when it comes to conservation, and shows that techno-eco-optimism is both misplaced and counterproductive for addressing society's great environmental challenges. Hence, we critique the ecologically dystopian future that would result from the strategies championed by techno-eco-optimists. Eco-optimism also disregards the broader ethical ramifications of species extinctions, being a strategy of denial. We support here an eco-realistic vision, presenting arguments for conservation grounded in ecological ethics.

The Scope of Techno-Eco-Optimism

We live in an age when anthropogenic impacts have markedly degraded global ecosystems. This has been called ecocide[13] as well as the environmental crisis, and the extent of human impact has been described as the "Anthropocene."[14] Society has pushed ecosystems beyond sustainable ecological limits,[15] causing an unprecedented mass extinction and threatening to destabilize the climate.[16] Yet, not everybody sees the Anthropocene as a threat. Lomborg[17] claims that climate change and concomitant biodiversity loss are not nearly as bad as environmentalists paint them.

A parallel development has come from the so-called "environmental pragmatists."[18] Spash refers to "new environmental pragmatism,"[19] which is focused on methods and concepts that are deemed to be effective. Shellenberger and Nordhaus do not deny the severity of climate change and biodiversity loss outright, but promote a "post-environmental approach" to climate change.[20] They consider environmental warnings to be out of touch with reality and propose techno-optimistic "pragmatic" strategies. They warn environmentalists to "stop trying to scare the pants off of the American public," and to realize that "the solution to the ecological crises wrought by modernity, technology, and progress will be more modernity, technology, and progress."[21]

In a similar manner, Kareiva et al.,[22] Thompson,[23] and Pearce[24] suggest that worries about species extinction are exaggerated. A related assertion is that humanity can create new and properly functioning novel ecosystems[25] that would benefit wealth creation. This changes the focus of conservation into an enterprise that is only valuable if it contributes to the flourishing of humanity.[26] Porritt lashes out at environmentalists for being blind to other problems in the world, and for fighting causes that ultimately stop poor countries from developing their "natural wealth."[27] Environmentalists are thus accused of standing in the way of progress and social justice, and simultaneously framing preservation of species as an antiquated and doomed enterprise. By contrast, it is implied that the "new ecosystems" are perfectly suited for humanity's use and economic flourishing.[28] Riding the wave of sustainability optimism, "new conservationists," such as Marris[29] and Kareiva,[30] argue that "traditional conservationists" are naive in their romantic notions of wild nature. These self-labeled "pragmatic" optimists argue that instead of decrying the loss of wild places and saving every species we should embrace human-managed nature.[31]

However, while some researchers argue that the extinction of certain species has not directly affected human welfare,[32] it is not true of most species.[33] The impacts on humans from the extinction of other species may not show up immediately or directly, but degradation of "ecosystem services" to humans will nevertheless result in the longer term.[34] Also, this narrow focus on human welfare ignores the ethics of species extinctions and ecosystem degradation.

The "environmental pragmatism" that supports eco-optimism has deep roots in shallow ecology, positing that anthropocentric motivation is consistent with a high degree of protection for nonhuman nature.[35] This assumption is based on a claim that the protection of the natural world—including animals—is in the interests of humans.[36] The pragmatist thinkers such as Hui argue that anthropocentrism is unavoidable.[37]

However, enlightened anthropocentrism has failed to solve the environmental crisis.[38] In fact, anthropocentrism is not humanity's culturally universal worldview[39] but linked to modernity's industrialism. The latter obscures premodern or alternative cultures[40] that exist in the modern age but are not part of the industrial structures. Anthropocentrism is thus avoidable and can be replaced by altruism,[41] ecocentrism,[42] and ecojustice.[43]

Fighting Against a "Good Story"

We recognize that the optimistic story with its focus on the celebration of human ingenuity and nature's resilience is appealing. The reassuring narrative of "it is not that bad and we can carry on as usual"[44] is convenient for those interested in protecting the status quo. It also complements the pathological attachment to "progress" in industrial societies,[45] of which "sustainability" has fallen prey to.[46] We also recognize that making claims against the radiant hope of easy salvation is never a popular position.[47] Accordingly, statements that human activity is causing mass extinction, and that we must act quickly to halt this (via "transformative change"),[48] do not inspire universal enthusiasm. After all, when the choice between "fear and innovation" is posed,[49] many of us would rather choose to believe in innovation.

This optimism undergirds the visions of a smooth transition to ecotopia through technical optimism,[50] a form of denial of the real threat of ecosystem collapse that many do not wish to face.[51] Techno-eco-optimism not only downplays scientific evidence of an ongoing mass extinction,[52] but also ignores or denies ecocentric ethics.[53] We seek to replace such techno-eco-optimism with a more holistic vision of a just (social justice *and* ecojustice) future for the ecosphere.

Denial and "Non-Denier Deniers"

Denial is a major problem in regard to not just climate change but virtually all environmental problems.[54] Denial-based claims are persistent[55] even in the light of studies showing authors have cherry-picked their data to foster denial of climate change and biodiversity loss.[56] Cohen[57] describes a useful division of denial into three categories:

1. *Literal denial:* This is the assertion that something did not happen or is not true. For global warming, this form of denial is seen in the generation of counterclaims by fossil fuel industries that climate change is not happening.
2. *Interpretive denial:* Here, the facts themselves are not denied, but they are given a different interpretation. Euphemisms and technical jargon are used to dispute the meanings of events. Interpretive denial is what we commonly call "spin," and it is used widely in politics and business.

3. *Implicatory denial:* Here, what is denied are "the psychological, political, or moral implications . . . Unlike literal or interpretive denial, knowledge itself is not an issue, but doing the 'right' thing with the knowledge."[58] It is a failure to incorporate this knowledge into everyday life or transform it into social action.[59]

Denialists tend to use literal denial and interpretive denial; governments tend to use interpretive denial; and "we the people" tend to commonly adopt implicatory denial.[60] It is the last that eco-optimists tend to exploit. Eco-optimists also make use what has been called "non-denier deniers."[61] This starts with putting themselves forward as reasonable interpreters of the science. Next, they do not deny an environmental problem per se or even that humans are the cause. They then argue that it is too late, however, to stop, for example, global warming, and thus: we should adapt; warming might even be good, and we must balance action with "concern for the economy."[62]

Sharot[63] argues that we need to understand that humanity tends to operate on unsupported optimism. Research shows that there is a strong "optimism bias" in society. This optimism bias is "one of the most consistent, prevalent, and robust biases documented in psychology and behavioural economics."[64] Thus, eco-optimism is part of a deep denial of serious problems that afflicts society.

ETHICS AND OPTIMISM: THE REALITY
OF BIODIVERSITY LOSS

Thomas[65] argues that we do not have to be concerned about massive changes to ecosystems due to human actions. This relies on the claim that nonnative species are an adequate replacement for native species, or even the celebration of exotic species. In fact, eco-optimists seem to revel in this global homogenization, despite the evidence that if we continue as we are, more than half of terrestrial species may go extinct by the end of the century, or perhaps earlier.[66]

What makes this crisis even more severe is the fact that most of the Earth is affected by a global expansion of infrastructure.[67] As Crist has written:

Human gridding is effected through roads and highways, fences and walls, above- and below-ground infrastructures . . . Intrinsic to the nature of the grid is that it is always unfurling. Metaphorically (and literally) it is like the all-too-familiar town that is always under construction either to accommodate growth or just to accommodate always-being-under-construction.[68]

Thomas says, "Call me a dreamer, but if we're interested in the natural world, then we need a healthy and well-fed world population."[69] This statement ignores environmental indicators and the ethical implications of the impacts of human population for the rest of life[70] and future generations of humans,[71] as well as the enslavement of billions of domestic animals.[72] As Safina reflects on Thomas, "Maybe it would be simpler if Thomas and his comrades just said, 'We don't care about nature.'"[73]

Through an ecocentric lens, such losses of wild species and mistreatment of domesticated animals constitute moral wrongs.[74] Unless the intrinsic value of nonhumans is recognized, there will be no institutional guarantees that other species will be considered in decision-making, and so their interests will be neglected whenever it is inconvenient to incorporate them.[75] A moral stance that embraces an ecocentric, biocentric, or zoocentric position offers wider protection for the environment than anthropocentrism.[76]

Ecojustice and Eco-Democracy

Ecological justice[77] is more inclusive than environmental justice and is concerned with other species independent of their instrumental value for humans. Washington argues that it is a great moral crime to ignore nonhuman justice. The simplest definition of ecojustice is justice for nonhuman nature. Justice and injustice are applicable only to relations among creatures considered "moral equals."[78] Dobson[79] argues that ignoring nature in traditional theories of justice comes out of a desire to exclude nature, not from sound theoretical reasoning. Eco-optimism refuses to consider that nonhuman nature *also* has a right to justice.[80]

Our democracies similarly ignore providing any mechanism to consider the interests of the nonhuman.[81] *Ecodemocracy* (a contraction of ecocentric democracy) aims to achieve representation for nonhuman nature in decision-making processes.[82] A crucial element of eco-democracy, as established in the platform's mission statement, is ensuring that decision-making processes explicitly acknowledge the moral, and where established, the legal.[83] In eco-democracy, a key mechanism by which representation for nonhuman nature could be achieved is the appointment of *human proxies* that represent nonhuman nature politically. Such representation could be as a voice in deliberative discussions, through the granting of voting rights.[84]

KEEPING THE WEALTH OF GLOBAL BIODIVERSITY

Conservation is about protecting the wealth of global biodiversity into the future[85]; how can this be done in the face of a huge environmental crisis? The first thing is to reaffirm that conservation is about retaining *both* human and nonhuman life on Earth, *not* creating more benefits for humanity as groups such as "new conservation" and "critical social scientists" argue.[86] The second thing is the need to accept the reality of our predicament rather than deny inconvenient truths.[87] By addressing the key drivers of overshoot—overpopulation and overconsumption,[88] conservation work has the greatest potential to protect life on Earth. Third, there is a need for a clear vision, such as the "Half Earth" or "Nature Needs Half."[89]

The "Nature Needs Half" movement expresses three main tenets: habitat loss and degradation are the leading causes of biodiversity loss; current protected areas are not extensive enough to stem further loss of biodiversity; and it is morally wrong for our species to drive other species to extinction.[90] While in many parts of the world it is hard enough to protect existing parks and World Heritage Areas,[91] conservation of areas *outside* the reserve system might be needed. We also accept that climate change is happening at an unprecedented rate, threatening a lot of biodiversity. This raises the difficult issue of whether we should become "ecological engineers."[92] The key point here is the issue of moving native species (mostly plants) to habitats they may not reach naturally themselves (due to the speed of climate change).

Probably on balance the answer to whether translocation should occur is "yes" for us, if only because we are now in a *triage* situation[93] where we seek to get as many species as possible through the extinction bottleneck of climate change, habitat clearing, exotic species, and so on.

Eco-realism rather than techno-optimism seeks to underscore the *reality of the crisis* and then demonstrate that positive (if challenging) solutions do exist.[94] Eco-realism has the capacity to solve the environmental crisis, by rejecting denial and accepting that we have difficult decisions to make.[95] These decisions need to consider that overpopulation and overconsumption pressure are driving an unprecedented environmental crisis of mass extinction and climate change. Ethically speaking, this is a great moral crime against the current and future inhabitants of the ecosphere,[96] *both* human and nonhuman.

The extinction of species reduces the evolutionary potential of the Earth's living beings. Indeed, "death is one thing—an end to birth is something else."[97] Thus, extinction is a kind of "super-killing" that shuts down the generative process of life itself.[98]

AN ECO-REALISTIC VISION

Spash[99] has argued that capitalism itself was incompatible with ecological sustainability and suggested that a radical shift in values was required to deal with the problem. For conservation, as well as for broader and related issues of ecological sustainability, ways forward should break the denial dam and focus on realism.[100] Paul Dayton notes, "Reality is the final authority; reality is what's going on out there, not what's in your mind or on your computer screen."[101] We need to accept the reality of our predicament, then explain the positive (if challenging) solutions to move toward a sustainable future.[102] That means not pretending everything is fine when we (and our actions) are the major cause of ecocide and mass extinction. It also means embracing an ecological ethics[103] in terms of how we act as a society. An eco-realistic vision, therefore, embraces ecocentrism, ecojustice, and eco-democracy—in large part because this is a more practical worldview[104] and ethics if society is to transition to a sustainable future.

Techno-eco-optimism does not promote rational or compassionate action to address the environmental crisis. We consider that many techno-eco-optimists contribute to distorted science and a weakening of an ethics that embraces life on Earth. An ecologically sustainable future depends on accepting the reality of our problems and acting immediately to put in place solutions that will promote an ecologically just ecosphere—true eco-realism. Techno-eco-optimism, in its refusal to accept the seriousness of the environmental crisis, is part of a deep denial that ought to be contested both in academia and in broader society.

Keeping the wealth of global biodiversity into the future is a major undertaking. We accept that inevitably we will lose more species. The key question is the degree of our failure. If we break the denial dam and abandon misleading eco-optimism, then we can address overpopulation, overconsumption, and the endless growth mantra as the key drivers of ecocide. If we adopt the Nature Needs Half vision, this will assist us to retain the diversity of life on Earth. Most importantly, abandoning anthropocentrism and adopting an ecocentric worldview can help us to carry out a duty of care to conserve nature and uphold its right to ecojustice.

NOTES

1. IPBES, "Nature's Dangerous Decline 'Unprecedented'; Species Extinction Rates 'Accelerating'," *Press Release Intergovernmental Science-Policy Platform on Biodiversity and Ecosystem Services*, accessed April 9, 2020, https://www.ipbes.net/news/Media-Release-Global-Assessment; Gerardo Ceballos, Anne H. Ehrlich, and Paul R. Ehrlich, *The Annihilation of Nature: Human Extinction of Birds and Mammals* (Baltimore, MD: Johns Hopkins University Press, 2015).

2. Will Steffen et al., "Planetary Boundaries: Guiding Human Development on a Changing Planet," *Science* 347, no. 6223 (2015): 1259855.

3. Chris D. Thomas, *Inheritors of the Earth: How Nature is Thriving in an Age of Extinction* (London: Hachette, 2017).

4. Ibid., 186.

5. Emma Marris, *Rambunctious Garden: Saving Nature in a Post-Wild World* (New York, NY: Bloomsbury, 2011).

6. Jonathan Porritt, *The World We Made* (London: Phaidon, 2013).

7. Louise Fresco, "De Strijd Tussen Angst en Vernieuwing," *NRC*, September 6, 2017, https://www.nrc.nl/nieuws/2017/09/06/de-strijd-tussen-angst-en-vernieuwing-12850811-a1572369.

8. Holmes Rolston, *A New Environmental Ethics: The Next Millennium for Life on Earth* (London: Routledge, 2012).

9. Chelsea Batavia and Michael Nelson, "For Goodness Sake! What is Intrinsic Value and Why Should We Care?" *Biological Conservation* 209 (2017).

10. Alexander Pyron, "We don't Need to Save Endangered Species. Extinction is Part of Evolution," *The Washington Post*, November 22, 2017, https://www.washingtonpost.com/outlook/we-dont-need-to-save-endangered-species-extinction-is-part-of-evolution/2017/11/21/57fc5658-cdb4-11e7-a1a3-0d1e45a6de3d_story.html.

11. Paul Ehrlich and Anne Ehrlich, *Betrayal of Science and Reason: How Anti-Environmental Rhetoric Threatens our Future* (New York, NY: Island Press, 1996), 63.

12. Polly Higgins, *Eradicating Ecocide* (London: Shepheard Walwyn Publishers, 2012).

13. David Zierler, *The Invention of Ecocide: Agent Orange, Vietnam, and the Scientists Who Changed the Way We Think About the Environment* (Athens, GA: University of Georgia Press, 2011).

14. Paul J. Crutzen and Eugene F. Stoermer, "The Anthropocene," *Global Change Newsletter* 41 (May 2000): 17–18.

15. Steffen et al., "Planetary Boundaries."

16. Ceballos, Ehrlich, and Ehrlich, *The Annihilation of Nature.*

17. Bjørn Lomborg, *The Skeptical Environmentalist: Measuring the Real State of the World* (Cambridge: Cambridge University Press, 2003).

18. Bryan G. Norton, "Environmental Ethics and Weak Anthropocentrism," *Environmental Ethics* 6, no. 2 (1984).

19. Clive L. Spash, "The Shallow or the Deep Ecological Economics Movement?" *Ecological Economics* 93 (2013).

20. Michael Shellenberger and Ted Nordhaus, "The Death of Environmentalism," *Global Warming Politics in a Post-Environmental World*, 2004, https://s3.us-east-2.amazonaws.com/uploads.thebreakthrough.org/legacy/images/Death_of_Environmentalism.pdf.

21. Ted Nordhaus and Michael Shellenberger, "The Long Death of Environmentalism," *Breakthrough Institute*, February 25, 2011, https://thebreakthrough.org/issues/energy/the-long-death-of-environmentalism.

22. Peter Kareiva, Robert Lalasz, and Michelle Marvier, "Conservation in the Anthropocene: Beyond Solitude and Fragility," *Breakthrough Journal* 2 (Fall 2011).

23. Ken Thompson, *Do We Need Pandas? The Uncomfortable Truth about Biodiversity* (London: Green Books, 2011).

24. Fred Pearce, *The New Wild: Why Invasive Species Will Be Nature's Salvation* (Boston, MA: Beacon Press, 2016).

25. Nordhaus and Shellenberger, "Long Death," 9.

26. Kareiva et al., "Conservation in the Anthropocene."

27. Porritt, *The World We Made.*

28. Marris, *Rambunctious Garden.*

29. Ibid.

30. Kareiva et al., "Conservation in the Anthropocene."

31. Marris, *Rambunctious Garden.*

32. Thompson, *Do We Need Pandas?*

33. Haydn Washington, *Demystifying Sustainability: Towards Real Solutions* (London: Routledge, 2015).

34. Ibid.

35. Katrina Hui, "Moral Anthropocentrism is Unavoidable," *The American Journal of Bioethics* 14, no. 2 (2014): 25.

36. Andrew Light, "Compatibilism in Political Ecology," in *Environmental Pragmatism*, ed. A. Light and E. Katz (New York, NY: Routledge, 1996).

37. Hui, "Moral Anthropocentrism."

38. Haydn Washington, *A Sense of Wonder Towards Nature: Healing the Planet Through Belonging* (London: Routledge, 2018).

39. Eleanor Shoreman-Ouimet and Helen Kopnina, "Reconciling Ecological and Social Justice to Promote Biodiversity Conservation," *Biological Conservation* 184 (2015): 320–6.

40. Eileen Crist and Helen Kopnina, "Unsettling Anthropocentrism," *Dialectical Anthropology* 38, no. 4 (2014).

41. Mikko Manner and John Gowdy, "The Evolution of Social and Moral Behavior: Evolutionary Insights for Public Policy," *Ecological Economics* 69, no. 4 (2010): 753–61.

42. Haydn Washington et al., "Why Ecocentrism is the Key Pathway to Sustainability," *Ecological Citizen* 1 (2017).

43. Haydn Washington et al., "Foregrounding Ecojustice in Conservation," *Biological Conservation* 228 (2018).

44. Ingolfur Blühdorn, "Sustaining the Unsustainable: Symbolic Politics and the Politics of Simulation," *Environmental Politics* 16, no. 2 (2007).

45. John Foster, *After Sustainability: Denial, Hope, Retrieval* (London: Routledge, 2014).

46. Washington, *Demystifying Sustainability.*

47. Michael Sitka-Sage et al., "Rewilding Education in Troubled Times; Or, Getting Back to the Wrong Post-Nature," *Visions for Sustainability* 8 (2017).

48. IPBES, "Nature's Dangerous Decline."

49. Fresco, "De Strijd."

50. Sitka-Sage et al., "Rewilding Education."

51. Haydn Washington and John Cook, *Climate Change Denial: Heads in the Sand* (London: Routledge, 2011).

52. Helen Kopnina et al., "Anthropocentrism: More than Just a Misunderstood Problem," *Journal of Agricultural and Environmental Ethics* 31, no. 1 (2018a).

53. Washington et al., "Why Ecocentrism"; John Piccolo et al., "Why Conservation Scientists Should Re-Embrace Their Ecocentric Roots," *Conservation Biology* 32, no. 4 (2018): 959–61; Washington et al., "Foregrounding Ecojustice."

54. Ehrlich and Ehrlich, *Betrayal of Science*; Naomi Oreskes and Erik Conway, *Merchants of Doubt: How a Handful of Scientists Obscured the Truth on Issues from Tobacco Smoke to Global Warming* (New York, NY: Bloomsbury Publishing USA, 2011); Washington, "Denial."

55. Foster, *After Sustainability.*

56. Peter Jacques, Riley Dunlap, and Mark Freeman, "The Organisation of Denial: Conservative Think Tanks and Environmental Skepticism," *Environmental Politics* 17, no. 3 (2008): 349–85; Oreskes and Conway, *Merchants of Doubt*; Riley Dunlap and Robert Brulle, eds., *Climate Change and Society: Sociological Perspectives* (Oxford: Oxford University Press, 2015).

57. Stanley Cohen, *States of Denial: Knowing About Atrocities and Suffering* (Hoboken: John Wiley & Sons, 2013).

58. Ibid., 9.

59. Kari Marie Norgaard, *Living in Denial: Climate Change, Emotions, and Everyday Life* (Boston, MA: MIT Press, 2011).

60. Washington and Cook, *Climate Change Denial.*

61. James Hoggan, *Climate Cover-Up: The Crusade to Deny Global Warming* (Vancouver: Greystone Books Ltd., 2009).

62. Ibid.

63. Tali Sharot, "The Optimism Bias," *Current Biology* 21, no. 23 (2011).

64. Ibid.

65. Thomas, *Inheritors of the Earth*, 186.

66. Edward O. Wilson, *The Future of Life* (New York, NY: Vintage, 2002); Eric Chivian and Aaron Bernstein, eds., *Sustaining Life: How Human Health Depends on Biodiversity* (Oxford: Oxford University Press, 2008).

67. William Laurance, "The Thin Green Line: Scientists Must do More to Limit the Toll of Burgeoning Infrastructure on Nature and Society," *The Ecological Citizen* 3 (2019), https://www.ecologicalcitizen.net/pdfs/thin-green-line.pdf.

68. Eileen Crist, "Let Earth Rebound! Conservation's New Imperative," in *Conservation: Intergrating Social and Ecological Justice*, ed. Helen Kopnina and Haydn Washington (Cham: Springer, 2020).

69. Richard Lea, "Chris D. Thomas: We Can Take a Much More Optimistic View of Conservation," *The Guardian*, July 13, 2017, https://www.theguard ian.com/books/2017/jul/13/chris-d-thomas-conservation-inheritors-of-the-earth-in terview.

70. Philip Cafaro and Eileen Crist, eds., *Life on the Brink: Environmentalists Confront Overpopulation* (Athens, GA: University of Georgia Press, 2012).

71. Eileen Crist, Camilo Mora, and Robert Engelman, "The Interaction of Human Population, Food Production, and Biodiversity Protection," *Science* 356, no. 6335 (2017).

72. Eileen Crist, "Abundant Earth and the Population Question," in *Life on the Brink: Environmentalists Confront Overpopulation*, ed. Philip Cafaro and Eileen Crist (Athens, GA: University of Georgia Press, 2012); Tara Garnett et al., "Sustainable Intensification in Agriculture: Premises and Policies," *Science* 341, no. 6141 (2013): 33–34.

73. Carl Safina, "In Defense of Biodiversity: Why Protecting Species from Extinction Matters," *Yale Environment* 360 (2018), https://e360.yale.edu/features/in-defense-of-biodiversity-why-protecting-species-from-extinction-matters.

74. Batavia and Nelson, "For Goodness Sake!"

75. Washington et al., "Why Ecocentrism"; Kopnina et al., "Anthropocentrism"; Piccolo et al., "Why Conservation."

76. Washington, *A Sense of Wonder*; Helen Kopnina and Brett Cherniak, "Neoliberalism and Justice in Education for Sustainable Development: A Call for Inclusive Pluralism," *Environmental Education Research* 22, no. 6 (2016).

77. David Schlosberg, "Reconceiving Environmental Justice: Global Movements and Political Theories," *Environmental Politics* 13, no. 3 (2004); Brian Baxter, *A Theory of Ecological Justice* (London: Routledge, 2004).

78. Washington et al., "Foregrounding Ecojustice."

79. Andrew Dobson, *Justice and the Environment: Conceptions of Environmental Sustainability and Theories of Distributive Justice* (Oxford: Oxford University Press, 1998).

80. Washington et al., "Foregrounding Ecojustice."

81. Robyn Eckersley, "Liberal Democracy and the Rights of Nature: The Struggle for Inclusion," *Environmental Politics* 4, no. 4 (1995); Robyn Eckersley, *The Green State: Rethinking Democracy and Sovereignty* (Cambridge, MA: MIT Press, 2004); Joe Gray and Patrick Curry, "Ecodemocracy: Helping Wildlife's Right to Survive," *ECOS* 37, no. 1 (2016).

82. Robyn Eckersley and Jean-Paul Gagnon, "Representing Nature and Contemporary Democracy," *Democratic Theory* 1 (2014).

83. GENIE, *Global Ecocentric Network for Implementing Ecodemocracy*, accessed March 1, 2020, https://www.ecodemocracy.net/.

84. Ibid.

85. Michael E. Soulé, "What is Conservation Biology?" *BioScience* 35, no. 11 (1985): 727–34; Piccolo et al., "Why Conservation"; Helen Kopnina and Haydn Washington, *Conservation: Integrating Social and Ecological Justice* (New York, NY: Springer, 2020).

86. Helen Kopnina et al., "The 'Future of Conservation' Debate: Defending Ecocentrism and the Nature Needs Half Movement," *Biological Conservation* 217 (2018b): 140–8.

87. Washington and Cook, *Climate Change Denial*.

88. Paul R. Ehrlich, "Conservation Biology and the Endarkenment," *Ambio* 43, no. 7 (2014); Washington, *Demystifying Sustainability*.

89. Cafaro et al., "If We Want a Whole Earth, Nature Needs Half: A Response to Büscher et al.," *Oryx* 51, no. 3 (2017): 400.

90. Ibid.

91. James Allan et al., "Recent Increases in Human Pressure and Forest Loss Threaten Many Natural World Heritage Sites," *Biological Conservation* 206 (2017).

92. Howard T. Odum et al., "Experiments with Engineering of Marine Ecosystems," *Publications of the Institute of Marine Science* 9 (1963).

93. Madeleine Bottrill et al., "Is Conservation Triage Just Smart Decision Making?" *Trends in Ecology & Evolution* 23, no. 12 (2008).

94. Lester Brown, *World on the Edge: How to Prevent Environmental and Economic Collapse* (London: Routledge, 2012).

95. Washington and Cook, *Climate Change Denial*.

96. Philip Cafaro and Richard Primack, "Species Extinction is a Great Moral Wrong," *Biological Conservation* 170 (2014): 1–2.

97. Michael Soulé and Bruce A. Wilcox, "Conservation Biology: Its Scope and its Challenge," in *Conservation Biology: An Evolutionary–Ecological Perspective*, ed. Michael Soulé and Bruce Wilcox (Sunderland, MA: Sinauer, 1980).

98. Rolston, *A New Environmental Ethics*.

99. Spash, "The Shallow or the Deep."

100. Washington, *Demystifying Sustainability*.

101. Paul Dayton, quoted in Richard Louv, *Last Child in the Woods: Saving Our Children From Nature–Deficit Disorder* (New York, NY: Algonquin Books, 2005), 161.

102. Washington, *Demystifying Sustainability*.

103. Patrick Curry, *Ecological Ethics* (Cambridge: Polity, 2011).

104. Washington, *A Sense of Wonder*.

BIBLIOGRAPHY

Allan, James R., Oscar Venter, Sean Maxwell, Bastian Bertzky, Kendall Jones, Yichuan Shi, and James E. M. Watson. "Recent Increases in Human Pressure and Forest Loss Threaten Many Natural World Heritage Sites." *Biological Conservation* 206 (2017): 47–55.

Batavia, Chelsea, and Michael P. Nelson. "For Goodness Sake! What is Intrinsic Value and Why Should We Care?" *Biological Conservation* 209 (2017): 366–76.

Baxter, Brian. *A Theory of Ecological Justice*. London: Routledge, 2004.

Blühdorn, Ingolfur. "Sustaining the Unsustainable: Symbolic Politics and the Politics of Simulation." *Environmental Politics* 16, no. 2 (2007): 251–75.

Bottrill, Madeleine C., Liana N. Joseph, Josie Carwardine, Michael Bode, Carly Cook, Edward T. Game, Hedley Grantham, et al. "Is Conservation Triage Just Smart Decision Making?" *Trends in Ecology & Evolution* 23, no. 12 (2008): 649–54.

Brown, Lester. *World on the Edge: How to Prevent Environmental and Economic Collapse*. London: Routledge, 2012.

Cafaro, Philip, and Eileen Crist, eds. *Life on the Brink: Environmentalists Confront Overpopulation*. Athens, GA: University of Georgia Press, 2012.

Cafaro, Philip, and Richard Primack. "Species Extinction is a Great Moral Wrong." *Biological Conservation* 170 (2014): 1–2.

Cafaro, Philip, Tom Butler, Eileen Crist, Paul Cryer, Eric Dinerstein, Helen Kopnina, Reed Noss, et al. "If We Want a Whole Earth, Nature Needs Half: A Response to Büscher et al." *Oryx* 51, no. 3 (2017): 400.

Ceballos, Gerardo, Anne H. Ehrlich, and Paul R. Ehrlich. *The Annihilation of Nature: Human Extinction of Birds and Mammals.* Baltimore, MD: Johns Hopkins University Press, 2015.

Chivian, Eric, and Aaron Bernstein, eds. *Sustaining Life: How Human Health Depends on Biodiversity.* Oxford: Oxford University Press, 2008.

Cohen, Stanley. *States of Denial: Knowing About Atrocities and Suffering.* Hoboken, NJ: John Wiley & Sons, 2013.

Crist, Eileen. "Abundant Earth and the Population Question." In *Life on the Brink: Environmentalists Confront Overpopulation.* Edited by Philip Cafaro and Eileen Crist, 141–51. Athens, GA: University of Georgia Press, 2012.

Crist, Eileen, and Helen Kopnina. "Unsettling Anthropocentrism." *Dialectical Anthropology* 38, no. 4 (2014): 387–96.

Crist, Eileen, Camilo Mora, and Robert Engelman. "The Interaction of Human Population, Food Production, and Biodiversity Protection." *Science* 356, no. 6335 (2017): 260–4.

Crist, Eileen. "Let Earth Rebound! Conservation's New Imperative." In *Conservation: Intergrating Social and Ecological Justice.* Edited by Helen Kopnina and Haydn Washington, 201–17. Cham: Springer, 2020.

Crutzen, Paul J., and Eugene F. Stoermer. "The Anthropocene." *Global Change Newsletter* 41 (May 2000): 17–18.

Curry, Patrick. *Ecological Ethics.* Cambridge: Polity, 2011.

Dobson, Andrew. *Justice and the Environment: Conceptions of Environmental Sustainability and Theories of Distributive Justice.* Oxford: Oxford University Press, 1998.

Dunlap, Riley E., and Robert J. Brulle, eds. *Climate Change and Society: Sociological Perspectives.* Oxford: Oxford University Press, 2015.

Eckersley, Robyn. "Liberal Democracy and the Rights of Nature: The Struggle for Inclusion." *Environmental Politics* 4, no. 4 (1995): 169–98.

Eckersley, Robyn. *The Green State: Rethinking Democracy and Sovereignty.* Cambridge, MA: MIT Press, 2004.

Eckersley, Robyn, and Jean-Paul Gagnon. "Representing Nature and Contemporary Democracy." *Democratic Theory* 1 (2014): 94–108.

Ehrlich, Paul R., and Anne H. Ehrlich. *Betrayal of Science and Reason: How Anti-Environmental Rhetoric Threatens our Future.* New York, NY: Island Press, 1996.

Ehrlich, Paul R. "Conservation Biology and the Endarkenment." *Ambio* 43, no. 7 (2014): 847–8.

Foster, John. *After Sustainability: Denial, Hope, Retrieval.* London: Routledge, 2014.

Fresco, Louise. "De Strijd Tussen Angst en Vernieuwing" ["The Battle Between Fear and Innovation"]. *NRC,* September 6, 2017. https://www.nrc.nl/nieuws/2017/09/06/de-strijd-tussen-angst-en-vernieuwing-12850811-a1572369.

Garnett, Tara, Michael C. Appleby, Andrew Balmford, Ian J. Bateman, Tim G. Benton, Phil Bloomer, Barbara Burlingame, et al. "Sustainable Intensification in Agriculture: Premises and Policies." *Science* 341, no. 6141 (2013): 33–34.

GENIE. *Global Ecocentric Network for Implementing Ecodemocracy*. Accessed March 1, 2020. https://www.ecodemocracy.net/.

Gray, Joe, and Patrick Curry. "Ecodemocracy: Helping Wildlife's Right to Survive." *ECOS* 37, no. 1 (2016): 18–27.

Higgins, Polly. *Eradicating Ecocide*. London: Shepheard Walwyn Publishers, 2012.

Hoggan, James. *Climate Cover-Up: The Crusade to Deny Global Warming*. Vancouver: Greystone Books Ltd., 2009.

Hui, Katrina. "Moral Anthropocentrism is Unavoidable." *The American Journal of Bioethics* 14, no. 2 (2014): 25.

IPBES. "Nature's Dangerous Decline 'Unprecedented'; Species Extinction Rates 'Accelerating'." *Press Release: Intergovernmental Science-Policy Platform on Biodiversity and Ecosystem Services*. Accessed April 9, 2020. https://www.ipbes .net/news/Media-Release-Global-Assessment.

Jacques, Peter J., Riley E. Dunlap, and Mark Freeman. "The Organisation of Denial: Conservative Think Tanks and Environmental Scepticism." *Environmental Politics* 17, no. 3 (2008): 349–85.

Kareiva, Peter, Robert Lalasz, and Michelle Marvier. "Conservation in the Anthropocene: Beyond Solitude and Fragility." *Breakthrough Journal* 2 (Fall 2011): 29–37.

In Love Your Monsters: Postenvironmentalism and the Anthropocene. Edited by Michael Shellenberger and Ted Nordhaus. Oakland: Breakthrough Institute, 2011.

Kopnina, Helen, and Brett Cherniak. "Neoliberalism and Justice in Education for Sustainable Development: a Call for Inclusive Pluralism." *Environmental Education Research* 22, no. 6 (2016): 827–41.

Kopnina, Helen, Haydn Washington, Bron Taylor, and John J. Piccolo. "Anthropocentrism: More than Just a Misunderstood Problem." *Journal of Agricultural and Environmental Ethics* 31, no. 1 (2018a): 109–27.

Kopnina, Helen, Haydn Washington, Joe Gray, and Bron Taylor. "The 'Future of Conservation' Debate: Defending Ecocentrism and the Nature Needs Half Movement." *Biological Conservation* 217 (2018b): 140–8.

Kopnina, Helen, and Haydn Washington. *Conservation: Intergrating Social and Ecological Justice*. New York, NY: Springer, 2020.

Laurance, William. "The Thin Green Line: Scientists Must Do More to Limit the Toll of Burgeoning Infrastructure on Nature and Society." *The Ecological Citizen* 3 (2019). https://www.ecologicalcitizen.net/pdfs/thin-green-line.pdf.

Lea, Richard. "Chris D. Thomas: We Can Take a Much More Optimistic View of Conservation." *The Guardian*, July 13, 2017. https://www.theguardian.com/books /2017/jul/13/chris-d-thomas-conservation-inheritors-of-the-earth-interview.

Light, Andrew. "Compatibilism in Political Ecology." In *Environmental Pragmatism*. Edited by A. Light and E. Katz, 161–84. London: Routledge, 1996.

Lomborg, Bjørn. *The Skeptical Environmentalist: Measuring the Real State of the World*. Cambridge: Cambridge University Press, 2003.

Louv, Richard. *Last Child in the Woods: Saving Our Children From Nature–Deficit Disorder*. New York, NY: Algonquin Books, 2005.

Manner, Mikko, and John Gowdy. "The Evolution of Social and Moral Behavior: Evolutionary Insights for Public Policy." *Ecological Economics* 69, no. 4 (2010): 753–61.

Marris, Emma. *Rambunctious Garden: Saving Nature in a Post-Wild World*. New York, NY: Bloomsbury, 2011.

Nordhaus, Ted, and Michael Shellenberger. "The Long Death of Environmentalism." *Breakthrough Institute*. Published February 25, 2011. https://thebreakthrough.org/issues/energy/the-long-death-of-environmentalism.

Norgaard, Kari Marie. *Living in Denial: Climate Change, Emotions, and Everyday Life*. Boston, MA: MIT Press, 2011.

Norton, Bryan G. "Environmental Ethics and Weak Anthropocentrism." *Environmental Ethics* 6, no. 2 (1984): 131–48.

Odum, Howard T., Walter L. Siler, Robert J. Beyers, and Neal Armstrong. "Experiments with Engineering of Marine Ecosystems." *Publications of the Institute of Marine Science* 9 (1963): 374–403.

Oreskes, Naomi, and Erik M. Conway. *Merchants of Doubt: How a Handful of Scientists Obscured the Truth on Issues from Tobacco Smoke to Global Warming*. New York, NY: Bloomsbury Publishing USA, 2011.

Pearce, Fred. *The New Wild: Why Invasive Species Will Be Nature's Salvation*. Boston, MA: Beacon Press, 2016.

Piccolo, John, Haydn Washington, Helen Kopnina, and Bron Taylor. "Why Conservation Scientists Should Re-Embrace Their Ecocentric Roots." *Conservation Biology* 32, no. 4 (2018): 959–61.

Porritt, Jonathan. *The World We Made*. London: Phaidon, 2013.

Pyron, R. Alexander. "We don't Need to Save Endangered Species. Extinction is Part of Evolution." *The Washington Post*, November 22, 2017. https://www.washingtonpost.com/outlook/we-dont-need-to-save-endangered-species-extinction-is-part-of-evolution/2017/11/21/57fc5658-cdb4-11e7-a1a3-0d1e45a6de3d_story.html.

Rolston III, Holmes. *A New Environmental Ethics: The Next Millennium for Life on Earth*. London: Routledge, 2012.

Safina, Carl. "In Defense of Biodiversity: Why Protecting Species from Extinction Matters." *Yale Environment* 360 (2018). https://e360.yale.edu/features/in-defense-of-biodiversity-why-protecting-species-from-extinction-matters.

Schlosberg, David. "Reconceiving Environmental Justice: Global Movements and Political Theories." *Environmental Politics* 13, no. 3 (2004): 517–40.

Sharot, Tali. "The Optimism Bias." *Current Biology* 21, no. 23 (2011): R941–5.

Shellenberger, Michael, and Ted Nordhaus. "The Death of Environmentalism." *Global Warming Politics in a Post-Environmental World*. https://s3.us-east-2.amazonaws.com/uploads.thebreakthrough.org/legacy/images/Death_of_Environmentalism.pdf.

Shoreman-Ouimet, Eleanor, and Helen Kopnina. "Reconciling Ecological and Social Justice to Promote Biodiversity Conservation." *Biological Conservation* 184 (2015): 320–6.

Sitka-Sage, Michael D., Helen Kopnina, Sean Blenkinsop, and Laura Piersol. "Rewilding Education in Troubled Times; Or, Getting Back to the Wrong Post-Nature." *Visions for Sustainability* 8 (2017): 1–19.

Soulé, Michael E., and Bruce A. Wilcox. "Conservation Biology: Its Scope and its Challenge." In *Conservation Biology: An Evolutionary–Ecological Perspective.* Edited by Michael Soulé and Bruce Wilcox, 1–8. Sunderland, MA: Sinauer, 1980.

Soulé, Michael E. "What is Conservation Biology?" *BioScience* 35, no. 11 (1985): 727–34.

Spash, Clive L. "The Shallow or the Deep Ecological Economics Movement?" *Ecological Economics* 93 (2013): 351–62.

Steffen, Will, Katherine Richardson, Johan Rockström, Sarah E. Cornell, Ingo Fetzer, Elena M. Bennett, Reinette Biggs, et al. "Planetary Boundaries: Guiding Human Development on a Changing Planet." *Science* 347, no. 6223 (2015): 1259855.

Thomas, Chris D. *Inheritors of the Earth: How Nature is Thriving in an Age of Extinction.* London: Hachette UK, 2017.

Thompson, Ken. *Do We Need Pandas? The Uncomfortable Truth about Biodiversity.* London: Green Books, 2011.

Washington, Haydn. *Demystifying Sustainability: Towards Real Solutions.* London: Routledge, 2015.

Washington, Haydn. *A Sense of Wonder Towards Nature: Healing the Planet Through Belonging.* London: Routledge, 2018.

Washington, Haydn, and John Cook. *Climate Change Denial: Heads in the Sand.* London: Routledge, 2011.

Washington, Haydn, Bron Taylor, Helen Kopnina, Paul Cryer, and John J. Piccolo. "Why Ecocentrism is the Key Pathway to Sustainability." *Ecological Citizen* 1 (2017): 35–41.

Washington, Haydn, Guillaume Chapron, Helen Kopnina, Patrick Curry, Joe Gray, and John J. Piccolo. "Foregrounding Ecojustice in Conservation." *Biological Conservation* 228 (2018): 367–74.

Wilson, Edward O. *The Future of Life.* New York, NY: Vintage, 2002.

Zierler, David. *The Invention of Ecocide: Agent Orange, Vietnam, and the Scientists Who Changed the Way We Think About the Environment.* Athens, GA: University of Georgia Press, 2011.

Chapter 10

The Horse in the Room

The Denial of Animal Subjectivity and Agency in Social Science Research on Human–Horse Relationships

Reingard Spannring and José De Giorgio-Schoorl

The title of this chapter alludes to *the elephant in the room,* a metaphor of silence and denial in everyday life.[1] The elephant can stand for alcoholism or sexual abuse in families, political and military atrocities, fraud, scheming, or any other "open secret," which is uncomfortable because it generates pain, fear, shame, and embarrassment. The elephant's conspicuous size should make it impossible not to see it. Yet, the collective denial seems unsurmountable because people are unwilling to publicly acknowledge it or quickly learn that they are not supposed to talk about it. What is ignored or avoided in everyday life is also often ignored or avoided in academia.[2] This is also true for the silence on horse agency in much of the social science literature on human–horse relations. Despite multiple invocations of equine subjectivity and agency, they are not made visible nor are the equestrian practices that limit horse agency critically discussed. These practices remain unquestioned in a paradigm of "naturecultures"[3] in which the use of the animal is "natural, normal, and necessary."[4] Changing the species in this metaphor, this chapter proposes that the horse refers to the silence on equine subjectivity and agency. However, in this case, the picture is complicated by the fact that this silence is veiled by many anthropocentric and speciesist discourses on horses.

In the contemporary Western world, human–horse relationships are largely presented through a discourse of love, care, and cooperation. However, it is unclear why the horse should benefit from this love. While there is a growing awareness of the animal question—talk about empathically interpreting and understanding the horse as a sentient being and intentional subject[5] and a focus on communication and improvement of human–horse relationships as principles for horse training and welfare[6]—welfare problems and vulner-abilities associated with the changeable economic, social, and emotional value of the horse continue.[7] Both sides are aspects of the same coin, namely the animal welfare approach. Even the "humanized," "loving" side of the relationship remains within the confines of the speciesist and anthropocentric conviction that humans can legitimately use nonhuman animals for their purposes and desires. That relationship thereby continues to determine the horses' existence and obscures and excludes the horses' own subjectivities, intentions, and projects. Applying the metaphor of the horse in the room, the cultural change toward a humanized and loving approach to horses can be described as dressing up rather than acknowledging the horse, since it denies the possibility of a non-speciesist relationship between a horse and human individual.

Research on human–horse relationships in the social sciences reflects the equestrian approach and the difficulties described earlier. It has provided ethnographic insights into the culture of the equestrian world,[8] particular equestrian subcultures and discourses,[9] concepts and communities of practice with respect to horse management and human–horse communication.[10] It has further addressed questions of social class and gender,[11] as well as ethical considerations within a welfare discourse.[12]

The equestrian frame consolidates the invisibility of the horse in the room in two fundamental ways. First, most of the literature treats horse subjectivity and agency en passant or as a conceptual projection. It remains an aspect of *human* culture that does not deserve scholarly attention in itself. The denial of the question how horses experience their *own* world and express their *own* curiosity and preferences confirms the general objectification and com-modification of nonhuman others as well as their reduction to species repre-sentatives.[13] Second, the failure to question the equestrian paradigm and its anthropocentrism naturalizes the confinement, training, and use of horses for human ends. It also obscures the negative impacts it has on equine subjectiv-ity and agency and the fact that other kinds of coexistence with horses are possible and, indeed, ethically desirable. The reproduction and legitimization of the dominant equestrian beliefs and practices have the effect of obligating the horses into simply reacting. Consequently, they are not able to experience and/or be aware of their own actions in a socio-cognitive way.[14] Only "[w]hen the concept of moral agency is connected to the concept that a subject is not a body for the use by someone else but, instead, has a body useful to itself, [does] it provide space for other theories of animality."[15] In this chap-ter, we seek to name and exemplify some major veils in the social science literature on human–horse relationships by bringing the work of activist and cognitive ethologist Francesco De Giorgio into dialogue with the disciplinary approaches, concepts, and research practices used in studies of human–horse relations. We thereby offer an ethical and practical frame for uncovering equine subjectivity and agency and open up space for the horse's liberation as protagonists of their own life, and with that considering an evolving perspective of them, also *within* our relationship and in research.

FORMS OF DENIAL

Acknowledgment of and respect for nonhuman animals' subjectivity and agency have fundamental implications for them as its denial renders any animal ethical discussion obsolete. In the social sciences, equine subjectivity and agency are primarily veiled by authors' unwillingness or inability to look beyond the equestrian paradigm. As Dashper writes with almost disarming honesty:

> Our reluctance to fully acknowledge the moral status and importance of other species is . . . perhaps not surprising, as it would entail drastic changes to our existing lifestyles. Many of us are just not ready for this, including most people within the horse world who would be reluctant to drastically alter their relationships with horses.[16]

In addition to outright denial, however, there are features peculiar to social scientific approaches, such as disciplinary blinkers, misleading concepts of agency, and the uncritical acceptance of power relationships in multispecies ethnography, which further veil animal subjectivity and agency.

Denial through Disciplinary Blinkers

One veil for seeing animal subjectivity for what it is pertains to disciplinary blinkers in the natural and in the social sciences. On the one hand, the prevailing image of nonhuman animals is largely the result of biological research in the positivist and reductionist tradition that tends to view nonhuman animals as passive and measurable objects or mechanisms. The vehement objection to subjectivist and anthropomorphic approaches to nonhuman animals not only limits the range of possible research questions,[17] as is the case in studies that measure the similarity to humans, such as mirror tests, the trainability of nonhuman animals, or behavioral patterns using ethograms. More fundamentally, the subject–object approach of the biobehavioral paradigm produces biologically deterministic and mechanistic understandings of nonhuman animals which are consequently reduced to "objects or vehicles that are acted upon and thought and felt about" and stripped of their subjectivity.[18] One study on horses exemplifying this reduction to reactions and behavioral patterns explored "the effect of different human approach styles on the behaviour of naive and experienced horses."[19] It measured the flight response of feral, semi-feral, and trained horses to different kinds of movement involving components such as speed, body posture, gestures, and eye contact. Very often—as in this case and more generally in applied animal behavior science and equestrian science—the data produced serve the more effective management and use of nonhuman animals. They not only objectify the horses but also expose them to an oppressive research setup that reproduces the speciesist culture and anthropocentric perspective.[20]

The social sciences, on the other hand, are exclusively interested in human structures, culture, and meaning-making. Where nonhuman animals are part of the research, they remain "raw material for human acts, thoughts, and feelings" which fits into human culture and structures without informing the research about their own subjectivities, socialities, and cultures.[21] The lack of adequate ethological knowledge further compounds the problem as it is simply replaced by naive anthropomorphism, as for example when the horse box is described as the horse's "personal bedroom,"[22] or by the application of anthropocentric "horsemanship wisdom."[23] Although researchers of human–horse relations empathically reject the human–animal and culture–nature dualism, there remains an unbridgeable gap in their research practice due to the lack of a research methodology that starts from the horses' subjectivities, their own preferences, motivations, pleasures, and expressiveness.[24]

Denial through Concepts of Agency

The second veil obscuring animal subjectivity and agency is the concept of agency as it is understood in the social sciences and applied in research on human–horse relationships. Very generally, agency is the capacity to act in a given situation, to engage with social structures, and affect other actors. In the Enlightenment tradition, it is associated with free will and instrumental and normative rationality, which presuppose conscious intentionality, reflexivity, and morality. In the classical subject philosophy, agency is exclusively oriented to humans and interhuman relations and deemed the opposite of animal behavior. Human agency is acknowledged as meaningful, purposeful, and active, while the latter is supposedly unconscious, instinctual, and reactive. This dualism rests on the outdated but still widely accepted simplification that animal cognition is "merely instinctual." Consequently, the ascription of internal states such as subjectivity, meaning, and purpose as the basis of agency is a matter of course when it concerns humans but denounced as inappropriate anthropomorphism when it comes to nonhuman animals. More recently, however, biological knowledge on animal cognition has challenged this belief.[25] In fact, from a socio-cognitive point of view nonhuman animals are owners of their own experiences[26] and subjects of their lives.[27] All animals, including humans, share "the need and pleasure to nourish and nurture themselves with cognitive experiences," and to express their subjectivity through agency instead of simply reacting to stimuli.[28] At the same time, all animals, including humans, can experience conditions or situations that do not preserve their socio-cognitive skills but foster reactive behavior to external and internal stimuli.[29] From this perspective, agency is directly linked to ownership of cognitive experiences and stands in contrast to reactive behavior for humans and nonhumans alike.

The current dichotomization of human agency and animal (reactive) behavior leads to two common misrepresentations of nonhuman animal agency. First, the discomfort felt with regard to nonhuman subjectivity and socio-cognitive skills leads some animal studies scholars to switch to the notion of agency as "the faculty of an agent, or of acting; action"[30] that carries the connotation of mechanistic causation. This reduction also features in some posthumanist theorizations of riding as a process of "mutual becoming"[31] of horse and rider. Indeed this "mutual becoming" is a caricature of (animal) agency, since it is a product of training, which returns us to a behavioristic model and ignores subjective meaning and experience yet again.[32] It seems that a deeper understanding of animal subjectivity, intrinsic motivation, and socio-cognitive abilities is still necessary to constitute an agency-ethic. Such an ethic requires the development of a coexistence with nonhuman animals preserving their quality of life, as individuals, with their own subjectivity.[33] While this approach also decenters the human, it does not do so by adding to the invisibility of the horse but rather by foregrounding horse subjectivity and humans' coexistence with it.

The other misrepresentation of animal agency in the context of human–animal coexistence is linked to the notion of resistance. The social sciences have been questioning human agency, autonomy, and free will in light of power relationships, ideologies, and social structures since the nineteenth century. Taking up this tradition, Carter and Charles have very importantly pointed to the existence of "agentic conditions" for nonhuman animals. This means that they are "agents in relation to human dominated structures" and "profoundly affected by their locations within a distribution of resources that is deeply skewed towards human animals, where their habitats and ecologies are subject to human interests."[34] In such a context, the labeling of behavior that resists power structures as agency constitutes an ethically committed strategy to highlight social injustice and to give oppressed subjects a voice.[35] Animal protest is normally veiled by the belief that nonhuman animals are passive victims who cannot change their fate. Yet nonhuman animal resistance "represents a normal biological phenomenon with a significant evolutionary and even ethological value."[36] Interestingly, the literature on human–horse relations never names and critically analyzes the agential conditions for horses in the equestrian world, nor does it interpret equine resistance as protest. It describes resistance as a problem to be solved by more training and better management, rather than acknowledging it as a "precise and considered act" of opposition to oppression (even in its "humanized" form) and an expression of a "cognitive and proud life."[37] Animal activism indeed defines animal resistance as an expression of agency, such as the polar bear that escapes the confines of his zoo exhibit or the circus elephant that attacks her trainer.[38]

Notwithstanding the lack of acknowledgment of resistance, the focus on resistance as agency is too narrow for the purpose of this chapter to illuminate agency. It limits agency to behavior that runs counter to dominant norms and coercive structures and blinds us to the many forms of being in dialogue with specific social structures, cultures, and environments. While resistance can be more readily recognized, the multiplicity and subtlety of expressions of agency and its socio-cognitive foundation require a different viewpoint and an ethical stance. An understanding of agency as *an ability of* rather than *an attribution to* a subject and the commitment to preserve it is possible with an interpretative approach that focuses on the meaning of action from the actor's point of view. This research perspective requires treating the Other not simply as the object of our observation but as a subject who cocreates the world by developing his/her own understanding of the world. *Verstehen* in sociology and anthropology implies the process of understanding another culture or subculture on its members' own terms rather than imposing the terms of the researcher's own culture. While the interpretative and participative approach of ethnographic work has produced rich insights, ethnographies on human–horse relationships (or human–animal relationships more generally) are still disappointing in that they remain based on the observation of animal objects rather than an engagement with the equine subjects' *own* interests, understandings, projects, and expressions.

The animal turn in the social sciences allows the human to imagine what it is like to be, for example, a feline in a cat shelter,[39] or a horse "co-creating a language system with her rider."[40] However, these ethnographic studies do not tell us what it is like to be that particular cat or horse as owner of his/her own world. We cannot share Brandt's confidence in equine experiences of "rewarding interactions and successful partnerships"[41] in the same way as we do with the respective human experiences. As Fine criticized with respect to the Algers' cats, this implies a "bifurcated epistemology" that reads humans "from the inside out and [nonhumans] from the outside in."[42] Resisting this kind of anthropomorphism and the naturalization of the animal Others requires engaging in political and ethical practice and encountering them as protagonists of their own life[43]—as in any good interpretative research. This implies desisting from "impos[ing] anthropo-formative and homologizing forms"[44] on them and instead "contaminating"[45] ourselves with their alterity in encounters where all involved can be themselves. Unless we seriously realize these aspects in our research, any ethnography with nonhuman animals remains depoliticized and disengaged,[46] thereby reproducing the invisibility of animal subjectivity and agency.

Denial through the Equestrian Gaze in Multispecies Ethnography

The last veiling aspect sheds a specific light on the impact of the equestrian gaze within ethnographies of horse–human relationships. Ethnography is the classical method for gaining an understanding of the research subjects' meaning-making. Nevertheless, it is sometimes accused of "creat[ing] and perpetuat[ing] stigmatization in marginalized populations" by turning a blind eye on power relationships.[47] The neglect of power relationships negatively affects the researcher's understanding how her/his position in the setting influences what can be observed and how it is perceived. It also impinges on the research subjects' ability to make sense of and reflect on their world and sometimes leads to the silencing of their voices.[48] The researcher's privileged position and bias systematically undermines the understanding of the impact of decisive factors such as race, class, and gender on the knowledge production.[49] This is particularly true for speciesism and the equestrian gaze.

The development of animal rights theories and the animal turn in the social sciences have moved human and animal relationships to the center of attention of what has come to be known as multispecies ethnography.[50] Yet despite these moral and conceptual advances, speciesism has not disappeared—neither in society nor in multispecies ethnography. Over the years, it actually contributed to a more sophisticated colonization of the animal mind, emphasizing positive training to adapt others to society (human animals included), losing subjectivity, instead of creating a critical view on human–animal relationships. While colonialism, capitalism, or gender can enter the analysis, the researcher's "sympathetic gaze" predictably obscures the speciesist relations and their impact on nonhuman animal's subjectivity and agency.[51] It writes away *"real* difference and incommensurability" between human and nonhuman research subjects,[52] in fact it writes away a whole culture in its own right: the nonhuman animals' world. The attempt to grapple with the "speciesist gaze" might therefore benefit from anthropology's critical engagement with the "colonial gaze."

Mary Pratt provides us with a lens by deconstructing colonial travel writing as an "enactment of race and gender relations" in the "context of colonial subordination and resistance."[53] She alerts us to the perils of colonial meaning-making in the "contact zone," which stands for "the space of colonial encounters, the space in which peoples geographically and historically separated come into contact with each other and establish ongoing relations, usually involving conditions of coercion, radical inequality and intractable conflict."[54] Her critique of travel books from Europeans about non-Europeans that created the "domestic subject of Euroimperialism" for the benefit of the European elite can easily be transferred to the texts celebrating equestrian culture. Here, notions, such as contact zone, natureculture, and mutual becoming, also foreground aspects of copresence and interaction while ignoring the implications of the political dimension and seeking to secure the authors' "innocence in the same moment as they assert European [here: human] hegemony."[55]

However, a research journey beyond the colonial or speciesist gaze is demanding since colonial and speciesist subjectivities are steeped in political, social, and emotional relationships based on deeply held beliefs, projections, and passions. Oppressive structures are not simply an external phenomenon but constitutive of subjectivity with all their damaging social and psychic effects.[56] Narratives of subjectivity and agency in a colonial context easily gloss over the deep social and psychic scars that these power relations left and still leave behind on both colonized and colonizers by evoking notions of resistance, progress, and cultural change.

The same is true for the equestrian gaze that clings to the conjectural obligation to dominate and control, and reproduces stereotypes. It thereby locks humans as well as horses into projections, fixed positions, protocols, and "consumptive experiences."[57] Training in particular implies forming horses to fulfill certain roles and performance expectations, no matter if it is done through negative or positive reinforcement. All training methods fit into the behavioristic model of learning and force horses to disconnect from themselves and their environment to blindly react to stimuli. The horse is not born a stimulus-response machine but turned into one through training. The negative consequences of this approach are highly underestimated: it seriously destructs the horses' ability and possibility to pursue their own intrinsic motivation, to explore, process information, and understand a situation in their own time and way.[58] Under these circumstances, horse behavior cannot be interpreted as an authentic expression of subjectivity and agency.

UNVEILING HORSE SUBJECTIVITY AND AGENCY

The unveiling of the horse in the room requires a decolonization of the human mind that sees horses as born to serve human purposes and to fulfill human desires for a relationship with them. Consequently, the decentering of the human involves the understanding that humans are not the most important element of the horses' world, and that horses need to be able to preserve their own dialogue with the world. Humans have to take responsibility for perverting equine agency rather than piling up new veils on this distortion. Such an uncompromising act will contribute to a more general despeciesization of the human mind to build a new basis for questioning and transforming interspecies relations—far beyond the equestrian gaze.

Like carnism,[59] equestrianism is invisible as ideology and power structure, especially as the welfare discourse persuades us of the "happy, humanely treated horse." However, from an ethical and socio-cognitive point of view, this is analogous to the myth of the "happy slave"[60] in that it reproduces the appropriation and perversion of the subjectivity of the dominated. Researching equine behavior through the equestrian lens implies limiting observations and understanding to what the system of dominance produces. As long as horses cannot be owners of their experiences and responses to a situation, we are still only observing an automatic response. Thus, agency presupposes cognitive horses that can feel and understand themselves, their initiatives, each other, their environment, and their social context, for their own interest in life, not to become an improved instrument. They must be able to express themselves not in an agency-amputating culture, but in an understanding starting with horses born as a family, not as a human product.[61]

Academic concepts, such as natureculture, mutual becoming, and contact zone, fail to unveil the horse in the room as long as ethnographers resist deconstructing power relationships and their impact on equine subjects. In the social sciences, we further miss a concept of agency based on the socio-cognitive paradigm that allows agency to be more than an empty formula. Here, we could benefit from a collaboration with an anti-speciesist ethology that stops to see nonhumans as mere representatives of a species for good. Finally, an evolution in the study of human–horse relationships requires stepping from the pedestal of abstract and objectifying thought and the "equestrian gaze" with all its desires, beliefs, and projections down to the earthy ground of embodied curiosity for the horses' own world.

In a decentralized coexistence, in which we fully immerse ourselves in the context and subjective meaning of the equine Other, in an experience that restores and preserves alterity by emancipating the Other rather than fitting him/her into our world, authentic being and dialogue become possible: "Only when you give to Nonhuman Others the space, the context, and the time to create their own experience, their own learning, their own sharing, when you focus on their quality of life, and freedom of expression, will you see them for who they really are."[62]

Similarly, recovering and protecting the affiliative–cognitive abilities of horses and fostering their agency imply opening up and safeguarding their space to maintain their own dialogue and to ask their own questions, creating their own awareness of their body, sensations, and inner states and facilitating them to express attention, curiosity, and motivation in their relationships with equine, human, and other companions.[63] The aim and value of this developmental process therefore do not lie in the production of data for a better management of horses or in scientific proofs of agency. Rather, it lies in the unveiling and preservation of subjectivity and agency, as ethical commitment toward an evolved coexistence beyond speciesism that gives weight to an individual animal's needs, intrinsic motivations, and subjective pleasures, not for human benefit, but as essential for the nonhuman animal, bearer of her/his own intrinsic value.[64]

ACKNOWLEDGMENT

The finalization of this chapter would not have been possible without the funding of the Austrian Science Foundation (FWF) for the research project "Surviving the Anthropocene," grant number I 4342.

NOTES

1. Eviatar Zerubavel, *The Elephant in The Room: Silence and Denial in Everyday Life* (New York, NY: Oxford University Press, 2008).

2. Ibid., 13.

3. Donna Haraway, *When Species Meet* (Minneapolis, MN: University of Minnesota Press, 2007).

4. Melanie Joy, *Why We Love Dogs, Eat Pigs, and Wear Cows: An Introduction to Carnism* (Cork: Red Wheel Weiser, 2011).

5. See, for example, Nora Schuurman, "Conceptions of Equine Welfare in Finnish Horse Magazines," *Society & Animals* 23, no. 3 (2015).

6. Nikki Savvides, "Communication as a Solution to Conflict: Fundamental Similarities in Divergent Methods of Horse Training," *Society & Animals* 20, no. 1 (2012), doi:10.1163/156853012X614378.

7. World Horse Welfare and Eurogroup for Animals, *Removing the Blinkers: The Health and Welfare of European Equidae in 2015*, accessed February 2, 2017, http://www.worldhorsewelfare.org/Removing-the-Blinkers.

8. Katherine Dashper, *Human–Animal Relationships in Equestrian Sport and Leisure* (London: Taylor & Francis, 2016).

9. See, for example, Joanna Latimer and Lynda Birke, "Natural Relations: Horses, Knowledge, Technology," *The Sociological Review* 57, no. 1 (2009), doi:10.1111%2Fj.1467-954X.2008.01802.x.

10. See, for example, Schuurman, "Conceptions of Equine Welfare."; Keri Brandt, "A Language of Their Own: An Interactionist Approach to Human–Horse Communication," *Society & Animals* 12, no. 4 (2004), doi:10.1163/1568530043068010.

11. See, for example, Lynda Birke and Keri Brandt, "Mutual Corporeality. Gender and Human/Horse Relationships," *Women's Studies International Forum* 32, no. 3 (2009), doi:10.1016/j.wsif.2009.05.015.

12. Jonna Bornemark et al., *Equine Cultures in Transition. Ethical Questions* (Milton: Routledge, 2019).

13. Francesco De Giorgio, *Nel Nome dell'Animalità di Cavalli, Cani, Umani e Altri Animali*, Second edition (Torino, Italy: Lindau, 2020).

14. Francesco De Giorgio and José De Giorgio-Schoorl, *Equus Lost? How We Misunderstand the Nature of the Horse–Human Relationship* (North Pomfret, VT: Trafalgar Square Books, 2016).

15. Ibid., 172.

16. Dashper, *Human–Animal Relationships*, 25.

17. Colin Allen and Marc Bekoff, *Species of Mind: The Philosophy and Biology of Cognitive Ethology* (Cambridge, MA and London: MIT, 1999).

18. Barbara Noske, "Deconstructing the Animal Image: Toward an Anthropology of Animals," *Anthrozoös* 5, no. 4 (1992): 228, doi:10.2752/089279392787011269.

19. Lynda Birke et al., "Horses' Responses to Variation in Human Approach," *Applied Animal Behaviour Science* 134, no. 1–2 (2011), doi:10.1016/j. applanim.2011.06.002.

20. De Giorgio, *Nel Nome dell'Animalità*.

21. Noske, "Deconstructing the Animal Image," 228.

22. Dashper, *Human–Animal Relationships*, 50.

23. De Giorgio and De Giorgio-Schoorl, *Equus Lost?*

24. De Giorgio, *Nel Nome dell'Animalità*.

25. See, for example, Allen and Bekoff, *Species of Mind*.

26. Francesco De Giorgio, "Animal Subjectivity: Evolving Ethics in Animal Studies," in *Food Futures: Ethics, Science & Culture*, ed. I. Anna et al. (Wageningen, NL: Wageningen Academic Publishers, 2016).

27. Tom Regan, *The Case for Animal Rights* (Berkeley, CA: University of California Press, 1983).

28. De Giorgio, *Nel Nome dell'Animalità*.

29. Ibid.

30. Bob Carter and Nickie Charles, "Animals, Agency and Resistance," *Journal for the Theory of Social Behaviour* 43, no. 3 (2013): 323, doi:10.1111/jtsb.12019.

31. Haraway, *When Species Meet*.

32. Reingard Spannring, "Mutual Becomings? In Search of an Ethical Pedagogic Space in Human–Horse Relationships," in *Animals in Environmental Education: Interdisciplinary Approaches to Curriculum and Pedagogy*, ed. Teresa Lloro-Bidart and Valerie Banschbach (Cham, Switzerland: Palgrave McMillan, 2019).

33. De Giorgio and De Giorgio-Schoorl, *Equus Lost?* 170.

34. Carter and Charles, "Animals, Agency and Resistance," 331.

35. Julia Coffey and David Farrugia, "Unpacking the Black Box. The Problem of Agency in the Sociology of Youth," *Journal of Youth Studies* 17, no. 4 (2014), doi:10 .1080/13676261.2013.830707.

36. De Giorgio, *Nel Nome dell'Animalità*, 202.

37. Ibid., 128.

38. Jason Hribal, *Fear of the Animal Planet: The Hidden History of Animal Resistance* (Oakland, CA: AK Press, 2010).

39. Janet Alger and Steve Alger, *Cat Culture: The Social World of a Cat Shelter* (Philadelphia, PA: Temple University Press, 2003).

40. Brandt, "A Language of Their Own."

41. Ibid., 300.

42. Gary Alan Fine, "Review Essay: Rats and Cats." *Journal of Contemporary Ethnography* 33, no. 5 (2004): 642.

43. De Giorgio, *Nel Nome dell'Animalita*.

44. Roberto Marchesini, "Zoomimesis," *Angelaki* 21, no. 1 (2016): 181, doi:10.10 80/0969725X.2016.1163841.

45. Ibid., 177.

46. Noske, "Deconstructing the Animal Image."

47. Meghan F. Hollis and Ramiro Martinez, "Introduction to the Special Issue on Ethnography from the Margins. Why We Need to Understand the Relationship Between Power, Powerlessness, and Marginalization," *Sociological Focus* 50, no. 1 (2017), doi:10.1080/00380237.2016.1218211.

48. Ibid.

49. Victor M. Rios, "Beyond Power-Blind Ethnography," *Sociological Focus* 50, no. 1 (2016), doi:10.1080/00380237.2016.1218224.

50. Eben Kirksey and Stefan Helmreich, "The Emergence of Multispecies Ethnography," *Cultural Anthropology* 25, no. 4 (2010), doi:10.1111/j.1548-1360.2010.01069.x.

51. Helen Kopnina, "Beyond Multispecies Ethnography: Engaging with Violence and Animal Rights in Anthropology," *Critique of Anthropology* 37, no. 3 (2017), doi:10.1177/0308275X17723973.

52. Raymond Madden, "Animals and the Limits of Ethnography," *Anthrozoös* 27, no. 2 (2015): 289, doi:10.2752/175303714X13903827487683.

53. Mary Louise Pratt, *Imperial Eyes. Travel Writing and Transculturation* (New York, NY and London: Routledge, 2008), 5.

54. Ibid., 6.

55. Ibid., 7.

56. Amal Treacher, "On Postcolonial Subjectivity," *Group Analysis* 38, no. 1 (2016), doi:10.1177/0533316405049365.

57. Reingard Spannring, "Ecological Citizenship Education and the Consumption of Animal Subjectivity," *Education Sciences* 9, no. 41 (2019), doi:10.3390/educsci9010041.

58. De Giorgio and De Giorgio-Schoorl, *Equus Lost?*

59. Joy, *Why We Love Dogs*.

60. Sue Donaldson and Will Kymlicka, *Zoopolis. A Political Theory of Animal Rights* (Oxford: Oxford University Press, 2011).

61. De Giorgio and De Giorgio-Schoorl, *Equus Lost?*

62. Ibid., 40.

63. Ibid., 112.

64. De Giorgio, *Animal Subjectivity*.

BIBLIOGRAPHY

Alger, Janet, and Steve Alger. *Cat Culture: The Social World of a Cat Shelter.* Philadelphia, PA: Temple University Press, 2003.

Allen, Colin, and Marc Bekoff. *Species of Mind: The Philosophy and Biology of Cognitive Ethology.* Cambridge, MA and London: MIT, 1999.

Birke, Lynda, and Keri Brandt. "Mutual Corporeality. Gender and Human/Horse Relationships." *Women's Studies International Forum* 32, no. 3 (2009): 189–97. doi:10.1016/j.wsif.2009.05.015.

Birke, Lynda, Jo Hockenhull, Emma Creighton, Lisa Pinno, Jenny Mee, and Daniel Mills. "Horses' Responses to Variation in Human Approach." *Applied Animal Behaviour Science* 134, no. 1–2 (2011): 56–63. doi:10.1016/j.applanim.2011.06.002.

Bornemark, Jonna, Petra Andersson, and Ulla Ekström von Essen. *Equine Cultures in Transition. Ethical Questions.* Milton: Routledge, 2019.

Brandt, Keri. "A Language of Their Own: An Interactionist Approach to Human–Horse Communication." *Society & Animals* 12, no. 4 (2004): 299–316. doi:10.1163/1568530043068010.

Carter, Bob, and Nicki Charles. "Animals, Agency and Resistance." *Journal for the Theory of Social Behaviour* 43, no. 3 (2013): 322–40. doi:10.1111/jtsb.12019.

Coffey, Julia, and David Farrugia. "Unpacking the Black Box. The Problem of Agency in the Sociology of Youth." *Journal of Youth Studies* 17, no. 4 (2014): 461–74. doi:10.1080/13676261.2013.830707.

Dashper, Katherine. *Human–Animal Relationships in Equestrian Sport and Leisure.* London: Taylor and Francis, 2016.

De Giorgio, Francesco. "Animal Subjectivity: Evolving Ethics in Animal Studies." In *Food Futures: Ethics, Science & Culture*, 169–74. Edited by I. Anna, S. Olsson, Sofia M. Araújo, and M. Fatima Vieira. Wageningen, NL: Wageningen Academic Publishers, 2016.

De Giorgio, Francesco, and José De Giorgio-Schoorl. *Equus Lost? How We Misunderstand the Nature of the Horse–Human Relationship.* North Pomfret, VT: Trafalgar Square Books, 2016.

De Giorgio, Francesco. *Nel Nome dell'Animalità di Cavalli, Cani, Umani e Altri Animali*, Second edition. Torino, Italy: Lindau, 2020.

Donaldson, Sue, and Will Kymlicka. *Zoopolis. A Political Theory of Animal Rights.* Oxford: Oxford University Press, 2011.

Fine, Gary Alan. "Review Essay: Rats and Cats." *Journal of Contemporary Ethnography* 33, no. 5 (2004): 638–44.

Haraway, Donna. *When Species Meet.* Minneapolis, MN: University of Minnesota Press, 2007.

Hollis, Meghan E., and Ramiro Martinez. "Introduction to the Special Issue on Ethnography from the Margins. Why We Need to Understand the Relationship Between Power, Powerlessness, and Marginalization." *Sociological Focus* 50, no. 1 (2017): 1–6. doi:10.1080/00380237.2016.1218211.

Hribal, Jason. *Fear of the Animal Planet: The Hidden History of Animal Resistance.* Oakland, CA: AK Press, 2010.

Joy, Melanie. *Why We Love Dogs, Eat Pigs, and Wear Cows: An Introduction to Carnism.* Cork: Red Wheel Weiser, 2011.

Kirksey, S. Eben, and Stefan Helmreich. "The Emergence of Multispecies Ethnography." *Cultural Anthropology* 25, no. 4 (2010), 545–76. doi:10.1111/j.1548-1360.2010.01069.x.

Kopnina, Helen. "Beyond Multispecies Ethnography: Engaging with Violence and Animal Rights in Anthropology." *Critique of Anthropology* 37, no. 3 (2017): 333–57. doi:10.1177/0308275X17723973.

Latimer, Joanna, and Lynda Birke. "Natural Relations: Horses, Knowledge, Technology." *The Sociological Review* 57, no. 1 (2009): 1–27. doi:10.1111%2Fj.1467-954X.2008.01802.x.

Madden, Raymond. "Animals and the Limits of Ethnography." *Anthrozoös* 27, no. 2 (2015): 279–93. doi:10.2752/175303714X13903827487683.

Marchesini, Roberto. "Zoomimesis." *Angelaki* 21, no. 1 (2016): 175–97. doi:10.1080/0 969725X.2016.1163841.

Noske, Barbara. "Deconstructing the Animal Image: Toward an Anthropology of Animals." *Anthrozoös* 5, no. 4 (1992): 226–30. doi:10.2752/089279392787011269.

Pratt, Mary Louise. *Imperial Eyes. Travel Writing and Transculturation.* New York, NY and London: Routledge, 2008.

Regan, Tom. *The Case for Animal Rights.* Berkeley, CA: University of California Press, 1983.

Rios, Victor M. "Beyond Power-Blind Ethnography." *Sociological Focus* 50, no. 1 (2016): 99–101. doi:10.1080/00380237.2016.1218224.

Savvides, Nikki. "Communication as a Solution to Conflict: Fundamental Similarities in Divergent Methods of Horse Training." *Society & Animals* 20, no. 1 (2012): 75–90. doi:10.1163/156853012X614378.

Schuurman, Nora. "Conceptions of Equine Welfare in Finnish Horse Magazines." *Society & Animals* 23, no. 3 (2015): 250–68. doi:10.1163/15685306-12341268.

Spannring, Reingard. "Mutual Becomings? In Search of an Ethical Pedagogic Space in Human–Horse Relationships." In *Animals in Environmental Education: Interdisciplinary Approaches to Curriculum and Pedagogy*, 79–94. Edited by Teresa Lloro-Bidart and Valerie Banschbach. Cham, Switzerland: Palgrave McMillan, 2019.

Spannring, Reingard. "Ecological Citizenship Education and the Consumption of Animal Subjectivity." *Education Sciences* 9, no. 41 (2019). doi:10.3390/educsci9010041.

Treacher, Amal. "On Postcolonial Subjectivity." *Group Analysis* 38, no. 1 (2016): 43–57. doi:10.1177/0533316405049365.

World Horse Welfare and Eurogroup for Animals. *Removing the Blinkers. The Health and Welfare of European Equidae in 2015.* Accessed February 2, 2017. http://www.worldhorsewelfare.org/Removing-the-Blinkers.

Zerubavel, Eviatar. *The Elephant in the Room: Silence and Denial in Everyday Life.* New York, NY: Oxford Univ. Press, 2008.

Chapter 11

Still in the Shadow of Man?

Judicial Denialism and Nonhuman Animals

Opi Outhwaite

POSITIONING ANIMALS WITHIN LAW

Law and the "Animal Turn"

In the past decade, there has been an "animal turn" in the humanities and social sciences,[1] implying an increased scholarly interest in animals and in the institutional, cultural, social, ethical, and scientific perspectives that define human–animal relations and the place of animals in society. Drivers for the Animal Turn include developments in philosophical and ethical perspectives (particularly those following or succeeding Peter Singer and Tom Reagan)[2] and developments in the natural sciences which provide new understandings of, for instance, animal autonomy, agency, emotion, relationships, and cognition.

Examining and questioning the relationship between humans and animals is important not only as a matter of animal "rights" or welfare, however. The ways in which humans live together with other species is a key consideration for transitioning toward sustainable societies and economies in the Anthropocene: the epoch of large-scale, human-induced alteration or collapse of planetary systems including ecosystems.[3] The relationship between humans and animals has significant implications for decision-making in numerous areas including mitigation and adaption to climate change, land use, conservation, health and disease control, and food production.[4]

Law, as a discipline, has not ignored the animal turn entirely; indeed, "animal law" is a rapidly emerging field with epistemological roots in environmental law, human rights law and ethics. Peters et al. note that in law, the interest in animals seems to be in line with the increasing concern for vulnerable groups (women, ethnic minorities, children, disabled, LGBTQ+) and the development of refined legal tools to address those concerns.[5] "Animal Law" is now taught widely in North American universities and in several European and Australian universities. The Global Journal of Animal Law was launched in 2012 and "animal law" has begun to appear in leading environmental journals and elsewhere.[6]

Questioning legal constructions of and perspectives on animals marks a significant point of departure for the discipline: the prevailing regulatory paradigms for animals—those for agriculture, welfare, and conservation are rooted in historical economic concerns and scientific perspectives and frame animals as "things" or property except in the circumstances in which law has granted specific protections.[7] Much work in the emerging field of animal law seeks to promote (in the case of advocacy) or assess (in the case of academic work) the extent to which the law does or could achieve particular standards of animal health, welfare, or conservation and on the moral and ethical position of animals within given legal codes. This work has set out the potential for new international or global efforts to address animals or to describe and establish legal rights for animals.[8]

In parallel with these advances has been an emerging jurisprudence in which judicial decisions directly respond to questions of the legal status of animals and the way in which legal constructs are applied to them. Most notably, several cases have been brought in which the courts were asked to grant a writ of habeas corpus (explained later) in respect of individual nonhuman animals and thereby to engage directly with whether nonhuman animals can be "legal persons." There has to date, however, been relatively limited critical engagement with the judicial reasoning in these cases and limited analysis of the way that legal reasoning and legal constructs are used, beyond conventional "black-letter" approaches to understand the judgments.

Constructing Animals: The Role of Judicial Decision-Making and the Common Law

Critical engagement with these decisions and the judicial reasoning within them is crucial first because in common law jurisdictions judicial decisions are themselves a source of legal rules and, second, because the way that the law is interpreted and applied has direct implications for animals as well as shaping wider social attitudes toward animals.

In the common law tradition, judges develop the law in two ways. First, following the historical principle of stare decisis the decisions of a higher court in previously decided cases form binding precedent and are to be followed by all lower courts (and in some instances, courts of the same rank) in subsequent cases. This provides certainty in law, since the aim and general effect is that similar cases are dealt with in the same way.[9] Second, judges play a less direct role in developing the law through their constitutional role in applying and interpreting statutory law. In clarifying and elaborating on the meaning that should be afforded to given statutory provisions, judges further shape the law, even where it originates from the legislature.[10]

Despite the importance of understanding the role played by judges and the way that judges apply and interpret the law, this source of rules and authority is frequently treated as objective and neutral, akin to the application of rules in the natural sciences. This has implications beyond the application of rules in a particular judgment because law and law-makers are sources of authority and power in society and what they *say the law is and should be* also therefore shapes wider societal views.

Recognizing That the Law Is Not Neutral: Critical Perspectives on Judicial Decision-Making

As a counterpoint to the acceptance of law not only as legitimate but also as objective and neutral, the Critical Legal Studies movement that emerged in the 1970s recognized that "dominant legal doctrines and conceptions perpetuate patterns of injustice and dominance by whites, men, the wealthy, employers, and heterosexuals" and argued that "prevailing modes of legal reasoning pretend to afford neutral and objective treatment of claims while shielding structures of power from fundamental reconsideration."[11]

Of particular interest for the purposes of this chapter, within the critical tradition, the Feminist Judgments Project treated legal decisions as sources and included discourse analysis of judicial reasoning (rather than the more typical doctrinal analysis that prevails in law) with an emphasis on qualitative analysis to identify the ways in which reasoning in those cases differed. The project challenged the prevailing "ways of knowing" in law: "Within feminist legal scholarship, there has been a long-standing argument that legal method is impervious to feminist perspectives, that legal categories and frameworks limit and distort feminist agendas, and the law actively disqualifies women's experience and knowledge."[12] The analysis of key judgments highlighted previously excluded social experiences that were addressed in certain judgments and assumptions, stereotypes, and the accepted "common knowledge" that played a significant role in the selected cases.[13] For example:

> The feminist critique of liberal autonomy rejects the notion of the autonomous, bounded, self-determining, abstract individual in favour of a more plausible account of individuals as relational, always connected to and dependent upon others. It follows that legal rules should reflect this basic condition of human lives rather than being constructed around the fictional liberal individual.[14]

Elsewhere, critical legal perspectives have begun to emerge specifically within animal law. In particular, the collection edited by Otomo and Mussawir recognized the developing interest in animal law but saw that "the theoretical problematization of law and rights themselves has not necessarily followed a sustained critical account."[15] Of particular relevance here, Bevilaqua examines two cases—one Austrian, the other Brazilian—in which the courts were asked to consider the question that is also central to the cases discussed in this chapter; whether a writ of habeas corpus could be issued, and, therefore, whether the chimpanzees in question could be considered legal persons.[16] Bevilaqua draws attention to the uneasy positioning in the subsequent hearings of nonhuman animals, drawn as of the human world yet still subject to the possession of humans. The diligent focus of the courts on procedural matters and the ultimate avoidance of or refusal to engage with the substantive legal questions of the meaning of personhood (as in the cases discussed in this chapter) gives the hearings the feeling of a "fictional narrative": "in the end, nothing seems to have really happened."[17] Ultimately, Bevilaqua suggests that one corollary of the current person/nonperson legal distinction is the "homogenisation of difference: there is only one way to differ and, therefore, all forms of existence must fit on one side or the other."[18]

These works demonstrate the importance of critical interrogation of judicial decision-making processes and highlight how unseen and unspoken perspectives and assumptions define and create the rules about how animals are treated and the wider landscape of societal values that frequently determine how they will live and how they will die.

Similarly, to the work of the Feminist Judgments Project, and to Bevilaqua's analysis, this chapter treats legal documents as sources. The analysis is not concerned with the merits of the various legal arguments advanced, or the decisions of the courts per se but on the reasoning processes and language used by the judges in arriving at their decision. To better understand the ways in which legal reasoning, processes, and procedure are applied and interpreted in relation to the habeas corpus claims the analysis that follows focuses on documents related to the relevant cases. Specifically, this includes transcripts of hearings, where applicable, as well as the formal decision handed down by appellate courts.

DENYING LEGAL PERSONHOOD

Tommy, Kiko, Hercules, and Leo: Claiming Legal Personhood for Nonhuman Animals

The analysis in this chapter focuses on a series of cases that are similar in certain important respects. The cases were all brought by the Nonhuman Rights

Project (NhRP).[19] The aims of the project include changing "the common law status of great apes, elephants, dolphins, and whales from mere 'things,' which lack the capacity to possess any legal right, to 'legal persons,' who possess such fundamental rights as bodily liberty and bodily integrity."[20]

The cases were brought in the United States and in each case a writ of habeas corpus was sought. This raised a crucial question of whether animals can be *legal persons* for the purposes of the writ. There have been other cases in which claims were brought on behalf of nonhuman persons but the similarity of these cases, including the legal issues raised and the jurisdiction in which they were brought, provides clear parameters for analysis.

Habeas corpus is an "ancient writ" that, when granted by a court, provides for a prisoner or other detained person to be brought before a court that can then determine whether the individual's detention is lawful. Thus habeas corpus is recognized as a fundamental, historical mechanism for protection of personal liberty and protection against arbitrary detention. The writ is founded in English common law and in the United States the opportunity to seek relief in the form of habeas corpus is set out in various Federal statutes.[21]

To be the subject of the writ the applicant or the person on whose behalf the writ is sought must have *legal* personality—they must be a *legal person*. A legal person can undertake legal transactions—they can enter into contracts, they can sue and be sued, they can be subject to legal obligations. This does not mean that they must be a *human* person. Legal personhood is an accepted fiction, distinguishing between legal persons and natural persons. It is very well established in law that corporations and international organizations, for example, are legal persons.

In 2013, NhRP filed a number of petitions seeking the writ of habeas corpus on behalf of individual chimpanzees. The first petition was sought on behalf of Tommy, a chimpanzee. NhRP's account provides that when they first encountered Tommy "he was living alone in a cage in a shed on a used trailer lot along Route 30 in Gloversville, New York."[22] Having formerly been owned by an animal trainer, Dave Sabo, ownership of Tommy, passed to the Laverys on Sabo's death. In NhRP's summary, "Concrete walls painted to look like a jungle are the only intimation of a chimpanzee's natural habitat in Tommy's cage. A television is his only company."[23] Patrick Lavery told the Albany Times Union in 2013 that Tommy would "rather be by himself. He likes being by himself."[24]

The petition was denied and NhRP appealed the decision.[25] On appeal (2014), the State of New York Supreme Court, Appellate Division, also denied the petition on the basis that chimpanzees, unlike humans, cannot exercise legal duties, which are requisite for the recognition of legal rights.[26]

The case of Kiko followed a similar pattern. NhRP provides that at the time of application Kiko was understood to be "held in captivity in a cage in a cement storefront" and that "in photos, Kiko can be seen with a steel chain and padlock around his neck, which the Prestis [the owners] appear to use as a leash."[27] Kiko was a former animal actor who was identified as having suffered abuse at the hands of his handlers. In its 2013 petition, NhRP sought the transfer of Kiko to an appropriate sanctuary. The application was denied, with the court noting that it was not prepared to take the "leap of faith" that it deemed was required.[28] An application for leave to appeal was subsequently denied (2015), with the court citing improper use of habeas corpus because the application was not ultimately seeking Kiko's "freedom" but only to change the conditions of his confinement.[29]

A further petition was filed on behalf of Hercules and Leo, two chimpanzees who were held at Stony Brook University and were subjects of research experiments. The petition was dismissed without a hearing,[30] but NhRP filed a further application. This again was denied (2015) with the court citing the binding precedent of *Lavery* (discussed as Tommy and Kiko I later).[31]

In 2017, the First Judicial department ruled that the NhRP could not seek second writs of habeas corpus on behalf of Tommy and Kiko with the court noting that the application of fundamental legal rights for animals was better suited to the legislative process (than the courts).[32] This is a key decision because it forms binding precedent and is cited in subsequent cases.[33] In 2018, the New York Court of Appeals denied permission to appeal. In a concurring opinion, Judge Eugene M. Fahey recognized the unsatisfactory position of the law, the importance of the issues in question, and the possibility that earlier decisions may have been flawed while ultimately denying permission to appeal.[34]

Each of the applications ultimately failed. But in analyzing the decisions, it can be seen that while on one level it appears that the courts are seeking to address applicable legal questions, a deeper analysis suggests that legal procedures and constructs are referred to without the real possibility that they would be interpreted in favor of the applicants. On numerous occasions judges distance themselves from the possibility of this outcome—dismissing arguments without engaging with them or jumping to a different point—or else they appeal to a higher authority or use interpretation to avoid a particular outcome.

"Just Animals": Denialism as a Framework for Understanding Judicial Decision-Making

In his seminal work on the subject, Stanley Cohen defines denial as "the maintenance of social worlds in which an undesirable situation (event, condition, phenomenon) is unrecognized, ignored or made to seem normal."[35] In Cohen's work, many people know about abuse and oppression yet they are in denial—a state of "knowing and not knowing." In this way, denial is frequently not explicit (though it can be). Rather, a range of processes can be employed which have the effect of denial.

While Cohen's focus was on the relationship between denial and abuse in humans, including human rights abuses, more recent work has applied the processes and techniques of denial that he describes to explain how animals are maintained as "different" from people and to explore the ways in which animal suffering is maintained, even where individuals and societies profess a love of animals and desire to end or avoid animal suffering.

Sykes's and Matza's "techniques of neutralization" informs Cohen's sociological theory of denial.[36] In the context of *accounts* and *rhetorical devices*, Sykes's and Matza's classification describes the use of vocabulary to neutralize "the moral bind of the law."[37] Techniques used to achieve these denials and neutralizations include denial of responsibility, denial of injury, denial of the victim, condemnation of the condemners, and appeal to higher loyalties. Applying these ideas in the context of animals, Sollund describes the processes through which animals are kept apart from people through technological interventions such as social distancing which enable people to see animals as "different" and to experience them as "just animals."[38] This, Sollund argues, amounts to a form of neutralization, a denial of the victim, which is maintained through various techniques, such as minimizing.

Denying one's own part in animal abuse is argued by Sollund to constitute a form of interpretive denial:

> As researchers, farmers, slaughterhouse workers and consumers we do not deny what actually is taking place, but we deny its character. The animals do not feel pain or the pain is not important to us (Linzey, 1989). Such a denial may be defined as another of Sykes' and Matzas' (1957) techniques of neutralization: the appeal to higher loyalties. Based on religion, legislation and philosophy, humans can claim to be above animals and this right stems not from humans themselves but from a higher spiritual sphere. In a division of the interests of the human species, and the other species—the non-human animals—the humans are given a "righteous" priority.[39]

In the same way as in Sollund's examples, judges are not consciously intending to maintain animal suffering and are not necessarily mindful of the broader consequences of the legal status afforded to animals, partly as a result of judgments including their own. They may express a sincere wish to see the best outcome for the animal in question. Yet when it comes to making decisions about what the law is—how particular terms and concepts are to be defined and interpreted—judges appeal to higher loyalties or find themselves bound in other ways which mean they must decide against the application. They may sympathize with the situation of the animal but there is nothing they can do; their hands are tied because the law cannot be applied in any other way.

Denialism in the Habeas Corpus Judgments

Legalism

In part of his work on accounting for atrocities, Cohen identifies *legalism* as a form of interpretive denial. This form of denial "comes from the language of legality itself."[40] In this form, rather than "seeing" or "knowing" about the abuse in question the focus is on the strict meaning, scope, and application of the relevant legal clauses and definitions. "Magical legalism" can also be used; in Cohen's example to "prove" that an allegation could not be correct because the action is illegal: "torture is strictly forbidden in our country; we have ratified the Convention Against Torture, therefore what we are doing cannot be torture."[41]

Also achieving the kind of "othering" necessary to distance oneself from suffering, Nadler (referring to Zygmunt Bauman) identifies categorization as a means of denial: "Classification is all about inclusion and exclusion . . . This system of naming is a necessary precondition to a sociomental manifestation of denial where the 'other' is denied."[42] Law ultimately is always about categorization: does a particular thing, person, or circumstance fall within this definition, or rule, or does it not?

These forms of denialism, I argue, are evident in the habeas corpus judgments in the ways in which the courts address the question of whether a nonhuman animal can be granted a writ of habeas corpus. This crucially turns on the question of whether "a person," for the purpose of the writ, can mean a nonhuman person. Questions of categorization are the main preoccupation of law, so it is not surprising that this issue is often key in the various decisions. But what can be observed are the tactics employed which mean that the answer to the question is never affirmative. If it cannot be established that animals can be legal persons, or conversely if the writ can only be granted to human persons, then the decision cannot go in the applicant's favor. Putting aside that legal personality is a legal fiction, if animals cannot fall within this definition, we might expect some consistency in the reasoning but this is not the case.

In Tommy I,[43] legal precedent supporting the notion that a chimpanzee could be recognized as a legal person is dismissed out right, without consideration of its legal validity. In pursuing the possibility of granting the writ, the judge heard legal authority supporting the grant of habeas corpus to persons who at the time of the petition were deemed not persons, but property—to black slaves, before the abolition of slavery. The judge does not contemplate the case, noting that the court "is not even going to consider that as syn-onymous so you'll have to use your other cases."[44] While the analogy may have felt uncomfortable, the legal point was to illustrate precedent for the application of the writ to individuals deemed as property, not, at the time, as persons. Similarly, following legal argument that animals can be beneficiaries of a trust and therefore have legal personality, the argument is again ignored ("let's turn to the reason why you're here"[45]). This approach to categorization prevents the possibility that a writ could be granted.

In Tommy II,[46] the court again is unable to recognize that nonhuman ani-mals can be legal persons. On this occasion, the court emphasizes that legal personhood is consistently defined in terms of rights and duties. This ignores the fact that personhood has been recognized in other circumstances—a criti-cism raised in separate amicus curie briefs.[47] These circumstances include the so-called marginal cases, such as fetuses and newborns, adults lacking mental capacity, and adults with certain physical limitations including those who are in a coma or similar state. Faced with arguments about these marginal cases, the court shifts the parameters for this categorization. It recognizes that some human beings are less able to bear duties but in this case, "These differences do not alter our analysis, as it is undeniable that, collectively, human beings possess the unique ability to bear legal responsibility."[48] Here the court switches the basis for recognition from a capacity to bear rights and duties per se to an ability, collectively, to assume these. The exceptionalism of humans is in fact the characteristic that is the key to legal personality, despite persua-sive precedent recognizing otherwise. [49]

This argument resurfaces in Tommy and Kiko I where the petitioner argued that the ability to acknowledge a legal duty or legal responsibility should not be determinative of entitlement to habeas relief, since, for example, "infants cannot comprehend that they owe duties or responsibilities and a comatose person lacks sentience, yet both have legal rights."[50] Again, human exception-alism now becomes the legal requirement: "this argument ignores the fact that these are still human beings, members of the human community."[51] This is also a circular argument—or perhaps, a form of magical legalism. The court determines that being human even without being able to bear duties is suf-ficient to confer personhood for the purpose of Habeas Corpus. And the court does not in fact refer back to the relevant legal provision; Article 70 does not refer to humans, but only to persons.

Distancing

Sollund describes social distancing as a form of neutralization, enabling people to see animals as "just animals."[52] In the habeas corpus cases, judges engage in a form of distancing by frequently switching focus and failing to engage with the legal arguments presented, whether in a hearing or a decision. But in these cases, the tactics employed perhaps also portray a resistance to really face and consider the possibility that some arguments could ultimately be successful, in favor of the writ being granted.

We have already seen above the courts unwillingness to engage with the arguments about the application of the writ to nonnatural persons and in instances where the law at the time denied recognition of an individual's personhood. Responding to the argument that "person" need not mean "human," as evidenced by a river in New Zealand designated as a legal person, the court in Tommy and Kiko I holds that this "is not relevant to the definition of 'person' . . . here in the United States and certainly is of no guidance to the entitlement of habeas relief by nonhumans in New York."[53] In Tommy I, the court asks about relevant precedent regarding personhood but does not examine the issue further, after closing down the analogy related to black slaves.[54] It is certainly the case that those decisions, since they were decided in another jurisdiction, are not binding on the US courts but it is a stretch to say that they are of no relevance; certainly recognition of interpretations in other jurisdictions are often used to inform the courts decision-making. But this avoidance implies a reluctance to be brought closer to the legal option of granting the writ.

Elsewhere in the cases, judicial authority is used to move discussion to a different point or to make claims about evidence that are unsupported. This has the effect of distancing the legal argument from the possibility of finding in favor of the applicants. It is not possible to satisfactorily answer the judge's question because no answer is really sought, and it is simply a means of moving the argument along.

In Tommy I, the court distances itself from recognized scientific evidence. The court asks whether the petitioner is differentiating chimpanzees from other animals. The point being made, counsel asserts, is that chimpanzees are autonomous. The court states that "it is beyond your ken and my ken" to know this and that this claim could only be supported by expert testimony.[55] This directly overlooks the sworn affidavits of numerous primatologists and other experts presented by the Petitioners attesting to this very point.[56] Subsequently, after hearing again arguments about the applicability of Article 70, the court jumps again to a different point—"what's the standing?"[57]

In Kiko II, the court focuses on the fact that if the writ were granted then Kiko would not be "free" to go where he chooses but would still be in confinement, albeit in better conditions. The petitioner cites examples where this has been the case for humans. Ignoring this argument, the judge goes on to enquire about evidence for the condition of Kiko. Later, the court proposes that the self-determination relied on by the petitioner actually precludes the granting of the writ: "It's that self-determination itself that causing you problems [*sic*], because, if that's true, then a self-determination would not to be kept in another captive environment, it would be to be free."[58] Faced with the argument that children too are in this position, the court switches its focus: "How do we know he even wants to leave?"[59]

Turning later to the question of jurisdiction, we see the court repeatedly raising the bar. First, the court enquires into the authority of the court to grant the writ. Responding to case examples demonstrating such jurisdiction, the question shifts: "Are any of those, do any, are any of those cases New York authority?"[60] Responding again to examples demonstrating such jurisdiction, the court again shifts: "As the intermediate appellate court?" Again, there is both a shifting and a denial of the relevance of existing precedent.

Appeal to Higher Loyalties

An appeal to higher loyalties appears as one of the Syke's and Matza's techniques of neutralization and can be employed as a rhetorical device of denial. In the context of the habeas corpus cases, we frequently see such appeals; judges appeal to the authority of the legislature or assert a loyalty to the statutory provisions themselves which are granted a higher loyalty.

In Tommy and Kiko I, the court asserts that "While petitioner's avowed mission is certainly laudable, the according of any fundamental legal rights to animals, including entitlement to habeas relief, is an issue better suited to the legislative process."[61] This is a point that reappears elsewhere in the cases, despite the fact that the availability and scope of the writ has developed through the common law, as is extensively discussed in the cases. In Kiko I the court notes, in conclusion: "I'm not prepared to make this leap of faith and I'm going to deny the request for a petition for writ of habeas corpus. I think personally this is more of a legislative issue than a judicial issue."[62] In Tommy II, the court notes, in conclusion, that the petitioner "is fully able to importune the Legislature to extend further legal protections to chimpanzees."[63]

In the 2018 concurring opinion on Tommy and Kiko, permission to appeal is denied but the separate concurring opinion of Justice Fahey goes to some lengths to recognize the significance of the legal question at hand and expresses sympathy with the cause, going so far as to note that:

> The reliance on a paradigm that determines entitlement to a court decision based on whether the party is considered a "person" or relegated to the category of a "thing" amounts to a refusal to confront a manifest injustice. Whether a being has the right to seek freedom from confinement through the writ of habeas corpus should not be treated as a simple either/or proposition. The evolving nature

of life makes clear that chimpanzees and humans exist on a continuum of living beings. Chimpanzees share at least 96 percent of their DNA with humans. They are autonomous, intelligent creatures. To solve this dilemma, we have to recognize its complexity and confront it . . . The issue whether a nonhuman animal has a fundamental right to liberty protected by the writ of habeas corpus is profound and far-reaching. It speaks to our relationship with all the life around us. Ultimately, we will not be able to ignore it. While it may be arguable that a chimpanzee is not a "person," there is no doubt that it is not merely a thing.[64]

Despite an extensive critique of the Appeal Court's reasoning in *Lavery* (Tommy and Kiko I), and holding the view that "the question will have to be answered eventually," the court in this instance is bound by the earlier decision and so for Justice Fahey this, again, is now out of their hands, and there is no reason to grant permission to appeal.

Similarly, in Hercules II, Justice Jaffe rules that, despite the merits of the NhRP's case, she is bound to follow the decision in *Lavery* and must deny NhRP's habeas petition.[65] In a markedly different approach to the employment of distancing tactics seen elsewhere, the court addresses several of the arguments that had not been properly addressed in the hearings for Tommy, Kiko, Leo, and Hercules and does not find difficulty in confirming that the procedural requirements are met. Nonetheless, she concludes:

> Efforts to extend legal rights to chimpanzees are . . . understandable; some day they may even succeed. Courts, however, are slow to embrace change, and occasionally seem reluctant to engage in broader, more inclusive interpretations of the law . . . As Justice Kennedy observed in *Lawrence* v *Texas*, "times can blind us to certain truths and later generations can see that laws once thought necessary and proper in fact serve only to oppress." For now, however, given the precedent to which I am bound, it is hereby ordered that the petition for a writ of habeas corpus is denied.[66]

Despite the more positive position as regards the petition, the court finds, applying the principle of stare decisis, that it is bound by the decision of the higher court but crucially *even if it is not*—since the petitioners argued that this was not the case because *Lavery* had misapplied the law—the issue is best decided by the legislature or the Court of Appeals.[67] It is the case that lower courts are properly bound by the decisions of higher courts—as explained earlier—but the "hedging of bets" here speaks to a broader reluctance to allow for the possibility of finding in favor of the applicants. Again, the court sympathizes but the petition must be denied: it is not for *this court* to make this step.

"NOT PREPARED TO MAKE THAT LEAP": MAINTAINING THE NONHUMAN DISTINCTION IN LAW

Spannring and Grušovnik discuss forms of cultural denial in the context of animals arguing that through cultural practices, power relationships, and ideology "society provides 'cognitive traditions,' which establish what to pay attention to and what to ignore, and organize denial by setting rules of good manners and ethical obligations to 'look the other way.'"[68] For Sollund, cultural denial can help to explain the treatment of animals in captivity because even though in these circumstances animals suffer and die this is not seen as mistreatment and indeed becomes socially acceptable.[69] The historical development and framing of the law provides it with its own cognitive traditions that set the rules for judicial decision-making: animals are property, humans and animals are—and must be—different. Arguments that challenge these traditions are ignored or else the parameters of the legal term or concept are contorted to ensure that they do not fit. Given the precedents that exist and other arguments presented, it might feasibly be open to a court to decide that the writ *could* be granted in favor of a nonhuman animal. But as some decisions acknowledge directly, the step is too great. It might be open to the legislature to make law in this area but it is not open to the courts—despite the courts making decisions that develop the law in many areas, as part of the common law tradition.

In the analysis above, I have argued that beyond the prima facie application of legal rules, the reasoning and decisions in these cases reveal forms of denial that serve to prevent changes to the legal status of nonhuman animals, specifically related to their recognition as legal persons for the purpose of the writ of habeas corpus, and therefore also to the conditions in which these and other individual animals live. The animal living a solitary life in a cage is suffering; extensive scientific evidence supports an account of the animals in question that recognizes that their emotional, cognitive, and physical needs demand more than this.[70] A decision to grant a writ of habeas corpus might open the door to alleviate some of that suffering. But the door remains closed. This is not to suggest that the law should not be applied consistently and judiciously. But the language and reasoning used in the decisions discussed earlier imply an absolute truth and limit of the capacity of the court in any given case to respond, without proper recognition of the arguments that threaten to shatter this mirror.

Denial in these cases takes the form of legalism, distancing, and appeals to higher authority. While judges do not overtly seek to cause suffering or harm to animals—and indeed at times comment on the empathy they feel for the nonhuman animals in question—they nevertheless use legal constructs in such a way as to ensure that animals are always "different" and consequently cannot be protected by the law in the manner sought by the applicants. Judges deny their role in animal suffering by relying on the application of legal constructs that prevent animals from gaining legal recognition, even where this depends on tortuous interpretation. It is not that judges do not wish to help the cause of animal welfare but the proposed legal avenue is not available. It is not that animals do not feel pain, or that they are not suffering in their current conditions, but the law is helpless to respond. Judges would like to reach a different outcome, but this is a matter for the legislature.

Far from being an objective and neutral force, law maintains distinctions and power relations which reinforce the status quo; in this case, courts maintain a binary distinction between human and nonhuman animals. Through these decisions and the reasoning deployed therein, the social world in which the legal distinguishing of animals as nonlegal persons, and the consequences that follow that distinction, is maintained and made to seem normal. In this way, judges play a role in maintaining the suffering of animals which they both know and do not know.

NOTES

1. See Harriet Ritvo, "On the Animal Turn," *Daedalus* 136 (2007).

2. Peter Singer, *Animal Liberation: A New Ethics for Our Treatment of Animals* (New York, NY: New York Review, 1975); Tom Regan, *The Case for Animal Rights* (Berkeley, CA: University of California Press, 2004).

3. Donna Haraway, *Staying with the Trouble: Making Kin in the Chthulucene* (Durham, NC: Duke University Press, 2016); Will Steffen et al., "Planetary Boundaries: Guiding Human Development on a Changing Planet," *Science* 347, no. 6223 (2015).

4. Steffen et al., "Planetary Boundaries," 736; Brian Machovina, Kenneth Feeley, and William Ripple, "Biodiversity Conservation: The Key is Reducing Meat Consumption," *Science of The Total Environment* 536 (2015); Lisa Kemmerer, *Eating Earth: Environmental Ethics and Dietary Choice* (Oxford: Oxford University Press, 2014).

5. Anne Peters, Saskia Stucki, and Livia Boscardin, "The Animal Turn and the Law," *1st Annual European Animal Law Conference*, Law School of the University of Basel, Switzerland, April 4–5, 2014.

6. See especially the special issue in *Transnational Environmental Law* 5, no. 1 (April 2016), https://www.cambridge.org/core/journals/transnational-environmental -law/issue/BD60C629432A53F16C82739262F2BE7C.

7. Opi Outhwaite, "Neither Fish, nor Fowl: Honeybees and the Parameters of Current Legal Frameworks for Animals, Wildlife and Biodiversity," *Journal of Environmental Law* 2, no. 3 (2017).

8. See work including David Favre, "An International Treaty for Animal Welfare," *Animal Law* 18, no. 2 (2012); Oscar Horta, "Zoopolis, Intervention, and the State of Nature," *Law, Ethics & Philosophy* 1 (2013); Miyun Park and Peter Singer, "The Globalization of Animal Welfare: More Food Does not Require More Suffering," *Foreign Affairs* 91, no. 2 (2012); Miah Gibson, "The Universal Declaration of Animal Welfare," *Deakin Law Review* 16, no. 2 (2011); Anne Peters, "Global Animal Law: What It Is and Why We Need It," *Transnational Environmental Law* 5, no. 1 (2016).

9. Emily Allbon and Sanmeet Kaur Dua, *Elliott & Quinn's English Legal System* (London: Pearson, 2019).

10. See Patrick Hodge, "The Scope of Judicial Law-Making in the Common Law Tradition," *Max Planck Institute of Comparative and International Private Law Hamburg*, October 28, 2019, https://www.supremecourt.uk/docs/speech-191028.pdf.

11. Abram Chayes et al., "Materials on Legal Theory—Critical Theory: Overview," *The Bridge*, accessed June 22, 2020, https://cyber.harvard.edu/bridge/CriticalTheory/critical1.htm.

12. Rosemary Hunter, "The Feminist Judgments Project: Legal Fiction as Critique and Praxis," *International Critical Thought* 5 (2015): 501–8, doi: https://doi-org.stmarys.idm.oclc.org/10.1080/21598282.2015.1102075

13. Ibid.

14. Ibid., 505.

15. Yoriko Otomo and Ed Mussawir, *Law and the Question of the Animal: A Critical Jurisprudence* (New York, NY: Routledge, 2013), 1.

16. See Cimea Barbato Bevilaqua, "Chimpanzees in Court: What Difference Does It Make?" in *Law and the Question of the Animal*, ed. Yoriko Otomo and Ed Mussawir (New York, NY: Routledge, 2013).

17. Ibid., 79.

18. Ibid., 84.

19. See the NhRP website, https://www.nonhumanrights.org/; Steven M. Wise, "Legal Personhood and the Nonhuman Rights Project," *Law Review* 17, no. 1 (2010), https://www.animallaw.info/sites/default/files/lralvol17_1_1.pdf.

20. "Who We Are," *Nonhuman Rights Project*, accessed July 12, 2020, https://www.nonhumanrights.org/who-we-are/.

21. Jonathan Kim, "Habeas Corpus," *Legal Information Institute, Cornell Law School*, accessed June 22, 2020, https://www.law.cornell.edu/wex/habeas_corpus.

22. "Client, Tommy (Chimpanzee)," *Nonhuman Rights Project*, accessed June 22, 2020, https://www.nonhumanrights.org/client-tommy/.

23. Ibid.

24. "Client, Tommy (Chimpanzee)." The background to the Tommy case was widely reported in the news media, see, for example Charles Siebert, "Should a Chimp Be Able to Sue Its Owner?" *New York Times*, April 23, 2014, https://www.nytimes.com/2014/04/27/magazine/the-rights-of-man-and-beast.html.

25. "Nonhuman Rights Project On Behalf of Tommy v Patrick C. Lavery, Diane Lavery and Circle Trailer Sales Inc.," *Nonhuman Rights Project*, December 29,

2013, https://www.nonhumanrights.org/content/uploads/Petition-re-Tommy-Case-F
ulton-Cty-NY.pdf. Hereafter "Tommy I."

26. "People ex rel. Nonhuman Rights Project, Inc. On Behalf of Tommy v.
Lavery," *Nonhuman Rights Project*, January 30, 2015, https://www.nonhumanrights
.org/content/uploads/5.-Decision-and-Order-on-Motion-for-Permission-to-Appeal-to
-the-Court-of-Appeals.pdf. Hereafter "Tommy II."

27. "Client, Kiko (Chimpanzee)," *Nonhuman Rights Project*, accessed June 22,
2020, https://www.nonhumanrights.org/client-kiko/.

28. Nonhuman Rights Project Inc., on behalf of Kiko, v, Presti, 9 Dec 2013.
Hereafter "Kiko I." Available at http://www.nycourts.gov/courts/ad4/Clerk/Decisions/
2015/01-02-15/PDF/1300.pdf. Last accessed 22 June 2020.

29. *Nonhuman Rights Project, Inc. v Presti* (124 AD3d 1334), 1335 [4th Dept
2015], *lv denied* 126 AD3d 1430 [4th Dept 2015]. Hereafter "Kiko II."

30. "Nonhuman Rights Project, Inc., v Samuel L. Stanley, etc., et al." *Nonhuman
Rights Project*, April 3, 2014, https://www.nonhumanrights.org/content/uploads/4.-
Dismissal-of-Appeal-4-3-14-Hercules-Leo.pdf. Hereafter "Hercules I."

31. "Nonhuman Rights Project Inc., On Behalf of Hercules and Leo v. Samuel
Stanley and Stony Brook University, State of New York," *Nonhuman Rights Project*,
July 29, 2015, http://www.courts.state.ny.us/REPORTER/3dseries/2015/2015_25257
.htm. Hereafter "Hercules II."

32. "Nonhuman Rights Project, Inc., On Behalf of Tommy and Kiko v Lavery,"
Nonhuman Rights Project, June 22, 2017, http://www.nonhumanrights.org/content/
uploads/Footnotes-with-annotated-Tommy-Kiko-appellate-court-opinion-FINAL-6
-22-17.pdf. Hereafter "Tommy and Kiko I."

33. "Client, Happy (Elephant)," *Nonhuman Rights Project*, accessed June 22,
2020, https://www.nonhumanrights.org/client-happy/.

34. Eugene M. Fahey, "Concurring Opinion—Nonhuman Rights Project on Behalf
of Tommy v Patrick C. Lavery," May 8, 2018, http://www.nycourts.gov/ctapps/Deci
sions/2018/May18/M2018-268opn18-Decision.pdf.

35. Stanley Cohen, *States of Denial: Knowing about Atrocities and Suffering*
(Cambridge: Polity, 2001).

36. Lisa White, "Discourse, Denial and Dehumanisation: Former Detainees'
Experiences of Narrating State Violence in Northern Ireland," *Papers from the British
Criminology Conference* 10 (2010).

37. Cohen, *States of Denial*, 60.

38. Ragnhild Sollund, "Causes for Speciesism: Difference, Distance and Denial,"
in *Global Harms: Ecological Crime and Speciesism*, ed. Ragnhild Sollund (New
York, NY: Nova Science Publishers, 2008).

39. Ibid., 124.

40. Cohen, *States of Denial*, 107.

41. Ibid., 108.

42. Christina Nadler, *Denial: A Sociological Theory* (PhD diss., City University of
New York, 2017), 68, https://academicworks.cuny.edu/gc_etds/2126/.

43. Tommy I.

44. Ibid., para. 12: 14–21.

45. Ibid., para. 13: 20–21.
46. Tommy II.
47. See Laurence H. Tribe, "Amicus Brief in Support of Leave to Appeal," *Nonhuman Right Project*, accessed June 22, 2020, https://www.nonhumanrights.org/content/uploads/Tribe-Amicus-Curiae-Letter-Brief-FINAL.pdf.
48. Tommy II: 5.
49. Persuasive rather than binding.
50. Tommy and Kiko I.
51. Ibid.
52. See Sollund, "Causes for Speciesism."
53. Tommy and Kiko I.
54. Tommy I, para. 12.
55. Ibid., 16 and 17.
56. The point was also raised in Kiko II, with the court questioning whether autonomy could be confirmed in that specific case.
57. Tommy I, 23 at 22.
58. "Kiko Appellate Court Hearing Transcript," *Nonhuman Rights Project*, December 2, 2014, justice at 15:58, https://www.nonhumanrights.org/content/uploads/Kiko-Appellate-Court-Transcript-120214.pdf.
59. "Kiko Appellate Court Hearing Transcript," at 18:19.
60. Ibid., at 12:00.
61. Tommy and Kiko I.
62. "Transcript of Oral Argument—Nonhuman Rights Project, Inc. on behalf of Kiko v Carmen and Christie Presti," *Nonhuman Rights Project*, December 9, 2013: 15, 10–14, https://www.nonhumanrights.org/content/uploads/Transcript_of_Oral_Argument-_Niagara_County_12-9-13.pdf.
63. Tommy II, 6.
64. Fahey, "Concurring Opinion," 6–7.
65. Hercules II: 32–33. And see discussion in part G: stare decisis.
66. Tommy I: 32–33.
67. Ibid.: 31.
68. Reingard Spannring and Tomaž Grušovnik, "Leaving the Meatrix? Transformative Learning and Denialism in the Case of Meat Consumption," *Environmental Education Research* 25, no. 8 (2018): 1193.
69. See Sollund, "Causes for Speciesism."
70. In the habeas corpus cases discussed, numerous affidavits were submitted by the petitioners supporting these claims as made within the cases.

BIBLIOGRAPHY

Allbon, Emily, and Sanmeet Kaur Dua. *Elliott & Quinn's English Legal System.* London: Pearson, 2019.

Bevilaqua, Cimea Barbato. "Chimpanzees in Court: What Difference Does it Make?" In *Law and the Question of the Animal*, edited by Yoriko Otomo and Ed Mussawir, 71–88. New York, NY: Routledge, 2013.

Chayes, Abram, William Fisher, Morton Horwitz, Frank Michelman, Martha Minow, Charles Nesson, and Todd Rakoff. "Materials on Legal Theory—Critical Theory: Overview." *The Bridge*. Accessed June 22, 2020. https://cyber.harvard.edu/bridge /CriticalTheory/critical1.htm.

"Client, Happy (Elephant)." *Nonhuman Rights Project*. Accessed June 22, 2020. https ://www.nonhumanrights.org/client-happy/.

"Client, Kiko (Chimpanzee)." *Nonhuman Rights Project*. Accessed June 22, 2020. https://www.nonhumanrights.org/client-kiko/.

"Client, Tommy (Chimpanzee)." *Nonhuman Rights Project*. Accessed June 22, 2020. https://www.nonhumanrights.org/client-tommy/.

Cohen, Stanley. *States of Denial: Knowing about Atrocities and Suffering*. Cambridge: Polity, 2001.

Fahey, Eugene M. "Concurring Opinion – Nonhuman Rights Project on Behalf of Tommy v Patrick C. Lavery." May 8, 2018. http://www.nycourts.gov/ctapps/Deci sions/2018/May18/M2018-268opn18-Decision.pdf.

Favre, David. "An International Treaty for Animal Welfare." *Animal Law* 18, no. 2 (2012): 237–80.

Gibson, Miah. "The Universal Declaration of Animal Welfare." *Deakin Law Review* 16, no. 2 (2011): 539–67.

Haraway, Donna. *Staying with the Trouble: Making Kin in the Chthulucene*. Durham, NC: Duke University Press, 2016.

Hodge, Patrick. "The Scope of Judicial Law-Making in the Common Law Tradition." *Max Planck Institute of Comparative and International Private Law Hamburg*. October 28, 2019. https://www.supremecourt.uk/docs/speech-191028 .pdf.

Horta, Oscar. "Zoopolis, Intervention, and the State of Nature." *Law, Ethics & Philosophy* 1 (2013): 113–25.

Hunter, Rosemary. "The Feminist Judgments Project: Legal Fiction as Critique and Praxis." *International Critical Thought* 5 (2015): 501–8. doi:10.1080/21598282.2 015.1102075.

"Kiko Appellate Court Hearing Transcript." *Nonhuman Rights Project*. December 2, 2014. https://www.nonhumanrights.org/content/uploads/Kiko-Appellate-Court-Tr anscript-120214.pdf.

Kim, Jonathan. "Habeas Corpus." *Legal Information Institute, Cornell Law School*. Accessed June 22, 2020. https://www.law.cornell.edu/wex/habeas_corpus.

Nadler, Christina. *Denial: A Sociological Theory*. PhD diss., City University of New York, 2017. https://academicworks.cuny.edu/gc_etds/2126/.

"Nonhuman Rights Project Inc., On Behalf of Tommy v Patrick C Lavery, Diane Lavery and Circle Trailer Sales Inc." *Nonhuman Rights Project*. December 29, 2013. https://www.nonhumanrights.org/content/uploads/Petition-re-Tommy-Case-Fulton-Cty-NY.pdf.

"Nonhuman Rights Project, Inc., etc., v Samuel L. Stanley, etc., et al." *Nonhuman Rights Project*. April 3, 2014. https://www.nonhumanrights.org/content/uploads /4.-Dismissal-of-Appeal-4-3-14-Hercules-Leo.pdf.

"Nonhuman Rights Project, Inc. On Behalf of Kiko v Presti." *Nonhuman Rights Project*. January 2, 2015. http://www.courts.state.ny.us/REPORTER/3dseries/20 15/2015_00085.htm.

"Nonhuman Rights Project Inc. On Behalf of Hercules and Leo v. Samuel Stanley and Stony Brook University, State of New York." *Nonhuman Rights Project*. July 29, 2015. http://www.courts.state.ny.us/REPORTER/3dseries/2015/2015_25257.htm.

"Nonhuman Rights Project, Inc. On Behalf of Tommy and Kiko v Lavery." *Nonhuman Rights Project*. June 22, 2017. http://www.nonhumanrights.org/content/uploads/Foot notes-with-annotated-Tommy-Kiko-appellate-court-opinion-FINAL-6-22-17.pdf.

Otomo, Yoriko, and Ed Mussawir. *Law and the Question of the Animal: A Critical Jurisprudence*. New York, NY: Routledge, 2013.

Outhwaite, Opi. "Neither Fish, Nor Fowl: Honeybees and the Parameters of Current Legal Frameworks for Animals, Wildlife and Biodiversity." *Journal of Environmental Law* 2, no. 3 (2017): 317–41.

Park, Miyun, and Peter Singer. "The Globalization of Animal Welfare: More Food Does not Require More Suffering." *Foreign Affairs* 91, no. 2 (2012): 122–33.

"People ex rel. Nonhuman Rights Project, Inc. On Behalf of Tommy v. Lavery." *Nonhuman Rights Project*. January 30, 2015. https://www.nonhumanrights.org /content/uploads/5.-Decision-and-Order-on-Motion-for-Permission-to-Appeal-to -the-Court-of-Appeals.pdf.

Peters, Anne, Saskia Stucki, and Livia Boscardin. "The Animal Turn and the Law." *1st Annual European Animal Law Conference*, Law School of the University of Basel, Switzerland, April 4–5, 2014.

Peters, Anne. "Global Animal Law: What It Is and Why We Need It." *Transnational Environmental Law* 5, no. 1 (2016): 9–23.

Regan, Tom. *The Case for Animal Rights*. Berkeley, CA: University of California Press, 2004.

Ritvo, Harriet. "On the Animal Turn." *Daedalus* 136 (2007): 118–22.

Siebert, Charles. "Should a Chimp Be Able to Sue Its Owner?" *New York Times*. April 23, 2014. https://www.nytimes.com/2014/04/27/magazine/the-rights-of-ma n-and-beast.html.

Singer, Peter. *Animal Liberation: A New Ethics for Our Treatment of Animals*. New York, NY: New York Review, 1975.

Sollund, Ragnhild. "Causes for Speciesism: Difference, Distance and Denial." In *Global Harms: Ecological Crime and Speciesism*, edited by Ragnhild Sollund, 109–31. New York, NY: Nova Science Publishers, 2008.

Spannring, Reingard, and Tomaž Grušovnik. "Leaving the Meatrix? Transformative Learning and Denialism in the Case of Meat Consumption." *Environmental Education Research* 25, no. 8 (2018): 1190–9.

Steffen, Will, Katherine Richardson, Johan Rockström, Sarah E. Cornell, Ingo Fetzer, Elena M. Bennett, Reinette Biggs, et al. "Planetary Boundaries: Guiding Human Development on a Changing Planet." *Science* 347, no. 6223 (2015): 1259855.

"Transcript of Oral Argument—Nonhuman Rights Project, Inc. on behalf of Kiko v Carmen and Christie Presti." *Nonhuman Rights Project.* December 9, 2013. https:/ /www.nonhumanrights.org/content/uploads/Transcript_of_Oral_Argument-_Niag ara_County_12-9-13.pdf.

Transnational Environmental Law 5, no. 1 (2016). https://www.cambridge.org/core /journals/transnational-environmental-law/issue/BD60C629432A53F16C8273 9262F2BE7C.

Tribe, Laurence H. "Amicus Brief in Support of Leave to Appeal." *Nonhuman Right Project.* Accessed June 22, 2020. https://www.nonhumanrights.org/content/upload s/Tribe-Amicus-Curiae-Letter-Brief-FINAL.pdf.

White, Lisa. "Discourse, Denial and Dehumanisation: Former Detainees' Experiences of Narrating State Violence in Northern Ireland." *Papers from the British Criminology Conference* 10 (2010): 3–18.

"Who We Are." *Nonhuman Rights Project.* Accessed July 12, 2020. https://www.non humanrights.org/who-we-are/.

Wise, Steven M. "Legal Personhood and the Nonhuman Rights Project." *Law Review* 17, no. 1 (2010). https://www.animallaw.info/sites/default/files/lralvol17_1_1.pdf.

Index

Page references for figures are italicized

About the Contributors

Kristian Bjørkdahl is a rhetoric scholar and currently a Postdoctoral Fellow at the Centre for Development and the Environment (SUM), at the University of Oslo. He has previously done research on American pragmatism, science communication, the cultural history of meat, and the contemporary uses of Nordic history. His PhD, from the University of Oslo, was on Richard Rorty's "utopia of solidarity." Currently, he is doing research in two main areas: the first looks into how science communication is organized at Norwegian universities, and the other studies how the idea of Nordic colonial innocence is used rhetorically. He has been editor or coeditor of several volumes, including *Rhetorical Animals* (Lexington, 2017) and *Pandemics, Publics, and Politics* (Palgrave Pivot, 2019). Another coedited volume, on Scandinavian do-goodism, is forthcoming, as is a coedited Norwegian language volume on science communication.

José De Giorgio-Schoorl is cofounder of Learning Animals—institute for research and development of animal ethics, interspecies interactions, and an anti-speciesist ethology, based on the work of Dr. Francesco De Giorgio and his socio-cognitive model. Central in her work, as teacher at the institute, as external adviser, and in her research, is a paradigm shift referring to an inclusive coexistence and interspecies interactions, where "everyone can be understood for their own cognitive way of being in the world." Her focus is to work for a change in awareness and understanding of the relationship between human and other animals, taking a critical position toward animal objectification (human included) in modern society, which is reflected in her publications. In 2012, she wrote *The Cognitive Horse* together with Dr. Francesco De Giorgio, which was released in 2014 in Italy as *Comprendere il Cavallo* (Giunti) and in 2017 in the United States under the title *Equus Lost?*

(Trafalgar Square Books), and several published articles in the last decennium addressing Animal Subjectivity and the possibilities to evolve in our human coexistence with other animals.

Joe Gray is a field naturalist and eco-activist based in St. Albans, UK, who has published various papers in the field of ecological ethics. He is a cofounder of *The Ecological Citizen* (an ecocentric journal) and chair of GENIE (the Global Ecocentric Network for Implementing Ecodemocracy). Joe is also a knowledge advisor on ecological ethics for the United Nations' Harmony with Nature program.

Tomaž Grušovnik is associate professor of philosophy of education and senior research fellow at the Faculty of Education, University of Primorska, Koper, Slovenia. His main areas of research include environmental and animal ethics and philosophy of education. He was a Fulbright Visiting Colleague at the department of Philosophy, University of New Mexico (2009), and Guest Lecturer at the Centre for Development and the Environment, University of Oslo (2011). Since 2018, he serves as president of the Slovenian Philosophical Society. He has published two books on environmental and animal ethics, two books of essays (all in Slovenian), as well as a number of papers and essays in various fields of interest. He is coeditor (together with Eduardo Mendieta and Lenart Škof) of the volume *Borders and Debordering: Topologies, Praxes, Hospitableness* (Lexington, 2018).

Katja Maria Hydle is associate professor of Digital Innovation in the department of Informatics, University of Oslo. Her former positions were research professor in NORCE and senior researcher in SINTEF. Her main research interests include organizational practices, strategy, and innovation and she has conducted research in the oil and gas industry, the aquaculture industry, entrepreneurial firms, and multinational companies, with outlets in academic journals such as *Organization Studies*, *Human Relations*, and *Journal of Word Business*.

Helen Kopnina (PhD, Cambridge University, 2002) is currently employed at The Hague University of Applied Sciences (HHS) in The Netherlands, coordinating Sustainable Business program and conducting research in three main areas: environmental sustainability, environmental education, and biological conservation. Kopnina is the author of over 150 peer-reviewed articles and coauthor and coeditor of sixteen books.

Google scholar: https://scholar.google.nl/citations?user=pE0rWdgAAAAJ&hl=nl

Researchgate: https://www.researchgate.net/profile/Helen_Kopnina2

Academia: http://thehagueuniversity.academia.edu/HelenKopnina/h
.kopnina@hhs.nl

Karen Lykke Syse is an agronomist and ethnologist and holds a PhD in Cultural History from the University of Oslo. She was Chevening Scholar at St. Andrews University, working on her PhD on land use, landscape, environmental issues, and the contested nature of Scotland, UK. She is currently associate professor of Environmental history at the Centre for Development and the Environment at the University of Oslo. Her research interests pivot around the histories and ideologies of nature, focusing on environmental discourse and practice; agrarian and arboreal landscape studies; and social and cultural aspects of food. She has been coeditor of the volumes *Perceptions of Water in Britain from Early Modern Times to the Present* (2010) and *Sustainable Consumption and the Good life* (2015). Another coedited volume on changing meat cultures is forthcoming, as is a coauthored book on the cultural history of meat in Norway. Her ongoing projects are on the cultural history of locative technologies, and the historical and contemporary relationships with nonhuman animals as food.

Atsuko Matsuoka is a professor at the School of Social Work, York University, Canada. She teaches Animals and Social Work from a Critical Animal Studies perspective. Her research has addressed the importance of understanding intersectionality of oppression among immigrants, ethnic older adults, and humans–other animals. In promoting consideration for animal–human relationships in social work, her current research, which is supported by the Social Sciences and Humanities Research Council of Canada, examines trans-species social justice (social justice beyond human animals) and social work. With John Sorenson, she coedited *Dog's Best Friend?: Rethinking Canid–Human Relations* (2019), *Critical Animal Studies: Towards Trans-Species Social Justice* (2018), *Defining Critical Animal Studies* (2014), and *Ghosts and Shadows: Constructions of Identity and Community in an African Diaspora* (2001).

Martin Lee Mueller holds a PhD in Philosophy from the University of Oslo. Currently, he is a postdoctoral researcher at the department of Teacher Education and School Research at the University of Oslo. The stage adaptation of his Nautilus Book Award-winning debut, *Being Salmon, Being Human*, has been touring across Scandinavia, the United Kingdom, and North America since 2016, both in Norwegian and English-language adaptations. The book also inspired the Virtual Reality artwork "The Bone," which premiered at the Screen City Biennal, Stavanger, Norway, in 2019 and will premier in its Spanish translation in Chile 2020. His writing has been called "game-changing culture-shifting, ethical and eloquent, opening the way toward a more mature natural science." He interweaves moral philosophy, earth systems science, indigenous perspectives, ecoliteracy, and ecopoetry. Mueller's latest publications include essays for the books *Otherkind. Spirit, Science, and the Practices of Kinship* (ed. Robin Wall Kimmerer et al., forthcoming), as well as for *The Wonder of Water. Lived Experience, Policy, and Practice* (ed. Ingrid Stefanovic, 2019, University of Toronto Press). Mueller is a fellow of the nonprofit Small Earth Institute.

Opi Outhwaite is associate professor in law at the St Mary's University, Twickenham. Opi specializes in international law and governance and has worked extensively on international biosecurity, human rights, and environmental law. She is cochair of the IUCN Academy of Environmental Law Teaching and Capacity Building Committee and has undertaken research and consultancy for government bodies and nongovernmental organizations including the Intergovernmental Science-Policy Platform on Biodiversity and Ecosystem Services (IPBES), Electronics Watch, the EU, UK Defra, the Belize Agricultural Health Agency, the Ministry of Agriculture in Tanzania.

John Piccolo is professor of biology at Karlstad University, Sweden. He has broad interests in ecology, evolution, and the philosophy of nature. He is president-elect of the Europe Section of the Society for Conservation Biology, and a long-time advocate of human recognition of the intrinsic values of nature.

Adam See is a university lecturer in philosophy at the New Jersey Institute of Technology. He recently completed his doctorate at the City University of New York, Graduate Center; his dissertation was a critical genealogy of animal minds skepticism from ancient philosophy to the twenty-first century. His research and published work focuses on the philosophy of animal minds, animal ethics, ethology, and the philosophy of biology. He also has long-standing interests in American pragmatism and the philosophy of education. He is currently the Treasurer of Minding Animals International.

John Sorenson teaches courses in Critical Animal Studies in the department of Sociology at Brock University. He has written and edited numerous books and articles on animal rights and various aspects of human–animal relationships. Recent books are *Dog's Best Friend?: Rethinking Canid–Human Relations* and *Critical Animal Studies: Towards Trans-Species Social Justice* (both coedited with Atsuko Matsuoka).

Reingard Spannring is sociologist working at the Institute for Educational Science, University of Innsbruck, Austria. Her main areas of research include critical animal studies, environmental education, sociology of youth, learning theories, and philosophy of education. She has coedited two books in the human–animal studies and cowritten an introduction to human–animal studies in German, in the context of the research hub Human Animal Studies at the University of Innsbruck. Recent peer-reviewed articles include "Ecological Citizenship Education and the Consumption of Animal Subjectivity" (in *Education Science*, 2019, 9(1)) and "Leaving the Meatrix? Transformative learning and denialism in the case of meat consumption" (together with Tomaž Grušovnik, in *Environmental Education Research*, 2019, 25(8)).

Susanne Stoll-Kleemann is a university professor and currently works as chair of Sustainability Science and Applied Geography, University of Greifswald. Susanne does research on conditions for a real transformation to sustainability and individual and collective behavior change. Susanne studied Geography, Political Sciences, Psychology, and Educational Sciences and received her PhD in 1999 from the Technical University of Berlin (Faculty Environment and Society). She conducted some of her research on the Human Dimension of Climate Change and Biodiversity in Switzerland, at the Swiss Federal Institute of Technology, Zurich, in Germany at the Potsdam Institute of Climate Impact Research, Potsdam and at the Humboldt University of Berlin, Germany.

Craig Taylor is associate professor of Philosophy at Flinders University. His area of research expertise is moral philosophy and he has a longstanding interest in the philosophy of Ludwig Wittgenstein. He is the author of *Sympathy: A Philosophical Analysis* and *Moralism: A Study of a Vice*. He is a coeditor of three edited collections with academic presses and the author of numerous refereed journal articles in philosophy.

Arne Johan Vetlesen is professor of philosophy at the University of Oslo. He is the author of twenty-five books, including *Evil and Human Agency* (2005), *The Denial of Nature* (2015), and *Cosmologies of the Anthropocene: Panpsychism, Animism, and the Limits of Posthumanism* (2019). His research interests are in the fields of moral, political, and environmental philosophy. He is a prominent public intellectual in Norway with a column in several newspapers.

Haydn Washington is an environmental scientist and writer with a forty-year history in environmental science. He also writes extensively on ecological economics and ecological ethics. He is an Adjunct Lecturer in the PANGEA Research Centre, BEES, UNSW. His books include *Climate Change Denial: Heads in the Sand* (2011 with John Cook), *Human Dependence on Nature* (2013), *Demystifying Sustainability* (2015), *A Sense of Wonder Towards Nature* (2019), and *What can I do to Help Heal the Environmental Crisis?* (2020). He is the coeditor of the 2019 book *Conservation: Integrating Social and Ecological Justice* from Springer. Haydn is codirector of the NSW Chapter of the Center for the Advancement of a Steady State Economy and is the vice chair of the Colong Foundation for Wilderness. He is also on the Steering Committee of the new group "GENIE" (www.ecodemocracy.net).

www.ingramcontent.com/pod-product-compliance
Lightning Source LLC
Chambersburg PA
CBHW050641280326
41932CB00015B/2739